Modeling XML Applications with UML

The Addison-Wesley Object Technology Series

Grady Booch, Ivar Jacobson, and James Rumbaugh, Series Editors

For more information check out the series web site [http://www.awl.com/cseng/otseries/].

The Component Software Series

Clemens Szyperski, Series Editor

For more information check out the series web site [http://www.awl.com/cseng/csseries/].

Modeling XML Applications with UML

Practical e-Business Applications

David Carlson

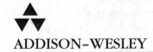

ADDISON–WESLEY

Boston • San Francisco • New York • Toronto • Montreal
London • Munich • Paris • Madrid
Capetown • Sydney • Tokyo • Singapore • Mexico City

Many of the designations used by manufacturers and sellers to distinguish their products are claimed as trademarks. Where those designations appear in this book, and Addison-Wesley, Inc. was aware of a trademark claim, the designations have been printed with initial capital letters or in all capitals.

The author and publisher have taken care in the preparation of this book, but make no expressed or implied warranty of any kind and assume no responsibility for errors or omissions. No liability is assumed for incidental or consequential damages in connection with or arising out of the use of the information or programs contained herein.

Figures 5-2, 5-3, and 11-7 courtesy of IBM; Figures 5-2, 5-3, 5-4, 11-3, and 11-7 courtesy of Sony Electronics, Inc.; Figure 5-6 copyright © Oracle Corporation. All rights reserved.

The publisher offers discounts on this book when ordered in quantity for special sales. For more information, please contact:

Pearson Education Corporate Sales Division
One Lake Street
Upper Saddle River, NJ 07458
(800) 382-3419
corpsales@pearsontechgroup.com

Visit AW on the Web: *www.awl.com/cseng/*

Library of Congress Cataloging-in-Publication Data
Carlson, David (David A.)
   Modeling XML applications with UML : practical e-business applications / David Carlson.
      p. cm. -- (The Addison-Wesley object technology series)
   ISBN 0-201-70915-5
   1. XML (Document markup language)   2. UML (Computer science)   I. Title.   II. Series.

   QA76.76.H94 C3685 2001
   005.72--dc21

                                                                                00-054325

Text printed on recycled and acid-free paper.
ISBN 0201709155
2 3 4 5 6 7 MA   04 03 02 01
2nd Printing   June 2001

To my parents for
nurturing my love for learning.

Contents

Foreword

While growing up I often heard the cliché, "a picture is worth a thousand words." In our media-driven culture we are constantly exposed to a stream of images that convey different meanings. We are truly creatures dependent on visualization for survival. How then does one apply this primary skill to concepts that have no innate shape or form? Early examples of solutions to this challenge can be found in the formation of ideographs and alphabets. Throughout the centuries, the capacity to visually express the nonvisual has been a key to transforming the world we live in. As each wave of scientific transformation has progressed, a key accelerator in that transformation has been the expression of a standardized notation and a vocabulary to visually communicate intent. Examples abound in the fields of electronics, engineering, physics, and music.

Software development is a field still in its infancy. We do not yet share many of the advantages that other, more mature disciplines have. One disadvantage is that we are still developing standard notations and vocabularies for our discipline. We currently have many choices, ranging from vocabularies that describe program execution like C++ and Java, to notations that describe database design like IDEF1x, to combined notational vocabularies like the Unified Modeling Language (UML), which attempt to define the entire context of a software development exercise.

As long as multiple notations and vocabularies exist it will be necessary to "map" concepts from one language to another so that people who think in different vocabularies can communicate, and the systems that they build can interoperate. This book helps satisfy that need. Although there are many books about UML and XML as independent vocabularies, a bridge between these two languages must be established so that XML developers can harness the visual power that the UML contains. After reading this book I think that you will agree with me that Dave does a great job of establishing a "translation guide" that, it is hoped, will serve as a primary input to eventual standardization.

So why spend time mapping UML and XML together? If one looks at current market dynamics the answer becomes clear. Over the last five years the UML has become established as the standard notation used to describe how systems are structured and how they should behave. The effect on software development has been profound. We have moved from a "Tower of Babel," where competing factions argued over how to visually express systems design, to an industry unified by a "lingua franca." In today's market it would be difficult, if not impossible, to deliver an enterprise application development tool that did not include UML-based visualization. The result has been an explosion of productivity as different groups and companies have mapped the UML into specific domains. Examples include UML profiles for Real-time systems, Data Modeling, Enterprise JavaBeans, and just about every modern implementation language. These mappings raise the level of abstraction that today's software development team works at.

Although the UML has become established as the standard notation for enterprise development, the very nature of enterprise development is changing in order to embrace the World Wide Web. The Web has changed the way systems are designed, and many new languages are spoken there. HTML and CGI led the first wave of Web applications, but the next wave is likely to be dominated by architectures based on the Java 2 Enterprise Edition and VS.Net. Because XML figures prominently in both architectural approaches, regardless of which path developers take, they will use XML to build solutions. A translation manual between the worlds of UML and XML is very helpful because it will accelerate the efforts of software developers who want to create Enterprise Web Applications.

Accelerating the efforts of today's XML developer is key because the demands they face are greater than ever. Brick and mortar companies are struggling to redefine themselves as "click and mortar" concerns and view software as critical to this effort. This sets up a "software paradox" where XML developers must deliver solutions more quickly than in the past (hence the term "internet time") and yet these solutions must be high quality because the customer interfaces with them directly. The fact that many business-to-customer and business-to-business solutions use XML as a communication language makes it imperative to accelerate the efforts of XML developers. By automating the process by which visual diagrams (in UML) become XML schemas and DTDs, we can accelerate e-business development while retaining a high level of quality in the resulting schemas.

Ironically, when I reviewed the draft of this publication our team at Rational had just delivered XML DTD support for Rational Rose. Any developer who has built a language generator for a UML tool (our team has built four to date) will tell you that the mapping is usually the critical part of this effort. Once a mapping is established the work goes pretty quickly. Because we had engaged in our own mapping exercise I was quite eager to see how our work stacked up. Although there were some small differences (for example, use of N-ary associations, and treatment of Entities), I was relieved to find that we had made most of the same connections that Dave has. If we'd had this text before we started, we would have had a great cheat sheet for our work. In particular, we found Dave's treatment of XPath, XPointer and XLink very useful for our continued work in evolving our own UML–XML support into the future. Based on our work in both the UML and XML community, our team feels that this book represents the best translation guide available for those looking to tightly bind the powerful expressiveness of UML and the ubiquity of XML together in a way that will help accelerate the delivery of enterprise Web applications. Enjoy!

Jeffrey Hammond,
Senior Product Manager,
Rational Software

Preface

Writing about XML and e-Business is a lot like taking a snapshot of a speeding train. And for those readers who are new to one or both of these subjects, it's a lot like attempting to jump onto that train. In writing this book, I've attempted to strike a balance between an introduction to these challenging subjects and a practical guide for designing realistic systems.

I make some assumptions about a basic prior knowledge of both XML and UML, but not so much that a motivated reader cannot easily meet these expectations with quick supplemental study. There are dozens of introductory books on both subjects but there is a lack of good explanation about how XML and UML can be combined in the analysis of complex systems. The goal of this book is not only to teach you *about* XML and UML but also how to *use* these technologies for practical applications.

Goals of This Book

Over the past twenty-five years of learning, teaching, and working, I have realized that there is a very significant difference between gaining knowledge about a subject and gaining *actionable* knowledge about that same topic. Knowledge is actionable when it directly and immediately affects what you do and how you do it. While writing this book, I had a note taped to the top of my computer monitor that read "Actionable Knowledge," so that it would continually prompt me to keep this focus in mind.

After reading this book, you will have learned the following actionable knowledge:

- Guidelines that you can use to gather key stakeholder input while developing your XML application.
- How you can integrate XML and UML in *current* design projects and what this means to achieving your e-business objectives.
- Steps and criteria to use in the visual analysis and design of XML vocabularies.
- A detailed guide to how you can generate XML DTDs and Schemas from those vocabularies, plus the trade-offs you must consider while doing so.
- Substantial, realistic examples to base your own work on.
- Concrete suggestions about how to apply recently adopted (or almost adopted) XML standards.
- A deep understanding that is based not on the marketing materials of individual vendors but on common practice that applies to all of them.
- A solid grounding about how to design XML applications now and many product or system releases in the future.
- An understanding of what's going to happen next!

Concepts of UML modeling and a streamlined Unified Process are woven throughout this book. e-Business examples demonstrate the breadth of UML modeling capabilities but without overwhelming the primary goal of creating successful applications using XML. As a means to this goal, this book focuses on a consistent, substantial example about the analysis and design of a product catalog application. An XML vocabulary for the Catalog Markup Language (CatML) is designed first in UML, then generated to both DTD and XML Schema languages.

This same catalog example is used to model requirements for the "MyCat" Web portal application, whose content is defined by the CatML vocabulary. An example MyCat portal is demonstrated using the Extensible Stylesheet Language Transformation (XSLT) to produce an HTML presentation from the XML documents, all based on the CatML vocabulary definitions. UML is used throughout the exercise to analyze the application requirements and the vocabulary design. Finally, XSLT is described as a language for transforming the CatML vocabulary to and from RosettaNet product catalog standards. Vocabulary transformation is an essential element in most e-business applications.

Who Should Read This Book?

This book is not a guide to programming XML applications; rather it focuses on the thoughtful analysis and design of XML vocabularies and their use within distributed systems. If you have a need to develop a system using XML, or if you are considering the value of such a system, then you will find this book helpful. Although their use is not restricted to e-business applications, those examples form the central theme throughout all chapters. These examples span the range of XML applied to the content of portal presentations to the specification and transformation of message content for system integration.

System architects will find many valuable points to consider when planning the use of XML. The use case analyses in Chapters 1, 4, and 5 build a business case for e-business integration and portal design using XML. These use cases are described from the perspective of key stakeholders who determine and evaluate the goals of a successful XML application. Each chapter concludes with a list of "Steps for Success" that are especially valuable to an architect.

Complex XML vocabulary definitions are often easier to comprehend and discuss with others when they are expressed graphically. Although a few existing tools provide some assistance in this regard, they are generally limited to a strict hierarchical view of the vocabulary structure. Complex structures may be represented in schemas that are more easily analyzed from an object-oriented perspective. These object-oriented models of schema definition are easily represented using UML class diagrams. This book is valuable to business analysts, who are responsible for the definition of business vocabularies that will be implemented using XML.

Those analysts often team with designers who fine-tune the vocabularies for generation to XML DTDs or Schemas. Chapter 8 provides a detailed comparison of XML DTDs with the new, much richer possibilities available in XML Schema definitions. Chapter 9 includes detailed design heuristics for generating both DTDs and Schemas from UML class models and describes trade-offs for specifying relaxed versus strict schema validation. These decisions are the daily work of XML designers.

Chapter 2 provides an overview of XML terminology using a simple real-world example that is relevant to the topics of this book. The Rich Site Summary (RSS) is described and compared with similar use of news content in HTML. For a more thorough introduction to XML, I recommend:

- Simon St. Laurent. *XML Elements of Style.* New York: McGraw-Hill, 1999.

If you are not familiar with UML, Chapter 3 includes a fast-paced overview of the essential diagrams that are used in this book. Those diagrams are applied to the same RSS XML example that is introduced in Chapter 2. For a good introduction to UML that is short and easy to read, I recommend:

- Martin Fowler, Kendall Scott. *UML Distilled: A Brief Guide to the Standard Object Modeling Language*, Second Edition. Boston: Addison-Wesley, 2000.

Chapters 10 and 11 include substantial examples of XSLT vocabulary transformations. XSLT is a very powerful but somewhat complex language whose detail is beyond the scope of this book. If you are new to XSLT, I recommend the following supplemental references:

- Neil Bradley. *The XSL Companion.* Boston: Addison-Wesley, 2000.
- Michael Kay. *XSLT Programmer's Reference.* Birmingham, UK: Wrox Press, 2000.

XMLModeling.com

Because no book covering the topics of XML and e-business can promise more than a snapshot of the speeding train, it's equally important to offer a first-class ticket for the ride into the future. A Web site has been especially prepared as the companion site for this book. It is available at *http://XMLModeling.com.*

The following information is available, organized in an easily navigated portal:

- Current XML news
- Quick links for XML and UML resources and tools
- Complete UML models and XML listings from this book's examples
- Tips and tools for generating XML schemas from UML models
- Case studies that apply these techniques

Acknowledgments

I am very grateful for the support of all my friends and colleagues at Gartner Solista in Boulder. I especially wish to thank Maryann Richards for providing detailed feedback on every chapter within days of its first draft. Her suggestions have made positive contributions to every chapter of this book. Also, Tim Johnson read the first versions of each chapter and helped keep me focused on the planned audience.

A special thanks to Kristin Erickson from Addison-Wesley for convincing me to write this book, then coaching me through the publication process and orchestrating a team of very busy reviewers. And of course I'm very grateful for the time and input of the anonymous reviewers who made significant contributions to these chapters.

And last, but certainly not least, the Bookend Café and the Trident coffeehouse in Boulder, Colorado, deserve honorable mentions. A substantial part of this book was imagined, written, or edited in those cafés while drinking many gallons of tea and eating more than a hundred chocolate-chip cookies.

David Carlson, Ph. D.
Boulder, Colorado

PART I
Foundations

Chapter 1

Convergence of Communities

e-Business is a catalyst for change. The change has been profound and fast as companies adopt the Internet as a primary channel for business interactions. Businesses initially used the Web as a one-way channel for communicating text and graphical information to consumers. The Web quickly became a platform for electronically processing orders and making catalog and real-time inventory available online. This consumer-oriented business transformation has now begun to impact the very heart of supply chain operations. Recent forecasts predict that business-to-business (B2B) transactions via the Internet will soon dwarf the other e-business conducted with consumers. Behind the scenes of this publicity, however, information-technology professionals are scrambling faster than ever. Yet, they are still falling behind in their efforts to interconnect all of the new and legacy systems required to fulfill this new electronic-business age.

e-Business requires integration of the information and processes needed to conduct business in real time. At the consumer level, this means that online catalogs must access the inventory database; also, credit authorization, order processing, and fulfillment must be integrated to deliver the goods to each buyer. Challenges have been encountered but were conquered, and the world moved on with this new, faster channel for sales. Then came B2B integration. Supply chain integration of manufacturers and distributors requires deeper introspection into sales forecasts, production scheduling, product configuration, and inventory management. The arrival of electronic marketplaces has created a "brave new world" of electronic bidding, auctions, reverse auctions, and a steady stream of never-before encountered business processes—all of which needs to be completed yesterday.

Finally, as if these challenges weren't difficult enough, all these new services must be delivered via personalized portals that can be accessed using Web browsers, personal digital assistants (PDAs), cell phones, pagers, interactive television, and automated shopping agents. These portals must become an extension of the core enterprise information infrastructure, not simply patched on as a Web sales channel. The portal becomes a secure conduit for basic operational data to be delivered to remote and mobile employees, key business partners, suppliers, and customers. The portal is a window into the B2B flow of information.

To satisfy these new demands, we must adopt a fundamental change in the way system integration is accomplished. This means an infrastructure that supports loose coupling of intra- and inter-enterprise information between widely disparate application designs, operating systems, databases, and application programming interfaces (APIs). The eXtensible Markup Language (XML) has become a solution for many of these needs. XML is not a magic wand that can solve all problems, but it does enable us to focus on the definition of shared vocabularies for exchanging information that can be processed easily by both human and computer systems. XML and its domain vocabularies are becoming the *lingua franca* for B2B communication.

An additional benefit of XML is that it was derived from a document-processing heritage for supporting both computer and human communication. As a result, it contains standardized stylesheet processing languages and tools for presenting XML documents to human users in many formats—print, multimedia, and synthesized voice. Through these technologies, XML has the potential to become the standard platform for convergence of information to all types of portals.

A complete coverage of how XML can address these e-business issues would require many volumes. This book adopts a more modest goal of addressing business-to-business vocabularies and portals using XML. Our main goal is to describe the use of the Unified Modeling Language (UML) as a technique for designing business vocabularies that can be deployed using XML for e-business integration.

Models for e-Business

By itself, XML is only a syntax for the exchange of data and text-oriented documents; yet we need more than a common syntax for successful communication. *Communication* requires shared models of both the underlying domain semantics, and the processes and policies used to engage in electronic commerce. These models are the very essence of B2B integration. They may be implicit in the applications that process the XML documents; or they may be explicit in definition of the model's concepts, relationships, and constraints. In practice, the models are defined both implicitly and explicitly.

We'll cover the following three aspects of modeling B2B communication.

- *Modeling system requirements with use cases.* These models define the roles of stakeholders and the use case actors who are involved in B2B interactions, plus the functional requirements of those stakeholders and actors.

- *Modeling processes and communication policies.* B2B interactions are not limited to sending a single message but require a coordinated sequence of activities and expectations of the business partners.

- *Modeling business vocabularies.* Each message exchanged within a communication process contains information content that may be short and simple or very long and complex. Each of these content documents is defined by a vocabulary that is shared by the parties engaged in the communication.

XML is becoming widely used for representing both the process and the content information when deploying models. Process information includes the messaging infrastructure and workflow control that guides the process execution. Many B2B processes are asynchronous and long running, so the XML-based message header information identifies the parties, process, and purpose of the message. The business vocabularies define the heart of the message—its content. Example product catalog vocabulary is developed in this book. The catalog data using this vocabulary will be exchanged in messages between business partners when aggregating catalogs from multiple suppliers or when responding to queries for product specification data.

An XML application is, however, much more than structured data! The application is part of a broader system context, including both architectural and process requirements. Most e-business applications contain requirements, from both business and technical stakeholders, which are distributed across an inter-enterprise system. Development of these systems benefits greatly from visual models and a process that encourages active communication. Let's face it—the business world revolves around graphical presentation, so anything that adds a visual component to XML specification is very helpful.

Stakeholder Communities

In the beginning stages of developing an e-business system, many stakeholders must contribute requirements, domain model details for the analysis, and specifications for design and implementation. This book does not attempt to cover the full development lifecycle but instead focuses on analysis and some parts of design, all with an eye toward the use of XML. Within this context, we must consider the needs of several diverse stakeholder communities. I have narrowed the focus for this book to five groups: consumers, business analysts, Web application specialists, system integration specialists, and content developers.

A complete analysis of an e-business system would require documenting many different use cases that describe the convergence of these stakeholder communities in B2B and business-to-customer (B2C) interaction scenarios. Figure 1-1 illustrates one high-level use case diagram that incorporates all five of the identified stakeholder communities. This high-level view spans the requirements from designing the product catalog structure and content to presenting personalized views of this catalog to consumers.

A use case specification identifies a set of "actors" that interact with each use case. Each actor represents the role of a user that works with the resulting system after it is deployed; a specific human user may fulfill several different roles. As shown in Figure 1-1, UML use case diagrams always represent an actor using a "stick person" icon. Each oval represents an individual use case that describes (in a separate document and/or diagram) the activity flow required to achieve the goal of that use case. The use case diagram presents an outside view (from the perspective of the actors) of the system without specifying *how* that functionality is designed or implemented.

I use the term *stakeholder* rather than actor in this description because of its broader meaning. A stakeholder represents all roles that have an interest in the goals of a use case, not only those who directly participate in performing the use case activities. Thus, a Consumer stakeholder provides requirements for the design of portals and business processes, although he or she may not have a direct role in performing the steps within those use cases.

Future chapters will decompose the individual use cases into scenarios illustrated with class diagrams, object diagrams, sequence diagrams, and activity diagrams that specify how XML fits into the overall e-business solution. But first, I'll describe the typical characteristics of each stakeholder community in a bit more detail.

Consumer

A consumer may be either a business customer in the supply chain (for example, a buyer of components for a manufacturer) or an end-user retail customer. I use the term *consumer* rather than customer to emphasize that consumption occurs at many points along the e-business supply chain. In many current situations, this consumer represents a human user who is interacting with the product catalog service. However, we will increasingly see automated consumer

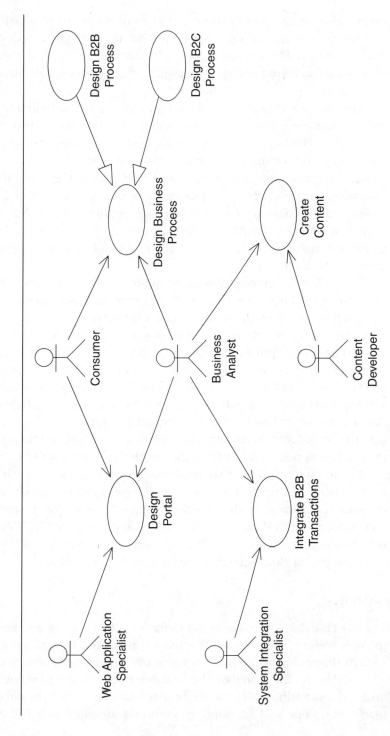

Figure 1-1 e-Business stakeholder interactions

agents, also called 'bots (a truncated form of the word robot), that fulfill the consumer role. A B2B consumer may be an automated order submission process triggered by the production schedule, or a retail consumer may be represented by an automated shopping agent that performs comparison shopping across sites.

The use case diagram shows the consumer as a stakeholder in both designing the business processes and in designing the portal's personalized views of the catalog. The business processes for business consumers are very different from those supporting retail customers. Therefore, the use case diagram includes two more specialized use cases that extend the general use case for designing business processes. During requirements analysis of a B2B service, representative consumers must be included, either in individual interviews or as part of larger focus groups. This input would be documented in text documents associated with the relevant use cases and in activity or sequence diagrams of the event flows.

The difference in requirements for human or 'bot consumers is unspecified in this high-level use case diagram. Their different requirements would need to be described in the individual use cases, or likely in additional sub-use cases that define the specialization. For example, both a human and an automated 'bot consumer require a personalized presentation of the catalog, but the means of personalization may be quite different. A human user would expect an HTML browser-based presentation that is tailored to his or her preferences and supports quick navigation without a lot of distracting, irrelevant information. On the other hand, a 'bot may expect a filtered subset of the catalog content that is tailored to its particular interests as a buyer. Of course, either of these kinds of personalization can be enabled by effective use of XML.

In the context of an XML application, consumers are both sources and recipients of communication. As a source, the consumer produces XML-based messages containing product catalog queries, requests for quotes, or orders. A consumer receives product catalog information encoded in XML documents, which is then presented in a Web browser or imported into the recipient's business system. Both scenarios are covered in later chapters.

Business Analyst

The use case diagram in Figure 1-1 depicts the business analyst as being central to implementing a successful e-business application. The analyst participates in each of the use cases, often as the integrative force and visionary for the overall system. The business analyst also collaborates with the content developer to create the domain model for the product catalog. Other stakeholders such as marketing, sales, and accounting would be included in a full requirements analysis. The analyst then works with the Web application specialist to design a dynamic, personalized Web site for this product catalog.

The business analyst uses this knowledge of the product catalog model to collaborate with the system integration specialists. System integration requirements include adaptation of legacy systems into this new e-business application at multiple stages of both B2B and B2C business processes, plus integration with other external systems such as credit authorization and shipping.

The business analyst uses his or her knowledge of the overall e-business environment to oversee the requirements gathering process for an integrated solution. He or she must understand the process for using the UML in use case and activity modeling and be able to facilitate design of the UML static structure models that represent the XML vocabularies for system integration and Web presentation. This last modeling responsibility is the central topic of this book.

Web Application Specialist

A Catalog Exchange Service (CatX) is analyzed as a sample application in this book. For the CatX system, Web application specialists are most often concerned with the portal server component and portal requirements and design. But this is no simple matter! We are still very early in the maturity of XML processing directly within Web browsers. So for the next year or two, it's likely that much of the Web application processing for XML content will be executed within application servers. For example, Java servlets may process the XML catalog content, using an XSLT transformation to produce HTML content for the e-marketplace portal interface.

There are many sub-roles within the community of Web application specialists. Dynamic server pages have become the mainstays of Web development; for example, the J2EE standard for JavaServer Pages (JSP), Microsoft's Active Server Pages (ASP), or Allaire's ColdFusion. These technologies are often used to process XML content for Web browser delivery. However, XML is also introducing new technologies into the Web developer's toolkit. The Extensible Stylesheet Language (XSL) is now used in combination with Cascading Style Sheets (CSS) to transform and format XML documents for presentation on the Web. These topics are discussed in later chapters as part of designing XML portals.

Jim Conallen's book [Conallen, 2000] examines the broader details and alternative architectures for designing Web applications. I focus attention on the analysis and design of XML content within e-business solutions. Chapters 2 and 5 explore the use of XML by Web application specialists and introduce the benefits of UML from their perspective.

There are also many exciting new developments in wireless Internet access via mobile phones, PDAs, and other specialized Internet devices. In most cases,

XML plays a significant, if not dominant, role in communicating information to and from these wireless devices. This new stakeholder role fits most closely with the skills of advanced Web application specialists but will also require development of new skills. I'll have more to say about this subject in later chapters, particularly regarding the use of XSLT to transform XML catalog content for presentation by the wireless world.

System Integration Specialist

System integration specialists play a very significant role in B2B e-commerce. It is almost a certainty that one will encounter several incompatible systems when integrating e-business processes across several organizations in a supply chain or marketplace. Prior to the availability of XML, the most common solutions were to attempt development of standard APIs using technologies like CORBA, RMI, or DCOM, or to adopt message-oriented middleware that supported reliable, asynchronous routing and delivery of data and events. These approaches proved difficult and expensive to implement in a widely distributed, heterogeneous environment using the public Internet for transport and did not have a good solution for formatting the large blocks of structured data contained in the message's body.

XML-enabled applications take a very different approach to integration. Instead of standardizing the APIs for system integration, the data format is standardized for text-based documents exchanged among participants. This is sometimes referred to as platform-independent data, which complements the Java programming language as platform-independent code for a complete, vendor-independent integration solution.

Use of XML for the content format allows these documents to be parsed and transformed with the use of standards-based tools that are very inexpensive, or often free. Thus, exporting and importing XML documents has become a common means for integrating otherwise incompatible systems. Many B2B integration solutions are now adopting a hybrid of message-oriented middleware, carrying XML structured content in the message body.

These are all primary tasks within the domain of system integration specialists. The use case diagram shown in Figure 1-1 includes one use case for integrating B2B transactions. Obviously, there are many details yet to be explored in these requirements. Chapters 3 and 4 introduce the use of UML for modeling business processes and the XML vocabularies required for B2B integration.

Content Developer

Within a large organization, hundreds of people may be involved in developing catalog content in the form of product specifications, price lists, white papers, frequently asked question (FAQ) lists, and so on. Since all of this content is potentially useful in a B2B service, the content developers must be involved in specification of the catalog vocabulary. These stakeholders will be consulted in upcoming chapters as we construct the UML models for the required behavior and structure of the XML documents.

Road Map for This Book

Figure 1-2 presents a road map for the topics in this book, and the following sections explain the contents of the three parts of the book. Each chapter concludes with a list of steps for success. The purpose of these steps is to distill general principles for modeling XML applications and to organize them along the guidelines of the Unified Process. Consider these steps as a supplement to rather than a replacement of the Unified Process. Their goal is to give you a road map that helps achieve successful completion of your own XML applications.

Part I. Foundations

Chapter 2 introduces XML by comparing it with a similar application of HTML. The example, using the Rich Site Summary (RSS) vocabulary for news headlines, builds a foundation for using the same vocabulary in future chapters. The chapter covers the center part of Figure 1-2 by describing XML documents and Document Type Definition (DTD) schemas, plus use of XSLT to transform XML into HTML for presentation.

Chapter 3 introduces UML models, thus covering the upper part of the road map. Each of the UML diagrams is described based on its role in an iterative development process using the RSS example from Chapter 2.

Chapter 4 analyzes the use case requirements for e-business integration. This chapter introduces the Catalog Markup Language (CatML) that is used throughout the remainder of the book. CatML was conceived and implemented strictly for the purposes of this book.

Chapter 5 analyzes the use case requirements for wired and wireless portals. "MyCat" is introduced as a personalized portal for our catalog exchange service example.

Part II. XML Vocabularies

Part II focuses entirely on the analysis and design of XML vocabularies using UML class diagrams. All examples are based on the CatML vocabulary.

Chapter 6 describes XML vocabulary design and works through seven design issues that must be considered when mapping UML class models to XML. UML object diagrams are used to describe the mapping scenarios.

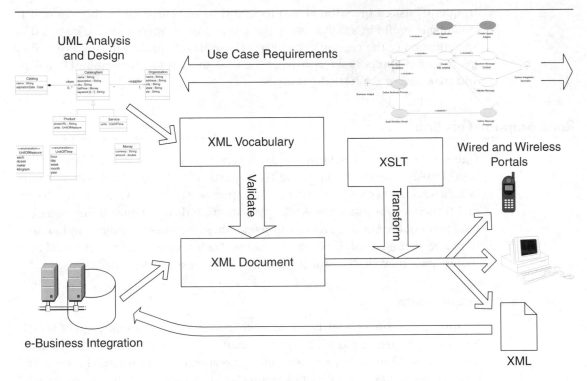

Figure 1-2 Components of an e-Business application

Chapter 7 takes the next step into distributed applications and describes four XML linking mechanisms used to map UML relationships into XML hyperlinks. This chapter completes our design specification for the CatML vocabulary.

Chapter 8 provides a detailed introduction and comparison of XML DTDs and Schemas.

Chapter 9 describes the criteria and production rules used to generate XML DTDs and Schemas from UML class diagrams. Alternative rules and trade-offs are analyzed for producing relaxed versus strict schemas. All examples are based on generating schemas for CatML.

Part III. Deployment

Chapter 10 returns to the e-business integration issues introduced in Chapter 4. Two detailed examples are described using XSLT to transform the CatML vocabulary to and from the RosettaNet standard XML vocabulary.

Chapter 11 probes deeper into deployment of the portal that was introduced in Chapter 5. XSLT is again used to transform CatML, but this time into HTML for presentation in the Apache Jetspeed portal framework.

Chapter 12 outlines the common features of current e-business architectures for deploying B2B applications. As part of the architecture, the Simple Object Access Protocol (SOAP) is introduced as an XML-based messaging standard for interconnecting distributed components.

Steps for Success

1. Identify e-business drivers. What strategies of your business are driving the need for integration? What are your customers' and suppliers' strategies? Where are your competitors headed?

2. Identify stakeholder communities. A successful XML application must consider the requirements of all major stakeholder communities, including consumers, suppliers, business analysts, system integrator specialists, Web application specialists, and content developers.

3. Create a high-level use case diagram for your system context.

4. For each use case, identify its primary goals and assumptions.

5. Identify an initial set of workflow processes among the stakeholders.

Chapter 2

What Is an XML Application?

Markup languages have existed in various forms since the early days of computing. The most fundamental characteristic of a markup language is its ability both to describe symbols or markers that are inserted into a text document and to define the meaning that those symbols bring to the associated text. Markup language can be applied to text-oriented documents intended for human use and to data-oriented documents used for storing or exchanging information by computer systems.

Although the history and use of markup languages is long and varied, most agree that HyperText Markup Language (HTML) brought these languages into everyday use and conversation. HTML was created in 1990 as a very simple technique for authoring and linking documents that are easily exchanged in a global information network [Berners-Lee, 1997]. No doubt this simplicity was essential to the Web's early success and exponential growth. But as HTML has evolved and matured in its design, much of this initial simplicity has been lost; our need for richer description and presentation of information content on the Internet has exceeded the capabilities of HTML. The eXtensible Markup Language (XML) was created specifically to overcome these limitations and to enable the next generation of global information exchange and e-business.

HTML, XML, and XHTML

Before exploring the details of XML, let's first quickly review the structure and use of HTML. We'll then be able to compare HTML's features with the much more general nature of XML and describe why XML is *not* simply the next

Listing 2-1   HTML news headlines

```
<!DOCTYPE HTML PUBLIC "-//W3C//DTD HTML 4.0//EN" "strict.dtd">
<HTML>
  <HEAD>
    <TITLE>UML Headlines</TITLE>
    <META NAME="managingEditor" CONTENT="editor@xmlmodeling.com">
  </HEAD>
  <BODY>
    <H1>UML Headlines</H1>
    <P>Recent news about the Unified Modeling Language (UML).</P>
    <UL>
      <LI><A HREF="http://www.omg.org">
           UML version 1.3 adopted by the OMG</A>
      </LI>
      <LI><A HREF="http://www.rational.com">
           Rational Rose 2000e released</A>
      </LI>
      <LI><A HREF="http://www.togethersoft.com">
           TogetherJ 4.0 released</A>
      </LI>
    </UL>
  </BODY>
</HTML>
```

generation of HTML. In fact, there are very good reasons for HTML and XML to coexist in peaceful harmony.

This book is filled with concrete, practical examples that illustrate how its concepts are applied. Each example is available for download on the companion Web site, as described in the Preface. We'll start with a short example of an HTML document that displays a list of news headlines. Listing 2-1 is a complete, valid example of HTML 4.0.

Even if you've had no prior experience with creating HTML documents, you probably can still understand the structure of these markup tags (although you might not know the precise detail of each tag's meaning). Let's discuss them in the order in which they appear.

A valid document must have exactly one root element named <HTML> that contains all others. The document's <HEAD> element contains metadata about the document, and the main body of the content is contained within <BODY>. Each element has a start tag and an end tag that surround its contents. The contents of each element may include other elements, possibly mixed with character text.

The <UL> element defines an unordered list that contains (in this example) three list items, as defined by the <LI> elements. Each <LI> element contains one hyperlink anchor, such as the following:

```
<A HREF="http://www.omg.org">Rational Rose 2000e released</A>
```

This anchor element contains only character text between start and end tags, but it also includes an attribute name/value pair as part of its start tag. The HREF attribute value specifies the URL destination of this hyperlink. HTML attributes (and XML attributes as we'll see in later chapters) are often used to define metadata or annotation for an element, where those attribute values are not part of the element content per se. So in this example, the attribute value is metadata about where to find additional information pertaining to the topic "Rational Rose 2000e released."

In fact, this HTML document could almost be parsed as a well-formed XML document were it not for the <META> tag, which violates XML's rules by not having a matching end tag. The vast majority of current HTML documents on the Web are not even close to being valid XML. There are two reasons this is the case. First, Web browsers are both notorious (but, ironically, praised) for accepting invalid HTML documents. That a browser attempts to produce a readable display of all documents retrieved can be seen as a positive characteristic, but such flexibility encourages bad habits by HTML authors. Second, even if a document is valid with respect to HTML 4.0, this standard is defined by an SGML document type definition (DTD),[1] which allows markup that cannot be parsed by XML applications.

Standard Generalized Markup Language (SGML) is the predecessor of XML, but its greater "generality" also made it too complex for widespread adoption on the Web. However, because XML is defined as a subset of SGML, any valid XML document is also a valid SGML document. (But the reverse is not true; one can create SGML documents and DTDs that cannot be processed by XML applications. This is the situation with HTML 4.0.)

One of the most common characteristics that prevent valid SGML documents, including HTML, from also being valid XML is the omission of end tags in a document. The preceding example could have omitted the </LI> end tag on each list item without sacrificing its SGML validity. This is because a parser would use the DTD to determine which end tags were omitted, based on the adjacent markup elements. XML standards strictly prohibit this practice. Every XML element must have a matching pair of begin and end tags; an XML element without content may use a shortened notation, such as the following line break element:

```
<BR/>
```

In a similar way, the previously mentioned invalid <META> tag in Listing 2-1 can be revised to valid XML by adding a closing '/>', as follows:

```
<META NAME="managingEditor" CONTENT="editor@xmlmodeling.com"/>
```

---

1. HTML 4.0.1 W3C Recommendation 24 December 1999. See *http://www.w3.org/TR/html4/*.

Most HTML documents use solo <BR> and <META> tags without a matching end tag. This is valid in HTML documents and conforms to the HTML 4.0 standard, but such markup can never be parsed by an XML application. Another point of significant difference is that SGML (and HTML) element names are not case sensitive, whereas XML element names are. Therefore, <LI>, <li>, and <Li>, equivalent in HTML, are three distinctly different tags in XML. Many HTML documents use a haphazard selection of upper- and lower-case element names, which would cause immediate failure by an XML application attempting to parse that document.

It's worth noting here that the common belief that "XML is the next-generation HTML" or "XML is HTML++" is very misleading. XML is a *meta-language* that defines other markup vocabularies, just as SGML defined the HTML 4.0 vocabulary. Both XML and SGML can be used to define new vocabularies for specialized application domains. HTML is just one specific vocabulary that is defined to support presentation of hyperlinked text and nontext content on the Web.

We have reviewed two of the characteristics that make HTML 4.0 incompatible with XML, namely case sensitivity and omission of end tags. A revision of HTML 4.0 has been standardized by the W3C that indeed *is* valid XML. This new standard, XHTML 1.0,[2] requires all tags to be lower case and to have an end tag or use the special empty tag syntax. XHTML can be viewed as a specific XML vocabulary used to create documents for hyperlinked presentations.

A primary objective of this book is to describe a process and design criteria for defining new XML vocabularies. Whereas HTML is a vocabulary intended for presentation, many other vocabularies are intended primarily for data exchange between applications. But even these data-oriented vocabularies may need to be presented to human users via the Web. The next two sections of this chapter first introduce an XML vocabulary for exchanging news headlines and then describe how that vocabulary also can be presented in current Web browsers.

XML Vocabularies

The HTML news headlines shown in Listing 2-1 are quite satisfactory for creating a simple display in a Web browser. But what if a portal service wants to present these same headlines in a radically different way (for example, within a table structure contained in a larger portal page)? How can these headlines be parsed and stored in a database? How can we add new non-displayed metadata about this news channel, such as the date of each headline or an optional image

---

2. XHTML 1.0 W3C Recommendation, 26 January 2000. See *http://www.w3.org/TR/xhtml1/*.

associated with the channel? HTML is severely limited in its ability to satisfy these requirements.

Over the past decade, many attempts have been made to parse HTML files and strip out the meaningful data, separating content from its presentation structure. But how do you associate the intended meaning with a paragraph or a list item? What is the purpose of the first paragraph in this news channel document from Listing 2-1? XML is designed to support these requirements and answer these questions.

The Rich Site Summary (RSS) is a simple XML vocabulary designed for exchanging news headline information without presentation markup. Netscape originally developed the RSS vocabulary for use on My Netscape Network, a customizable portal home page for Netcenter.[3] But use of RSS has grown far beyond its original application at Netscape.[4]

Simplicity was among the highest priority criteria guiding the design of RSS. The thought was that anyone should be able to create an RSS channel using only the simplest of tools, such as the Notepad editor in Windows. Using basic guidelines, an author can create a channel even with no direct knowledge of XML. Netscape's Web-based validation tool verifies that a RSS file has the correct structure, which improves productivity. A fundamental mantra of Web development can be summarized very simply: Keep it simple, provide free tools that leverage that simplicity, and users will adopt it. These were guiding principles of the original HTML, and they appear to be working for RSS also.

RSS is not currently sanctioned by a standards body but has evolved among a growing community of users. There are other more elaborate XML vocabularies designed for use by the news syndication industry,[5] but RSS is intended for widespread use by ordinary users. The current version used in early 2001 is 0.91, although a draft proposal for version 1.0 has been released.

A sample RSS document is shown in Listing 2-2. This is a valid XML document that contains all of the information from the HTML example in Listing 2-1, plus several additional elements that are required by RSS.

A couple of things should jump out at you. First, nothing in this document remotely resembles information about presentation. There are no paragraphs or lists, and the width and height elements contained by image are characteristics of the graphical image that *may* be used for formatting the display. This document's elements describe the meaning or purpose of the text or child elements that they contain.

---

3. The RSS specification for My Netscape Network is located at *http://my.netscape.com/publish/help/mnn20/quickstart.html.*

4. For more information on RSS, see *http://www.oreillynet.com/topics/rss/rss.*

5. The XMLNews specifications are available at *http://www.xmlnews.org/.*

Listing 2-2 RSS news headlines

```xml
<?xml version="1.0"?>
<!DOCTYPE rss PUBLIC "-//Netscape Communications//DTD RSS 0.91//EN"
            "http://my.netscape.com/publish/formats/rss-0.91.dtd">
<rss version="0.91">
  <channel>
    <title>UML Headlines</title>
    <description>Recent news about the
                Unified Modeling Language (UML).</description>
    <language>en-us</language>
    <link>http://xmlmodeling.com</link>
    <managingEditor>editor@xmlmodeling.com</managingEditor>
    <skipDays>
      <day>Saturday</day><day>Sunday</day>
    </skipDays>
    <pubDate>July 1, 2000</pubDate>

    <image>
      <title>UML Headlines</title>
      <url>http://xmlmodeling.com/images/xmlmodeling.jpg</url>
      <link>http://xmlmodeling.com</link>
      <width>88</width>
      <height>31</height>
    </image>

    <item>
      <title>UML version 1.3 adopted by the OMG</title>
      <link>http://www.omg.org</link>
      <description>The OMG's UML specification is the industry
        standard for analysis and design.</description>
    </item>
    <item>
      <title>Rational Rose 2000e released</title>
      <link>http://www.rational.com</link>
      <description>Rational announced the release of
        Rational Rose 2000e.</description>
    </item>
    <item>
      <title>TogetherJ 4.0 released</title>
      <link>http://www.togethersoft.com</link>
      <description>The Together 4.0 product line
        is now shipping.</description>
    </item>
  </channel>
</rss>
```

The root element <rss> includes an attribute that specifies which version of RSS is contained in this document (version 0.9 is also in moderately widespread use at this time). The root element contains one <channel>, which in turn contains several child elements that describe the channel, plus three <item> elements that describe the individual headlines. Each item is described by a title, link, and description.

But are these the only elements allowed by the RSS vocabulary? Exactly how can they be combined and in what order? How can we test whether a particular document instance is valid with respect to this vocabulary? In general, an XML vocabulary must define both the complete set of allowed terms as well as a grammar for how those terms may be combined. The XML 1.0 specification includes a Document Type Definition language that can help us answer each of these questions. The XML DTD specification was inherited from that used by SGML, but with several significant simplifications. One of the simplifications is not to allow omission of end tags in XML, as mentioned earlier in the HTML description.

The partial DTD for RSS 0.91 is shown in Listing 2-3. This is a majority subset of the RSS document structure. I have excluded several subelements of channel and a lengthy list of character constants defined in the official DTD.[6] I will not attempt to explain every detail of the DTD syntax in this example, nor do I encourage you to examine the details at this time (unless you are already familiar with DTD syntax). I include this example so that you can gain a general understanding of what a DTD contains. The details of DTDs are explained in Chapters 8 and 9 after we have examined the principles of XML vocabulary design.

The first four ELEMENT declarations define containers for other elements, and the remaining element definitions specify the innermost text values of an RSS document. The root element, rss, is allowed to contain exactly one channel; rss also has one attribute named version. A channel may contain any of nine element types, although this DTD implies an illusion of control that doesn't really exist. As defined, a channel may contain zero or more of each element, in any order. The '?' and '+' element cardinality constraints are ignored, given the way this declaration is constructed. This situation is fully explained in Chapter 8. The same situation exists for the image and item elements.

Most of the elements in the latter part of this DTD are defined with (#PCDATA) following the element name. This means that the element may contain parsed character data, or more simply, a string. But why aren't width and height defined as integer types, and why isn't pubDate restricted to a date? A DTD has no notion of these common primitive datatypes, so almost everything gets the same string type definition.

---

6. The complete DTD is available at *http://my.netscape.com/publish/formats/rss-0.91.dtd*.

Listing 2-3   RSS 0.91 Document Type Definition

```
<!ELEMENT rss (channel)>
<!ATTLIST rss
          version      CDATA #REQUIRED> <!-- must be "0.91" -->

<!ELEMENT channel (title | description | link | language
          | managingEditor? | pubDate? | image? | skipDays?
          | item+ )*>
<!ELEMENT image (title | url | link | width? | height?
          | description?)*>
<!ELEMENT item (title | link | description)*>

<!ELEMENT title (#PCDATA)>
<!ELEMENT description (#PCDATA)>
<!ELEMENT link (#PCDATA)>
<!ELEMENT language (#PCDATA)>
<!ELEMENT managingEditor (#PCDATA)>
<!ELEMENT pubDate (#PCDATA)>
<!ELEMENT url (#PCDATA)>
<!ELEMENT width (#PCDATA)>
<!ELEMENT height (#PCDATA)>
<!ELEMENT skipDays (day+)>
<!ELEMENT day (#PCDATA)>
```

These datatype restrictions and several other significant limitations of DTDs are described in much more detail in Chapter 8—but the solution is also introduced. The XML Schema[7] is a complete reconceptualization of XML document type definitions that includes a datatype definition language along with the structural specification language. The somewhat cryptic syntax of DTDs has been replaced with the use of XML itself to define the schemas for document types.

A DTD or XML Schema (or schema for either) is a very useful specification of the elements, attributes, and structures that are valid for a particular vocabulary. The schema provides documentation to authors, a template for computer-based authoring tools, and a specification used to validate the correctness of XML documents received in e-business messages. But a schema is not required by the XML standard. Many software developers create XML documents as part of their applications without ever defining a schema. In other cases, the definitions are written informally in design documents, which supports human communication but does not allow automated validation.

The main premise of this book is that the UML can be used very effectively for specifying XML vocabularies as well as other software designs. XML DTDs

---

7. For more information on XML Schema, see *http://www.w3.org/XML/Schema*.

and Schemas can be automatically generated from the UML model so that the entire software system is traced back to a common model of the application domain. Part II of this book describes the details of how this is done and the way in which the object-oriented analysis and design principles embodied by the UML are applied to improving the development of XML applications. One of the most obvious outcomes of this approach is that graphical diagrams can be created to illustrate the specification of XML vocabularies. These UML diagrams are introduced using the RSS vocabulary in Chapter 3.

XML Presentation

XML allows us to specify vocabularies that eliminate all presentation information—so how *do* we display XML document content to users? A stylesheet defines a marriage of content and presentation, for a particular user or purpose, so we might define one stylesheet for presenting RSS headlines alone on a Web page, another for summarizing them within an Internet portal, another for displaying them on a mobile phone, and yet another for presenting the content as part of a printed document. Each of these outputs might use a different presentation language (for example, HTML for the Web pages, WML for the mobile phone, and Postscript for the printed document).

A generalized stylesheet presentation architecture must enable a single XML document to be styled or transformed for each of these destinations, using the appropriate presentation language. I will introduce two stylesheet languages that are standardized by the W3C: Cascading Style Sheets and Extensible Stylesheet Language for Transformation (XSLT).

Cascading Style Sheets

The Cascading Style Sheets (CSS) specifications[8] were originally developed for use with HTML, prior to the creation of XML. However, the same principles apply to both HTML and XML, allowing a common technique and set of tools to be used. Listing 2-4 is an example of applying CSS to the HTML document in Listing 2-1.

This stylesheet is associated with an HTML document by adding one additional line within the HEAD element of that document. The following line was added to Listing 2-1:

```
<LINK REL="STYLESHEET" TYPE="text/css" HREF="rss-html.css">
```

---

8. For more information on CSS, see *http://www.w3.org/Style/CSS/*.

Listing 2-4   CSS stylesheet for HTML

```
BODY {
  font-family: "Times New Roman";
  font-size: 12pt;
}
H1 {
  font-family: Arial;
  font-weight: bold;
  text-align: center;
  color: blue;
  font-size: 14pt;
}
LI {
  font-family: "Arial";
  font-size: 10pt;
}
```

A CSS stylesheet may add presentation style information to any element type in an HTML document by selecting one or more elements (BODY, H1, and LI in this example) and listing one or more CSS styles that are associated with all elements of those types. These styles *cascade* down through the hierarchy of elements within one document, so the styles specified for BODY are also applied to H1 and LI because BODY contains them. But H1 may override any of the styles that it inherits, and it may also add additional styles that are applied to it and its children. An individual element can also specify styles that are uniquely applicable to that one element; for example, to highlight the third LI element, just rewrite as

```
<LI STYLE="color: red">
  <A HREF="http://www.togethersoft.com">
    TogetherJ 4.0 released</A>
</LI>
```

The current generation of Web browsers are finally improving on the extent to which they support CSS standards, but there are still gaps in compliance. You will also find some CSS support in non-PC devices, such as palm computers. But don't blindly apply the standard without reviewing current support by your target presentation clients. If client implementation is done generically, then the CSS styles can be applied to any document being presented, not just HTML. A CSS stylesheet will work whether it's applied to HTML elements or elements from some other nonpresentation XML vocabulary. The CSS stylesheet in Listing 2-5 provides rudimentary presentation of styling for the RSS vocabulary.

Listing 2-5   CSS stylesheet for RSS

```
rss, channel, item, title, description, link
{
  display: block;
}
image, language, managingEditor, pubDate, skipDays
{
  display: none;
}
channel title {
  font-family: Arial;
  font-weight: bold;
  text-align: center;
  color: blue;
  font-size: 14pt;
}
item title {
  font-family: Arial;
  font-weight: normal;
  text-align: left;
  color: black;
  font-size: 10pt;
}
item description {
  display: none;
}
link {
  text-decoration: underline;
  color: blue;
  margin-left: 1em;
}
```

The first style group specifies six elements that must be displayed as a `block` (that is, each one on a line by itself). Without this style, the text might all run together or have the browser defaults control its appearance in some other fashion. The second style group assigns {`display: none;`} to five elements, which effectively hides them in the presented view. Next we must handle the situation where the `title` element can appear in three different contexts within the document, as a child of `channel`, `image`, or `item`. In this stylesheet, we want the `title` within `channel` to appear with a larger font than that used for a `title` within `item`. This can be handled by CSS with a statement like

```
item title {font-size: 10pt;}
```

This means that `title` must be a *descendent* of `item` (that is, a child nested any number of levels beneath an `item`).

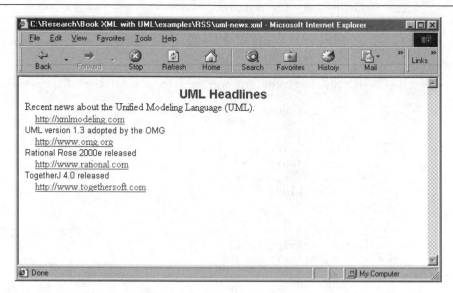

Figure 2-1 XML presented with CSS

When we apply this CSS stylesheet to Listing 2-2, the display in Figure 2-1 appears in Microsoft's Internet Explorer (version 5.5). There are, however, several major deficiencies when using CSS to present the RSS vocabulary. CSS cannot reorder the elements in a document, nor can it compute or otherwise derive new values by combining several elements and/or attributes from a source document. As shown in the figure, an `item`'s `title` and `link` values cannot be combined into one hyperlink, as would be used in an HTML document. Further, the underlined URL in the browser display is not really a clickable hyperlink. Finally, as if this weren't bad enough, the RSS Document Type Definition does not restrict the order in which `title`, `link`, and `description` elements are specified for an `item`. The second `item` might reverse the order of child elements used by the other two `item`s. A CSS stylesheet just takes them as they come.

Fortunately, we can resolve all of these issues by using a very straightforward XSLT stylesheet instead of CSS to present this document.

XSLT Stylesheets

The Extensible Stylesheet Language for Transformation (XSLT) specification[9] enables the creation of something much more powerful than CSS stylesheets.

---

9. XSL Transformations (XSLT) Version 1.0 W3C Recommendation 16 November 1999—see *http://www.w3.org/TR/xslt*.

But XML document presentation is only one goal of XSLT—it also can be used to transform a document from one vocabulary to a new XML document based on a different vocabulary. This would permit, for example, transforming a NewsML newsfeed document into the simpler RSS vocabulary for use in portals. This general transformation capability of XSLT is addressed in Chapter 10.

Transformation of an XML document to HTML is just one special case of an XSLT application. And unlike the use of CSS with XML, an XSLT stylesheet can produce an actual HTML document as its output rather than only assigning style information to existing XML elements. The stylesheet shown in Listing 2-6 will transform any RSS document into an HTML document. I won't attempt to

Listing 2-6   XSLT stylesheet for RSS

```
<?xml version="1.0"?>
<xsl:stylesheet
    xmlns:xsl="http://www.w3.org/1999/XSL/Transform"
    version="1.0" >

  <xsl:output method="html" version="4.0" indent="yes"
              doctype-public="-//W3C//DTD HTML 4.0//EN"
              doctype-system="strict.dtd"/>

  <!-- Match the <channel> element and process
      all <item> children. -->
  <xsl:template match="channel">
    <HTML>
     <HEAD>
        <TITLE><xsl:value-of select="title"/></TITLE>
        <META NAME="managingEditor" CONTENT="{managingEditor}"/>
        <LINK REL="STYLESHEET" TYPE="text/css" HREF="rss-html.css"/>
     </HEAD>
    <BODY>
       <H1><xsl:value-of select="title"/></H1>
       <P><xsl:value-of select="description"/></P>
       <UL>
         <xsl:apply-templates select="item"/>
       </UL>
    </BODY></HTML>
  </xsl:template>

  <xsl:template match="item">
    <LI>
      <A HREF="{link}">
        <xsl:value-of select="title"/>
      </A>
    </LI>
  </xsl:template>
</xsl:stylesheet>
```

Listing 2-7 HTML generated by XSLT

```
<!DOCTYPE html PUBLIC "-//W3C//DTD HTML 4.0//EN" "strict.dtd">
<HTML>
    <HEAD>
        <meta http-equiv="Content-Type"
              content="text/html; charset=utf-8">

        <TITLE>UML Headlines</TITLE>
        <META NAME="managingEditor" CONTENT="editor@xmlmodeling.com">
        <LINK REL="STYLESHEET" TYPE="text/css" HREF="rss-html.css">
    </HEAD>
    <BODY>
        <H1>UML Headlines</H1>
        <P>Recent news about the Unified Modeling Language (UML).
        </P>
        <UL>
            <LI><A HREF="http://www.omg.org">
                UML version 1.3 adopted by the OMG</A></LI>
            <LI><A HREF="http://www.rational.com">
                Rational Rose 2000e released</A></LI>
            <LI><A HREF="http://www.togethersoft.com">
                TogetherJ 4.0 released</A></LI>
        </UL>
    </BODY>
</HTML>
```

explain here the more complex syntax of XSLT; the details are covered in Chapters 10 and 11. The objective at this point is for you to gain an appreciation of what is possible using a very realistic and practical application.

When applied to the RSS document shown in Listing 2-2, this stylesheet produces the HTML document shown in Listing 2-7. (Notice that this output document is essentially identical to Listing 2-1, which was handwritten!)

When opened in a Web browser, this HTML document appears as shown in Figure 2-2. Notice that the XSLT stylesheet inserts a META tag reference to "rss-html.css," which contains the same content as Listing 2-4. This CSS stylesheet specifies font and layout styles for the HTML document, which is produced as output, and not for the XML source document. In general, this is a good design practice when writing XSLT stylesheets because the presentation style information may be the same as much of the Web site, thereby allowing CSS styles to be modified without changing the XSLT transformations.

We've come full circle with this last example. We reached this point by applying an XML vocabulary designed for exchanging news headline items that are independent of presentation style. The same RSS document could be read from or written to a database, presented within a larger Internet portal home page, or delivered to a wireless server gateway for display on mobile phones.

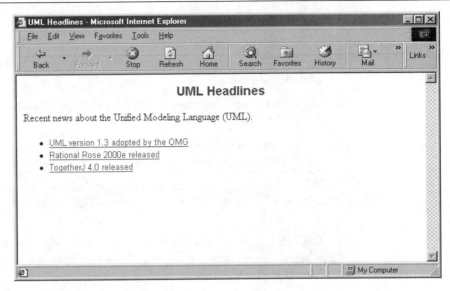

Figure 2-2   XML presented with XSLT

We created a minimal XSLT transformation from RSS to HTML that functions identically to the handcrafted Web page that began this journey. We also separated the final CSS styles so that, for example, users of a portal are able to choose their own font size and color preferences. Chapter 3 takes the next step into XML application design by introducing use of UML models.

Chapter Summary

- The simplicity and flexibility of HTML were critical factors in its rapid, widespread adoption and in the resulting growth of the Web.
- HTML was designed for presentation of text, not for description of data.
- Rich Site Summary (RSS) is a good example of a very simple XML vocabulary that has gained widespread use for describing news headline data.
- Cascading Style Sheets (CSS) allow presentation style information to be separated from both HTML and XML documents, but its use with XML has limitations.
- The Extensible Stylesheet Language for Transformation (XSLT) can be used to transform XML documents like RSS into HTML for presentation on the Web.

Steps for Success

1. Evaluate the HTML documents presented on your Web site to identify opportunities where their data content can be described independent of their presentation.

2. Search for existing vocabularies. Have XML vocabularies been created for this type of content (for example, RSS)?

3. Identify the information source. Does the data content come from existing databases or legacy applications, or is it authored by human writers?

4. When no existing XML vocabularies are available, consider the system-wide use and reuse of the information while you design the required vocabulary.

5. Develop CSS styles that are applied uniformly to your Web site, whether the content is directly authored in HTML or transformed from XML into HTML.

6. It's fine for some text information to be authored directly in HTML! Don't fall into the trap of thinking that every bit of information must be created using XML documents.

Chapter 3

What Is a UML Model?

The Unified Modeling Language (UML) defines a standard language and graphical notation for creating models of business and technical systems.[1] Contrary to popular opinion, UML is not only for programmers. In fact, UML defines several model types that span a range from functional requirements and activity workflow models, to class structure design and component diagrams. This book describes how these models are applied to specify the use of XML within the context of an e-business system. These models, and a development process that uses them, improve and simplify communication among an application's many diverse stakeholders.

UML has made great strides toward achieving its goal of a unified standard, and it is becoming the preferred language for describing business systems. The fact that UML has been accepted in practice and not just as a formal theoretical standard has spawned a rapid growth and healthy competition for UML modeling tools. UML-compliant products range from full software engineering suites to relatively inexpensive business-oriented requirements analysis tools. Several open source projects are also developing free UML tools.[2]

---

1. The UML specifications are found at *http://www.omg.org/technology/uml/*. The best introduction to UML is Fowler [2000].

2. A list of current UML tools is available on this book's Web site, at *http://XMLModeling.com*.

Models and Views

Distributed, inter-enterprise business systems are very complex beasts. Few people can fully comprehend all aspects of the system at one time. Instead, they must approach the problem as a set of subsystems, each of which is further decomposed into a set of alternate models and views. Each model deliberately ignores aspects of the system that are not relevant to its purpose. Building these models is similar to the way we cope with the complexity of everyday life by ignoring irrelevant details.

UML defines an abstract language for describing the structure and behavior of software systems. A standard graphical notation is also defined for creating views of the model elements in this language. Standard diagrams in the UML are discussed in the sidebar on this page [Booch, 1999].

■ Standard Diagrams in the UML

Structure Diagrams

Class (static structure)—Class diagrams illustrate the static design view of a system, including packages, classes, interfaces, collaborations, and their relationships.

Object—Object diagrams show static snapshots of instances of things found in the class diagrams, especially from the perspective of real or prototypical cases.

Component—Component diagrams illustrate the static implementation view of a system, showing a set of components and their relationships. A component represents a physical implementation of the logical abstractions in a model, such as classes and their interactions.

Deployment—Deployment diagrams illustrate the connectivity of physical nodes in an architectural view of the system. A node is a computational resource that provides a physical operating environment for executing one or more components.

Behavior Diagrams

Use Case—Use Case diagrams model the behavior of a system, subsystem, or a class by illustrating the relationships among a set of use cases and their actors.

Activity—Activity diagrams show the flow of activity within a system, including the sequential or branching flow from activity to activity and the objects that act or are acted upon by those activities.

Statechart—Statechart diagrams illustrate a state machine, consisting of states, transitions, events, and activities. These diagrams are most often used to model the event-ordered behavior of an object.

Sequence—Sequence diagrams illustrate the interaction among objects by emphasizing the time-ordering sequence of messages. The objects are typically instances of classes but may also represent other classifiers such as actors, components, or nodes.

Collaboration—Collaboration diagrams also show the interaction among objects but emphasize the structural organization of the objects that send and receive messages.

Note: Sequence and collaboration diagrams are alternative representations for the same model elements, so you can convert one to the other without loss of information.

Seven of these nine diagrams are used in this book to describe the analysis and design of XML applications. In the remainder of this chapter, each of these seven diagrams is introduced and then applied to modeling the structure and use of RSS vocabulary documents that were introduced in Chapter 2. Deployment and statechart diagrams are omitted, although they are often applicable to later process activities that specify design and implementation of e-business systems.

These seven diagrams could be described as independent artifacts defined by the UML modeling specifications. It's helpful, however, instead to introduce the diagrams within the context of a minimal software development process and to make the descriptions concrete using the RSS newsfeed application example. Additional references to complete software development processes compatible with the UML are provided in the References.

The next three sections describe requirements, analysis, and design workflows, and the diagrams are introduced in the order in which they are typically applied during a development project. These models would be created, extended, and modified during each iteration of the development process. You should interpret these diagrams as constituting the first iteration, where initial requirements are documented and early analysis models are created and refined with some additional design detail.

Requirements Workflow

Documentation of a system's requirements provides a focus for the scope of functionality, communication to designers, and a basis for testing whether the implementation satisfies those needs. The examples used in this chapter describe a typical iteration of system development and carve out a very narrow slice of a distributed news service that might be much larger. This is, however, a realistic scope for the first proof-of-concept iteration of a portal based on RSS news channels.

Use Case Diagram

A use case documents the interactions between the roles of a system's users (called actors) and subsets of system functionality. An actor represents a generic role of user, not necessarily an identifiable person or job title. An actor is often a human user, but also might be another system or automated software agent. A use case diagram captures a model of how several use cases depend on

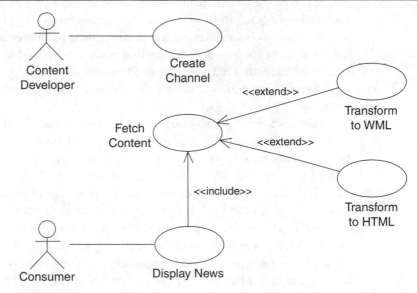

Figure 3-1 RSS channel requirements

one another and how one or more actors interact with those use cases. A simple diagram is shown in Figure 3-1.

A diagram such as this one can help guide the collection of system requirements by focusing attention on each actor and evaluating whether the associated use cases are sufficient to meet that actor's needs. In addition, if use cases not required by actors are present, then the inclusion of that functionality in the system may be questionable. Use case diagrams should enhance the communication of system requirements with each of the human users who fulfill the roles represented by these actors.

Each use case, rendered as an oval in the diagram, should be accompanied by a structured document capturing information such as a goal statement, priority, assumptions, preconditions, postconditions, and a list of activities describing how the actors fulfill the identified goal. The Create Channel use case would describe exactly how the news portal system supports a Content Developer in authoring channel content using the RSS format.

As shown in Figure 3-1, a dependency between use cases may be labeled as <<include>> or <<extend>>.[3] Display News includes Fetch Content, which

---

3. UML version 1.3 revised the standard to <<include>> and <<extend>> dependencies. You will see other books and UML tools that employ the deprecated standard names of <<uses>> and <<extends>>.

means that the first use case (referred to as the base use case) depends on the *results* or *outcome* of the included use case. This is a useful approach for factoring out common behavior that may be included by other use cases. In this situation, the Fetch Content use case does not contain any reference to the base use case but is described as an independent sequence of activities. Within the action sequence of Display News, the included use case is explicitly invoked and its results are used by the remaining steps.

Two use cases extend Fetch Content in this model. The extensions specify behavior that is optional or exceptional in the description and are not essential to the definition of the base use case, Fetch Content. In this situation, only the extension use cases knows of the relationship between the use cases. The base use case only knows that it has an extension point that may be used by other use cases.

The specification of Fetch Content must define an extension point as one of the steps in its action sequence. When the use case is executed and an extension point is reached, each of the extensions is evaluated to determine if its preconditions are met. If so, then that extension use case is executed. Any number of extension use cases may be specified as long as they cover all required circumstances in the news portal application. In this example, two extensions are specified that transform the news content into either the Wireless Markup Language (WML) or the HyperText Markup Language (HTML). This use case is analyzed in more detail with an activity diagram.

Analysis Workflow

After establishing the initial requirements, we can begin a more detailed analysis of the system structure and behavior. We'll do that by refining the use case activity flows, creating an initial structural model of the overall architecture, and diagramming the collaboration among classes that are distributed across the system.

Activity Diagram

Activity diagrams are most useful in two situations. The first situation is an activity diagram that represents a general business process workflow and often spans several use cases. These workflow diagrams are created in parallel with, or even before, the use cases are documented.

The second situation is an activity diagram created to document the flow within one use case. These are often more detailed than the workflow diagrams and sometimes represent rough pseudocode for the system logic. For example, if you needed to document the logic required for a new e-business promotional

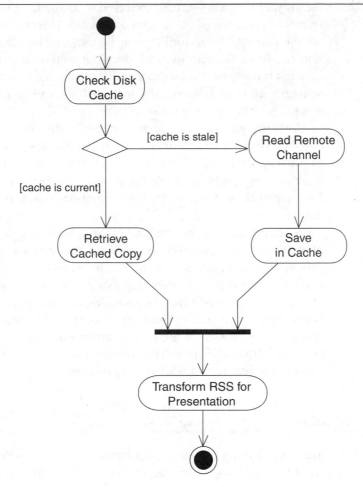

Figure 3-2   Analysis of Fetch Content use case

discount algorithm, an activity diagram would communicate these requirements to the design, implementation, and test teams.

The activity diagram shown in Figure 3-2 describes the caching requirements for the Fetch Content use case shown in Figure 3-1. This activity diagram
would supplement but not replace the text documentation for the use case.
Your inability to derive an activity diagram from the use case text description
would suggest that the text may be incomplete.

The final activity in this flow, "Transform RSS for Presentation," is the designated extension point in this use case. The extension use cases specify exactly
how the transformation should be performed, depending on the attributes of

the current actor when this use case is executed. For example, the actor would be designated as using either a wireless mobile phone browser or a desktop Web browser; this information determines whether to invoke Transform to WML or Transform to HTML.

An activity diagram has one start state, indicated by the solid circle at the top, and one or more end states represented by the bull's-eye at the bottom. This diagram includes five activities, one decision node, and one synchronization bar. Each of the transitions coming out of the decision node is labeled with a guard condition that specifies which transition is followed to the next activity. The synchronization bar requires that all inputs are received before the output transition is taken to the next activity.

Model Management Diagram

As we begin to analyze the high-level architecture for a distributed news, catalog, and portal system, we need to understand the major subsystems and their dependencies. A UML model management diagram, as shown in Figure 3-3, is the best way to approach this. A *package,* represented as a file folder icon on the diagram, is a static structure element in the UML, so this diagram is a close cousin of the class diagram. A package can contain any other model elements, including classes, use cases, activity diagrams, or other packages. But for now, we'll focus on the package as a collection of classes.

Each package in Figure 3-3 lists a subset of the classes it contains. At this early stage of analysis, class names represent a first estimate of each subsystem's responsibility without providing any detail about those classes or their relationships. In addition to the alignment of packages with subsystems, a UML model management diagram is also useful as part of a divide-and-conquer strategy for project management, especially during the early iterations of system analysis. In this case, a package represents the responsibility of one team within a larger development project.

The dependency arrows in this diagram indicate that the Portal Services subsystem depends on the other three packages, but those packages are each specified independent of the others. Both in this chapter and Chapter 2, we have reverse-engineered the RSS subsystem from existing implementations (but with limited specifications) available on the Web. Analysis and design of the Catalog subsystem is the subject of the remaining chapters of this book. The Portal Services and Personalization packages require substantial additional analysis and design, but we'll integrate them at only the highest level of interaction.

Collaboration Diagram

Having identified the architectural subsystems and a few primary classes within each package, we need next to specify how those classes collaborate in

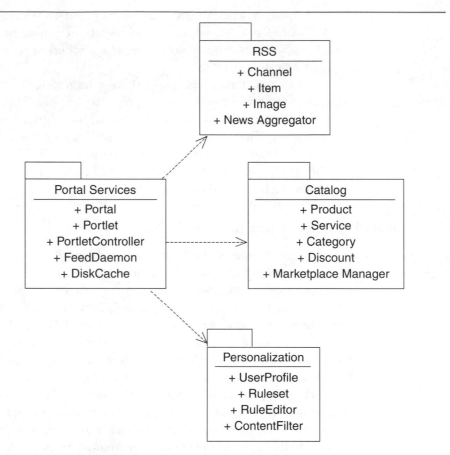

Figure 3-3 High-level subsystem packages

a distributed system. It's often useful to focus on a use case and analyze how a specific set of classes collaborate to fulfill the goal of that use case. This is referred to as the *realization* of a use case.

The collaboration diagram described here complements the activity diagram shown in Figure 3-2, and both of these diagrams specify the realization of the Fetch Content use case in Figure 3-1. The activity diagram specifies the realization as a flow of activities, whereas the collaboration diagram specifies a sequence of messages exchanged between objects. The FeedDaemon object controls the proactive refresh of the channel cache so that current content is always available for display to a user.

A UML collaboration diagram is shown in Figure 3-4. The FeedDaemon class within the Portal Services subsystem coordinates the timely update of news

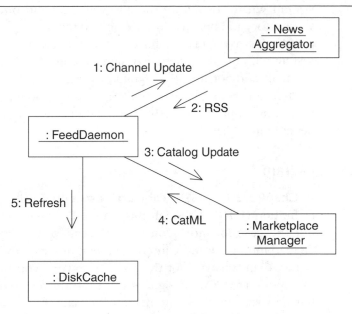

Figure 3-4 Object collaborations required for cache update

and catalog content and then automates update of the disk cache to assure optimal performance of the portal. The diagram illustrates four objects, each of which is an instance of the indicated class. In all UML diagrams, an object instance is shown with its name underlined. A series of five messages is shown being exchanged among these objects during execution of this scenario.

Our objective for using a collaboration diagram during the analysis stage is to document the role of XML documents for system integration. The Channel Update message is a request to a News Aggregator for a current copy of the channel, and the reply received is an XML document using the RSS vocabulary. Similarly, the Marketplace Manager replies with an XML document using the Catalog Markup Language (CatML) vocabulary.

As we move into the design workflow, the RSS vocabulary is specified in much more detail to prepare for implementation of the required XML processing. The CatML vocabulary design is specified in Part II of this book.

Design Workflow

The primary goal of design is to make the analysis models manageable in a realistic system. This is where the rubber meets the road when deciding whether a system will work within the allowed time and budget. Our current task is straightforward because we are specifying a design for existing systems that use the RSS vocabulary; later chapters will tackle the design of a new catalog system with more alternative designs to consider.

Four additional UML diagrams are introduced in the design workflow, all focused on specification of the RSS package shown in Figure 3-3. We begin to focus our emphasis on XML vocabulary design from this point onward in the development lifecycle.

Class Diagram

In Chapter 2, the RSS vocabulary is specified using an XML Document Type Definition (DTD). Although this simple DTD is easily understood, that's often not the case for more complex vocabularies. A large vocabulary might be divided into ten or more interdependent modules and use more advanced DTD syntax than was used for the RSS. These large vocabularies may be intelligible to experienced XML designers, but they are very difficult to share with other business stakeholders who need to evaluate the vocabulary's completeness for their requirements.

A UML class diagram can be constructed to visually represent the elements, relationships, and constraints of an XML vocabulary. With a little initial coaching (or a copy of this book), even complex vocabularies can be shared with business stakeholders. The RSS DTD from Listing 2-3 was manually reverse-engineered into the class diagram shown in Figure 3-5.

Part II explains vocabulary design using class diagrams, so I will not describe here why the model is constructed this way. Instead, I'll focus on describing the UML class diagram notation so that you'll be prepared for the analysis in later chapters. I devote far more attention to this diagram than to the others because class diagrams are of central importance when designing XML vocabularies.

This diagram contains seven UML *class* definitions (a UML class is the abstraction of a concept in the application domain). In more concrete terms, a class represents an entity such as a Channel or an Item that may be mapped into one or more tables in a relational database. A class may define a set of attributes, or properties, that represent its state and a set of operations that represent its behavior. A UML class thus maps directly to a class definition in object-oriented programming languages, such as Java, Smalltalk, or C++. UML defines a standard graphical notation specifying how these classes are presented on a diagram, independent of the implementation language.

As shown in the diagram, each *attribute* defines its type (for example, String, Date, or int). An attribute may also specify its default value, as is shown for the `version` attribute on `RichSiteSummary`. Each attribute has an optional

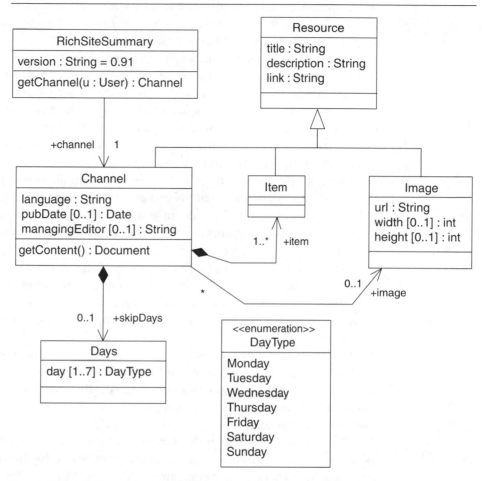

Figure 3-5 RSS vocabulary design

`multiplicity` specification that takes the form [m..n], where m is the minimum number of values allowed for an attribute, and n is the maximum number of values. A multiplicity of * represents zero or more, and a multiplicity of [1..1] may be specified using the shorthand value of [1]. An attribute with no multiplicity specification defaults to [1..1].

When examining other UML class diagrams, you'll see that attribute multiplicity constraints are quite uncommon. They are generally unspecified, meaning that the attribute is required [1..1]. However, when working with XML vocabularies you will often want to declare a child element as optional, so the multiplicity must be explicitly stated on the UML diagram as [0..1]. The diagram in Figure 3-5 declares four optional attributes and one whose multiplicity is [1..7]. You can have from one to seven attribute values for day, where each value is taken from the enumerated list DayType.

An *operation* defines its name, parameters, and return type. RichSiteSummary includes an operation named getChannel that requires a User object as its parameter and returns a Channel object. The operation signature is specified without regard for how it is implemented. For example, the returned Channel object might be produced either by simply reading a file or by a sophisticated rule engine that considers many attributes of the user's profile, target marketing rules, historical Web site visits, and so on.

Although the operations of a class are key elements of its behavioral specification in object-oriented analysis and design, they are not required when defining the *structure* of an XML document. For this reason, I will omit the operations on UML class diagrams from this point onward, but please bear in mind they are an essential part of a complete UML class diagram.

This model includes a *generalization* relationship from Channel, Item, and Image to Resource. In object-oriented modeling, generalization relationships are more commonly referred to as *inheritance*, composed of superclasses and subclasses, where the subclasses inherit their properties and behavior from their superclasses.

In this example, the three subclasses inherit the Resource attributes for title, description, and link. A subclass may also inherit the associations specified for its superclass. A subclass may then specify additional attributes, operations, and associations that are not applicable to the superclass—this is referred to as *specialization*.

The four *associations* in this diagram are unidirectional, meaning that the association is easily navigated in the direction indicated by the arrow. This does not mean that the association cannot be navigated in the other direction, but the directionality is a hint that implementations should make navigation in the primary direction convenient and efficient. One class knows about the existence of the other in the direction of navigation, but the reverse is not necessarily true.

Associations generally can be read in two directions, where the *role* on the association end describes how the related class is used. For example, in Figure 3-5, a Channel is associated with an Item using the role *item*, and a Channel is associated with Days using the role *skipDays*. In the case of unidirectional associations, I usually specify a role for only the destination end, leaving the origin role anonymous.

An association end also specifies the *multiplicity* of the destination class. So, also in Figure 3-5, a Channel contains one or more Item objects, and a RichSiteSummary has exactly one supplier Channel. The diagram notation for associations is identical to that used for attributes, except that the multiplicity expression is not enclosed by [ ].

The association from `Channel` to `Item` is a special *composition* type. Composition means that the lifetime of the associated objects is dependent on the life of their container (for example, the life of an `Item` is tied to the life of its containing `Channel`). The solid diamond on the `Channel` class association end designates this meaning. You can read this in two ways: that a `Channel` is composed of one or more `Items`, or that an `Item` is part of a `Channel`. When the object owning a composition is deleted, all if its members are deleted too. By comparison, the association form `Channel` to `Image` is not a composition, so the same lifetime dependency is not required.

Finally, the model includes a class named `DayType` that is annotated with an <<enumeration>> *stereotype*. Stereotypes are used to extend the core UML metamodel with additional modeling constructs and to visualize those extensions in a diagram. A set of related stereotypes might be grouped into a standard profile that is used to model a specialized application domain such as Web applications or real-time systems. Or, as in the case of <<enumeration>>, a set of common stereotypes is defined as part of UML specification. A UML extension profile for XML schemas is defined in Appendix C.

Enumerated types are part of many programming languages and are also useful when constructing a conceptual model of an application domain. In the RSS, we want to limit the selection of day attribute values to one of a predetermined list. By convention in UML, attributes are added to the enumeration class as a means to define the list of possible value tokens. No attribute types are necessary for these enumeration list values. In the RSS vocabulary, the day attribute of a `Days` object must have a value taken from this list.

Object Diagram

You'll find the object diagram refreshingly straightforward after working through the class diagram in the previous section! An object diagram represents instances of the classes defined in a class diagram. A separate object diagram is typically constructed for each scenario or prototype documented in a system specification. During system analysis and design, it's helpful to create a few object diagrams that document specific scenarios to be used for testing. Such object scenario diagrams provide concrete examples that facilitate communication between users, analysts, and developers.

Figure 3-6 illustrates an object diagram corresponding to the RSS document instance shown in Listing 2-2, which represents a simple news channel scenario. Notice that each *object* in this diagram includes the attributes defined by its class (for example, `Channel` defines `language`, `pubDate`, and `managingEditor`)

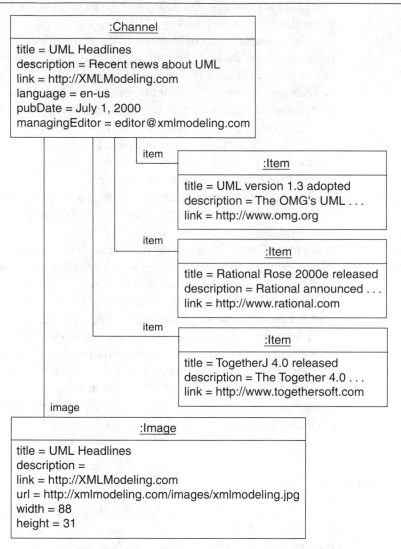

Figure 3-6 An RSS scenario of channel objects and links

plus all attributes inherited from its superclasses (for example, `Resource` attributes are `title`, `description`, and `link`). Because `Item` has no locally defined attributes, it contains only the inherited attributes. This diagram includes *links* from a `Channel` object to three `Item` objects and one `Image` object. Each link represents an instance of an association defined in the class diagram. If there is no association defined between the classes, then there cannot be a link between the instances.

It's important to emphasize that the object instance diagram is created without any knowledge or dependence on the XML vocabulary for RSS. In fact, the object instances might never be written to an XML document because they are simply objects with attribute values defined by a UML class diagram. They may, however, be written to a relational database, displayed in a Java applet, or handled in a myriad of other possible ways.

When reviewing the rules for mapping UML objects to XML documents described in Chapters 6 and 7, you will notice that object instance diagrams are used to define the scenario of each example. Those examples show that a number of different strategies exist for creating XML documents from objects.

Sequence Diagram

A significant benefit of object-oriented analysis and design is that system responsibility is assigned to classes rather than being mixed into a bunch of procedural programs or scripts. The difficult thing about object-oriented analysis and design, however, is understanding how all of the objects collaborate to satisfy some higher level goal! Both activity diagrams and sequence diagrams can help to sort out these interactions.

The use case diagram shown in Figure 3-1 defined a "Display News" use case. We partially specified the required behavior of this use case in the activity diagram shown in Figure 3-2. This activity diagram describes the caching behavior required for improved system performance. Now that we have completed initial package and class diagrams for our system, we can begin to specify how these objects will collaborate to fulfill the use case goals. Sequence diagrams are used to illustrate object interactions required for a specific scenario.

The diagram in Figure 3-7 shows how a Consumer actor initiates a sequence of messages between three objects that result in the HTML display of a news channel. Each of the vertical lines represents one object instance of the designated class, so we have a Consumer instance interacting with instances of three other classes. A primary purpose of this diagram is to show the integration of classes from the three different architectural packages that Figure 3-3 specified.

This sequence diagram is specified at a relatively high level of generality and abstraction during the first iteration of development. Some of the messages between objects are described using unstructured labels, such as "display." Other messages use operations on the target objects as specified in the class diagram, such as the getContent() message for Channel. The getChannel(User) message sent to ContentFilter specifies that the User object should be supplied as a parameter for filtering the channel contents in a personalized response. The final implementation of how these classes interact may be different or include more message interactions, but the diagram's purpose at this

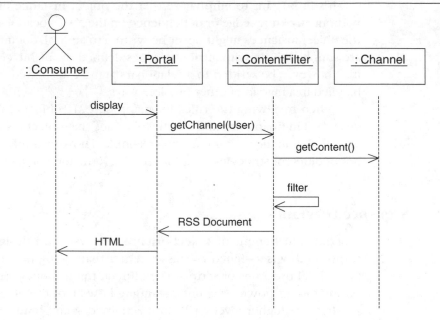

Figure 3-7   Scenario for channel display in a portal

early stage is to define approximate dependencies before the details are worked out.

Component Diagram

After designing the classes and significant interactions, we need to begin thinking about how those classes will be implemented by reusable components. This is referred to as the *realization* of a component by one or more classes.

Specification of components is a transitional task between design and implementation workflows of a project. Proper component specification and its relationship to class specifications must be considered early in the lifecycle for a good modular, reusable design. A designer must consider the relatively tight coupling of classes within a logical component, and the loose coupling that interfaces allow between components. But components also define the units of implementation, so their specification has a strong dependency on the technology platform. For example, Enterprise JavaBeans (EJB) implementation imposes a different component framework than does Microsoft's Component Object Model (COM).

These implementation level decisions are beyond the scope of this book, but we can still gain some insight from UML component diagrams as we con-

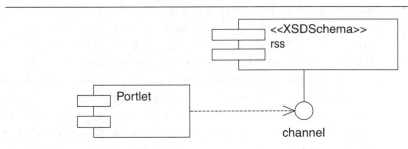

Figure 3-8   Component dependencies for RSS implementation

sider the integration of XML-based components with other components that process those XML documents. Figure 3-8 depicts two components using the standard UML notation.

The lollipop icon attached to the rss component represents an *interface*, named channel, defined by the component. An interface serves as a point of connection to its owner from other components in the system. A dashed line arrow represents a *dependency* between two model elements in a UML model. In this case, the arrow specifies a dependency of the Portlet component on the channel interface.

As part of UML specification, one or more classes are assigned to each component. In this example, all of the classes from the RSS package are assigned to the rss component. The Portlet component is undefined so far but would be realized by classes specified in the Portal Services package.

In some UML tools, code generation is controlled by component definitions in the model and by the classes that are assigned to those components. To further specify this code generation, the rss component has a stereotype label, XSDSchema, that is similar in concept to the enumeration stereotype used on the DayType class in Figure 3-5. In this case, the presence of the stereotype instructs the code generator to produce an XML Schema from the assigned class specifications. This topic is covered in great detail in Chapter 9 and in Appendix C.

The Unified Process

Seven different UML diagrams were introduced within three workflows that form the basis for a simple software development process, but a much more complete process definition is required for most applications. The Unified Process forms a general, adaptable framework for software development [Jacobson, 1999]. The Unified Process is not one specific software development process but rather a family of related processes that represent the current evolution of at least two decades of software engineering practices. It is beyond the scope of this book to describe a process in detail, but a few pointers are provided for additional reference. The Unified Process also provides a framework for the remaining chapters in this book.

A fundamental characteristic of the Unified Process is that it is iterative and incremental. On the surface, this iterative approach is a natural evolution from the sequential waterfall processes that were popular in the 1970s and 1980s. But there's more to it than that. The iterative approach is better suited to object-oriented analysis and design where a system is naturally decomposed into encapsulated classes and packages that are extended via inheritance. The incremental approach is also necessary for responding to the demands for ultra-fast development in the Web-based world of e-business.

A widely known specialization of the Unified Process is sold as a product by Rational Software. An introduction to the iterative process and a summary of the Rational Unified Process (RUP) appear in a recent book [Kruchten, 2000]. In fact, the simple view of three process workflows that forms the basis for describing the UML in this chapter is drawn from RUP. A generic iterative development process as described by RUP is summarized in Figure 3-9.

A core idea of the Unified Process and RUP is that other more specific variations can and should be defined for your industry, your company, or your unique problem domain. For example, this process has been specialized for the development of Web applications, as described by Conallen [2000]. Other books provide a more focused, detailed description of a use case-driven requirements workflow [Schneider, 1998], which is only one of six software engineering workflows defined by RUP.

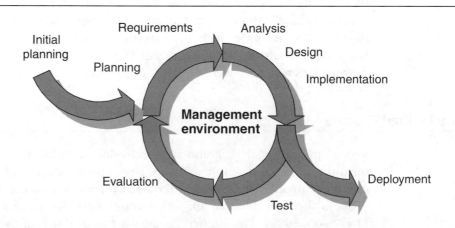

Figure 3-9   Iterative and incremental process [from Kruchten, 2000, p. 7]

This book is organized around a streamlined process for the analysis and design of XML applications. Although it does not attempt to describe a complete view of the process workflows required for a full iteration, the approach and use of UML artifacts may be applied as a specialization of the analysis and design workflow within RUP.

Chapter Summary

- The UML is a general-purpose language and graphical notation for modeling business and technical systems. It is not limited to programming and code generation.

- A large inter-enterprise system must be decomposed into several subsystem models and views so that the full range of details, abstractions, and dependencies can be shared with all relevant stakeholders.

- UML models are broadly classified into structure diagrams and behavior diagrams. Although the structure diagrams are most relevant for modeling XML vocabularies, the behavior of those vocabularies must also be analyzed in the full system context.

- UML models are applicable to each workflow within a system development process, but one type of diagram is not exclusively used in a single workflow. Class diagrams may be developed with more or less detail, activity diagrams may model either business processes or the flow of an algorithm, and so on.

- A particular system requirement should be traceable through all lifecycle workflows and through all UML models created during those workflows.

Steps for Success

We need critical input from the five stakeholder groups identified in Chapter 1 while developing the XML applications. But what development process should we follow to ensure successful completion? How can we truly achieve convergence of these stakeholder communities?

There are three principal dimensions to this convergence.

1. Convergence of requirements. As illustrated in Figure 1-1, input from all stakeholder communities is needed to determine the collective system requirements. These requirements are primarily documented as use cases and high-level activity diagrams. These diagrams drive the requirements workflow of the iterative process. Chapters 4 and 5 focus on use case models for the product catalog example.

2. Convergence of analysis and design. For B2B XML applications, there are three primary outcomes of analysis and design that require contributions from multiple stakeholder communities.

   ■ Process models of the B2B workflow, documented as UML activity diagrams

   ■ Interaction models of exchanges among B2B partners, documented as UML collaboration and sequence diagrams

   ■ Vocabulary models of the message content, documented as UML class diagrams

3. Convergence of design and implementation. The existing UML and XML technology communities must converge upon a common (or at least complimentary) approach for design and development. This convergence is enabled by the XML Metadata Interchange (XMI) standard. Part II of this book is dedicated to this topic.

Chapter 4

e-Business Integration with XML

The XML application described so far—exchanging news headlines—succeeded because of its simplicity and flexibility for distributing content that is independent of presentation format and device. The RSS vocabulary enables a basic form of e-business integration where the collaborating parties do not need to agree on an application programming interface (API) but must agree only on the content vocabulary of messages. An XML document conforming to the RSS vocabulary is all that is needed for successful communication.

The second key to this simplicity is that no special messaging infrastructure is required to exchange RSS documents. Ubiquitous HTTP Web servers are used to distribute the XML documents.[1] No reply is required or expected by the news distributor, and use of the standard port 80 on the news channel URL assures little or no problems with security firewalls that might be between the sender and receiver.

But can we scale this integration concept to large e-business applications? The exchange of news headlines requires no particular coordination between a news distributor and a recipient. The RSS vocabulary modeled as a class diagram in Figure 3-6 allows for "skipDays" that specify days of the week when the channel is not updated; however, any actor can read the channel any time it likes. More complex B2B exchanges require workflow, protocol, and security agreements in addition to vocabulary agreements.

---

1. To try a simple example, retrieve an RSS channel of current news headlines from CNN using the following URL: *http://cnn.com/cnn.rss*.

e-Business integration must therefore support the following general requirements.

- Actors agree on message content vocabularies, not APIs.
- Documents are validated against a known vocabulary but should allow for extensions.
- Message content can be transformed from one vocabulary to another.
- Workflow processes and communication protocols are defined for document exchange.
- Legacy system adapters are created that import and export XML documents.

e-Business integration should be separated from presentation of the exchanged documents. XML documents may be exported and imported from legacy systems and databases, or they may be authored as structured content without ever rendering that content for human use. The requirements described in this chapter focus exclusively on integration without presentation; Chapter 5 describes the requirements for building portal applications using the same content vocabularies.

Use Case Analysis

An analysis of e-business integration is presented at a generalized level that can be applied to many different XML applications. I describe their application to RSS integration and introduce a new distributed product catalog example. These requirement specifications can also be used as a vendor-independent specification to guide product evaluations. This use case model might be extended or modified to suit your particular application environment.

The requirements for e-business integration are divided into three categories: shared business vocabularies, process workflow and messaging, and application integration. The use cases corresponding to these requirements are illustrated with a UML use case diagram in Figure 4-1, where the three categories are differentiated using shaded icons. This diagram represents the next level of detail for two use cases that were introduced in Figure 1-1.

Four use cases in Figure 4-1 are related to the design of shared business vocabularies and schemas; these use cases are illustrated with no shading. The business analyst is responsible for defining one or more business vocabularies that are then used by the system integration specialist. The XML schemas are generated from the vocabulary definition, and those schemas are used as the basis for transforming and validating XML message contents. Because the XML

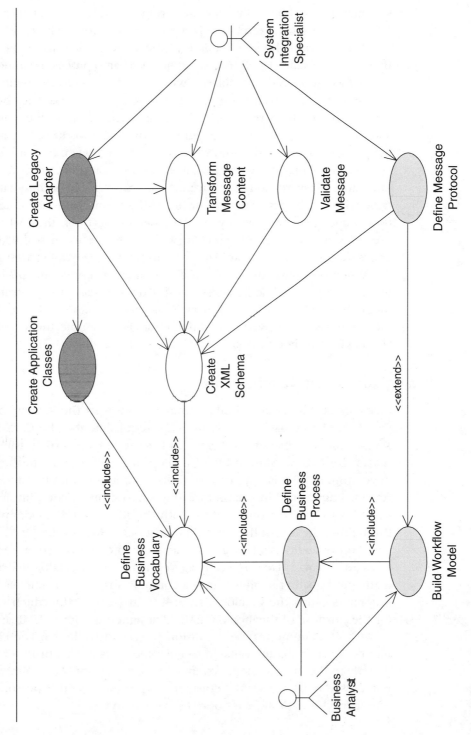

Figure 4-1 e-Business integration use case diagram

schemas are automatically generated from the UML model, that particular use case does not show a direct interaction with an actor in Figure 4-1.

The use cases shown with light gray shading are all related to process workflow and messaging. In a B2B application, the shared process definitions are as important as the shared vocabularies when coordinating the activities of business partners. The business process definition describes how and when business documents (based on the shared vocabularies) are exchanged, and the workflow model automates those processes by assigning activities to workers. Message protocols define agreements used to control conversation between two or more agents.

The use cases shown as dark gray represent requirements for application integration. The creation of application classes often can be automated, based on either the vocabulary definition or the XML schema. Although detailed description of code generation is beyond the scope of this book, the goals of these two use cases are summarized in relationship to the core use cases. Additional references for these topics are available on this book's companion Web site.

When reviewing the overall use case diagram, notice that *all* requirements depend on the "Define Business Vocabulary" use case. In application environments where the XML vocabulary is provided by an outside entity, development activities are driven by that definition. For example, the RSS news vocabulary has already been defined.

Catalog Vocabulary Requirements

I have created a fictitious B2B e-commerce business, the Catalog Exchange Service (CatX), to illustrate these use case requirements. The CatX scenario describes concrete examples of how XML is used in a realistic business situation. It also shows how UML and the Unified Process contribute to the incremental development of this application. Unlike the RSS vocabulary model that was reverse-engineered in Chapters 2 and 3 based on existing implementations, CatX is developed from scratch. Both the RSS and CatX examples are used throughout the rest of this book, but most of the focus is on CatX.

A bit of additional background: an e-commerce marketplace (also referred to as an e-marketplace) typically aggregates product catalog information from many participating suppliers into a common format and schema. This catalog schema is called the Catalog Markup Language (CatML), which was invented for the purpose of this book. CatML is designed using the UML and generated as an XML document type definition (DTD) and Schema. The catalog documents are then made available to customers via a Web browser interface or directly to the procurement system of a customer's business. When the catalog is accessed in a browser, the consumer is presented with a personalized portal interface. Our CatX system's portal is named MyCat.

The CatX example is limited to requirements for catalog aggregation and presentation. A complete marketplace solution would also include routing of purchase orders and invoices, payment authorization, and perhaps more advanced services like auctions and a workflow for processing requisitions, quotes, and price negotiation. However, aggregating product catalog data from hundreds or thousands of businesses is a nontrivial problem that's especially difficult when (as is generally the case) each participating business has its own internal representation for catalog data. Yet, these participants are highly motivated to make their products available to the millions of customers registered with our CatX service. Remember that focus as you study the following use case summaries.

Shared Business Vocabularies

The topics covered in this book focus significantly on the four use cases related to vocabulary definition. As is evident from the diagram, the rationale for this emphasis stems from the fact that all other requirements are dependent on the definition of business vocabularies and schemas.

Define Business Vocabulary

A vocabulary definition is the heart and soul of an XML application; but, as with many system requirements, there is no single right or wrong way to define the vocabulary. Also keep in mind that many applications have not just one vocabulary but rely on interdependencies and extensibility of modular vocabulary definitions. In fact, this modularity of XML vocabulary design is essential for reuse across a range of applications, just as good object-oriented design is essential for class and component reuse. It is much easier to apply similar concepts of reuse to both XML and object technology when XML vocabularies are designed using UML class diagrams.

Although a vocabulary defines the dictionary of terms that are necessary for two parties to communicate, a simple list of terms is not enough. A vocabulary must define the semantics of those terms in sufficient detail to ensure unambiguous communication between parties in a B2B application. Those semantics must define first the relationships that are allowed (or not allowed) between terms and second additional constraints on datatypes and the multiplicity of property values or members of a relationship. As described in Chapter 3, especially in Figure 3-6, these are fundamental characteristics of a UML class diagram. In addition, the modularity and interdependencies of vocabularies are well suited to UML package diagrams, as illustrated in Figure 3-4. Part II of this book is devoted to the subject of vocabulary design using UML.

There are other critical considerations when designing XML vocabularies. How will the vocabulary or set of modular vocabularies be used? Are they for exclusive use in system-to-system data interchange? If so, are other non-XML data interchange standards such as EDI already in use? As a vocabulary designer, you must consider the ease of interoperability and common terminology with these other data formats. The interoperability may be achieved by vocabulary transformation (as described in another use case), but the possibility for transformation must be considered when the new vocabulary is designed.

Another more subtle requirement in vocabulary design is consideration of user requirements when the vocabulary is applied by human document authors in addition to (or instead of) automated data interchange. As a result of reviewing thousands of messages posted to XML mail discussion lists, I can often classify an analyst or designer as either text-centric or data-centric based on his or her view of XML. (These viewpoints fall into the content developer or system integration specialist roles summarized in Chapter 1.) However, an application may not always fall neatly into one or the other categories. Be sure to consider the appropriate set of stakeholder requirements. Both stakeholder roles may need to be part of your vocabulary analysis and design, although it is possible for one person with sufficient breadth of experience to fulfill both roles.

It's common to illustrate the realization of a use case action flow using a UML activity diagram. The activities and decision branch points for this use case are shown in Figure 4-2.

I intentionally specified CatML vocabulary requirements that would be relevant to all stakeholders. The catalog data is exchanged between systems when aggregating catalogs and when synchronizing product category structures. Also, especially for data interchange, the vocabulary must specify datatype and referential integrity constraints with enough detail to support validation of XML documents received from other parties. XML documents might be transformed between CatML and other related vocabularies, such as RosettaNet. Vocabulary definition should support generation (or at least partial generation) of application program classes and/or legacy system adapters.

The CatML catalog content may also be authored directly by humans using a word processor-like interface, such as SoftQuad's XMetaL. This topic is further described in Chapters 5 and 8. Finally, documents based on CatML are presented in portals that are viewed by a range of wired and wireless client devices.

Create XML Schema

A vocabulary defines the terms, relationships, and constraints required to support communication in a particular application domain. But the UML model that defines this vocabulary is independent of the schema that implements

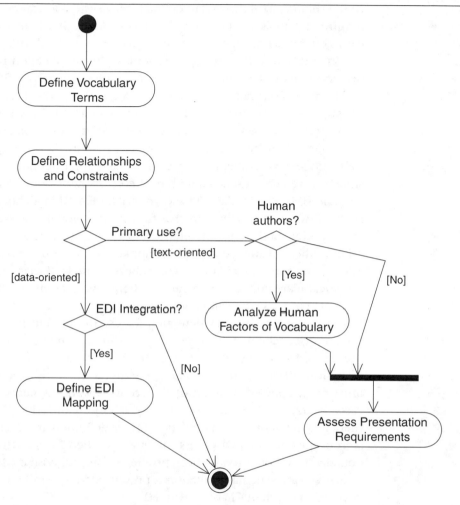

Figure 4-2 Activity flow of vocabulary definition

XML applications. The word *schema* is used here to include either an XML DTD or an XML Schema as introduced in Chapter 2. (When I use *schema* beginning with a lower-case s, I am referring to this group of XML schema languages and not just to the W3C XML Schema recommendation.) Several other schema languages have been created in the past two years, but the W3C recommends only these two.

Your application requirements will determine whether you need to use a DTD or an XML Schema in your implementation. Or you may require both types of schemas in different subsystems of your application; for example, an

XML Schema might be used to define legacy system adapters, whereas a DTD is required for tools used by human authors. But both schemas may be automatically generated from the same vocabulary definition in UML.

In addition to the choice of schemas, your application requirements also determine how strict those schemas must be in their specification of element and attribute constraints. It's sometimes preferable to use a schema with relaxed constraints that permit elements to appear in any order within an XML document, perhaps to make document creation easier. Or it's sometimes necessary to exchange document fragments that are not valid by themselves but are intended to be merged with other fragments into a base application model. Either of these situations requires a schema with relaxed constraints for order or multiplicity.

The UML activity diagram shown in Figure 4-3 highlights the key decisions required when generating schemas from a class model. The synchronization bar in the middle of the diagram indicates that once you select one or both types of schema, the remaining decisions are applied to the result of that choice.

Try to represent all known constraints in the UML class model that defines the vocabulary and then generate a schema with strictness that is appropriate for that schema's use. You might also generate both strict and relaxed schemas from the same vocabulary definition for use in different parts of your application. A strict schema will always define XML documents that are also valid for the relaxed schema (but not the other way around).

These design choices regarding generation of relaxed or strict schema must be supported by additional stereotypes and tagged values in the UML class diagram. UML stereotypes were very briefly introduced in Chapter 3, but there is much more depth available in their definition and use. A cohesive set of stereotypes and tagged values that are specified for a particular application domain are referred to as a UML profile. A comprehensive UML profile for customizing XML schema generation is presented in Appendix C. These topics are covered in depth in Chapters 8 and 9.

When vocabularies and their generated schemas are used for system-to-system data interchange, it's possible (and desirable) to produce schemas based on a relatively formal, albeit verbose, markup structure. This is true for message brokers and enterprise application integration (EAI) middleware. However, these more formal schemas may be too awkward or nonintuitive for use by human document authors. Historically, DTDs have been handcrafted and optimized for human use, but these handcrafted DTDs are often more difficult to integrate as business objects within a larger system design. We need an approach that defines a shared vocabulary definition in UML but still allows generation of schemas from the vocabulary that are intuitive for human use.

This section summarized schema and vocabulary design choices; the solution is in Chapter 9 and Appendix C.

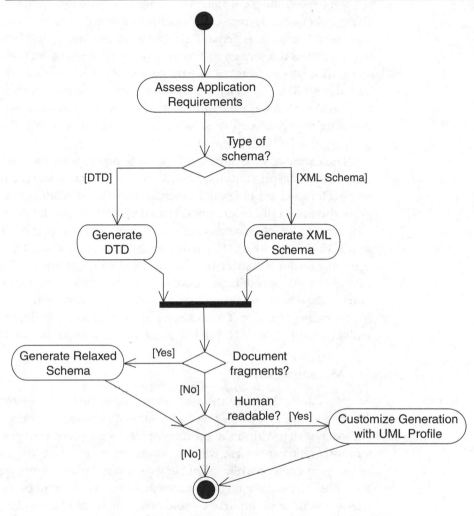

Figure 4-3   Activity flow for schema generation

Validate Message

Review the use case diagram in Figure 4-1 to establish the context for the use case named Validate Message. Validate Message depends on the schema generated from the previous use case, which in turn includes the vocabulary definition from the first use case described. The business analyst is shown as the actor role responsible for defining the vocabulary, and the system integration specialist is the key actor responsible for message validation.

So, what *is* message validation? The term *message* refers to one of the exchanges between system components in a distributed B2B application. A message, which is often represented as an XML document, has header information that identifies the sender and receiver parties, message identity, datestamp, and so on. But this use case is mostly concerned with the *message content* that includes an XML document based on a schema for the corresponding business vocabulary. Message validation in this context means to assure that the XML document conforms to its schema. This conformance is called *validation* in XML applications.

The extent of validation that is possible depends on the schema strictness, as described in the previous use case. A relaxed schema is lenient about which documents it passes as being valid, whereas the strictest schema validates documents using the full set of constraints specified in the UML model for this vocabulary. A requirement for schema-based validation is specified as part of the XML standard, so it is built into most XML parsing tools. Thus, validation of message content is generally a simple matter of parsing the document with validation activated. However, validation of large documents and complex schemas can be computationally expensive. It is therefore important to clearly state in your application requirements when, or if, a message must be validated during its processing. It's unlikely that you need to validate a document at each step of a process.

Transform Message Content

As with Validate Message, this use case includes the result of Create XML schema. Looking ahead, it appears that the results of message transformation may be included as a step within the creation of legacy adapters. It's very likely that a system integration specialist will encounter more than one vocabulary for related application content while assembling a distributed e-business application. This is due either to alternative vocabularies designed by different business partners in a B2B scenario or to differences between your vocabulary and a generic industry standard vocabulary that has been created for document exchange.

A common transformation required for e-business integration is the conversion of message content from a proprietary vocabulary such as CatML to an industry standard vocabulary like RosettaNet. The RosettaNet consortium was created to define standard vocabularies and processes used for computer product distribution, and its scope is expanding into the supply chain for computer assembly.[2] A transformation like this one can be defined and implemented

---

2. For more information on RosettaNet, see *http://www.rosettanet.org*.

using XSLT. XSLT was introduced in Chapter 2 as a means to produce HTML from XML documents, but it has more general use as a language for transforming an XML document between two vocabularies. Chapter 10 is dedicated to this subject.

It's helpful to relate this XSLT transformation back to the overall roadmap diagram shown in Figure 1-2. In that figure, an XML document is shown transformed to a variety of output types, including HTML and XML. The XML document result may be fed back into a different legacy system within the same organization or that of a business partner. That system could export its own XML document using a different schema, and the same integration cycle would be repeated with other systems.

The specifications for all of these e-business integration requirements and designs can be created using UML, as illustrated in Figure 1-2. The use case requirements span the full integration and presentation cycle. UML static structure diagrams are used to specify the various proprietary and industry standard vocabularies that enable sharing information across this global information network. Those class structure diagrams also provide the specifications required for defining transformations between vocabularies.

Process Workflow and Messaging

Process definition and vocabulary definition are equally important in successful e-business integration. Either one by itself is insufficient for automating large-scale cooperation among loosely coupled business partners. Historically, the process definitions were established as informal or contractual agreements managed as human procedures, or they were hard-wired into applications. Many EAI middleware vendors are currently including process definition and workflow components as key features of their middleware products. Although these topics are not examined in detail within this book, the next three use cases summarize high-level requirements and emphasize the role of UML in their specification.

Define Business Process

As with other UML analysis models, a business process definition can, and should, be specified independent of its implementation. The separation of this use case from the next (Build Workflow Model) reflects this separation of analysis from implementation. Our primary objective in business process definition is to model the roles of users involved in the process and identify the document types that are exchanged during the process.

A UML activity diagram is the best analysis diagram both for specifying the process steps required by each participant and illustrating the document types and vocabularies that are required for communication. An activity diagram for the CatX system specification is shown in Figure 4-4. This figure illustrates one additional standard feature of UML activity diagrams that was not described in Chapter 3. The diagram includes four swimlanes that separate responsibility of the activity flow by actor roles and vocabularies. The term *swimlane* is a carryover from common terminology used in business process diagrams developed prior to creation of the UML standard. In UML, no particular semantics are assigned to a swimlane; it serves instead as a generic partition for the diagram elements.[3]

This process flow specifies the need for transforming our CatML catalog vocabulary to a RosettaNet vocabulary before sending the update to a B2B marketplace. RosettaNet defines a large family of related vocabularies, each one dedicated to a particular Partner Interface Process (PIP). This diagram specifies the required PIP vocabulary and shows that a receipt acknowledgment is returned from the marketplace to the original supplier who initiated the process. Although this diagram is not taken from a PIP specification document, it is similar in scope and purpose to those specifications.[4]

Build Workflow Model

A workflow model specifies the instantiation of a process definition, principally by assigning workers to each role and by refining the timing and message flow required for a particular situation. A worker is not necessarily a human participant; more likely, a worker is a system component that can fulfill the requirements of an activity specified in an activity diagram like that shown in Figure 4-4.

The separation of process definition from workflow model instantiation is often not clearly delineated in vendor product implementations. However, even if a product does not allow separate definitions, the UML activity diagrams should be created as part of the use case-driven requirements analysis. Although it's desirable to import a UML activity diagram definition into a workflow management product, I have not yet seen a product that can support this. Many of the previous generation of workflow management systems have been updated to support more modular designs that depend on XML documents for integration between systems. In addition, some of these products use an XML document to

---

3. Similar activity diagrams are used to specify each Partner Interface Process in the RosettaNet standards. See *User's Guide: Understanding a PIP Blueprint* at *http://apps.rosettanet.org/ library/pipvoting.nsf/docid/rost-4bavbt*.

4. You can download a wide array of RosettaNet PIP documents from *http://www.rosettanet.org*.

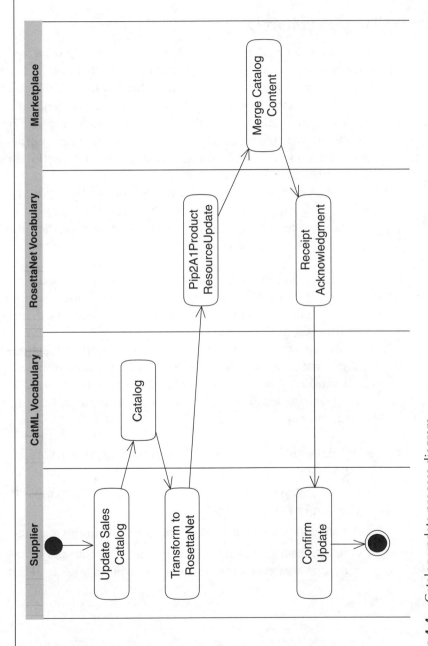

Figure 4-4 Catalog update process diagram

63

store the process definitions, so it might be possible to import or export UML activity diagram specifications through the use of XSLT transformation.

Define Message Protocol

The process definition and workflow models specify what activities are to be performed, by whom, and using which objects as input and output. An actor involved in a process might be either a human user of the system or an automated system interface. Many of the system components are automated for e-business integration, but a human decision-maker might be required, for example, to approve a purchase requisition or release an order for shipment. But we haven't yet specified requirements about how the messages will be exchanged between system actors.

The message protocol used for integration might be based on existing non-XML middleware such as BEA's Tuxedo, IBM's MQSeries, or Active Software's ActiveWorks server.[5] Experience has shown, however, that pure XML messaging has advantages over these other products when integrating systems between thousands of loosely coupled business partners, such as those found in many B2B e-marketplaces. A pure XML message protocol defines the XML message envelope structure that contains identifiers and routing information as well as the content being communicated. The content is represented using vocabularies such as RSS and CatML.

There are several proposals and prototype implementations for open XML message protocols, but most commercial implementations are proprietary or nonstandard as of early 2001. The W3C has recently formed an XML Protocol Working Group[6] whose initial charter requirements are to design the following four components:

- An extensible envelope structure for encapsulating XML data transferred between parties
- A convention for using the envelope content as a Remote Procedure Call (RPC) mechanism
- A convention for serializing application data in the message content
- A mechanism for using HTTP as the network transport for XML protocol messages that also allows for other transports, such as SMTP.

---

5. Most middleware products, including those listed here, have added support for XML message content but are still based on a proprietary message routing infrastructure.

6. W3C XML Protocol Activity, September 2000; see *http://www.w3.org/2000/xp/*.

This W3C working group will likely build on prior specifications such as the Simple Object Access Protocol (SOAP)[7] that has gained substantial industry attention. It's worth noting that a standards group did not produce the SOAP specification; it is instead the result of collaboration among several key software vendors.

Additional application level protocols may be built on the results of this work to address such issues as security, transactions, and message exchange patterns. The message exchange patterns would specify, for example, when a business partner must acknowledge receipt of a message. These types of application level message patterns define the policies of B2B e-commerce.

Application Integration

The third major category of use case requirements for e-business integration is focused on application integration. As shown in Figure 4-1, these two use cases depend on the results of three other use cases from the shared business vocabularies.

Create Application Classes

There is a growing collection of software tools available that don't require the development of custom programs for processing XML documents. For example, XSLT may be used for a wide range of transformation and presentation tasks, and several scripting languages are able to process any XML document by using the Document Object Model (DOM) interface. However, it's unlikely that an entire XML application can be built using only these general-purpose tools. Instead, application class libraries are produced from a vocabulary model, most often using the Java language. Those classes provide convenient programming interfaces for working with the business objects represented by XML documents.

There are several different ways to approach this requirement. The most common approach has been to handcraft an XML DTD or XML Schema, then run the schema through a conversion tool that generates the corresponding Java class library. Other parts of the application can be designed using the UML and generating to Java; yet other components can be written in Java. This process is shown in a UML activity diagram in Figure 4-5.

The central argument presented in this book is that all of the core application models should be designed using the UML and that both XML schemas and Java class libraries should then be generated from those same models. A revised

---

7. For more about the Simple Object Access Protocol, see *http://www.w3.org/TR/SOAP/*.

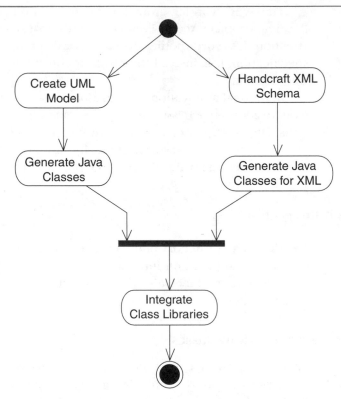

Figure 4-5 Activity diagram for split process

process depicting this approach is shown in Figure 4-6. In this case, the first activity, "Create UML Model," must specify an integrated model for the XML vocabulary and other application classes. The same classes used to represent elements of the vocabulary are also used to produce business objects in the target programming language.

Regardless of which process is followed, the application classes should be able to write and read XML documents; those documents contain elements that represent objects from the application model. This is referred to as *serialization* of the objects into XML and *deserialization* of the XML documents to recreate object instances. If you refer back to the use case for Define Message Protocol, you will see that this serialization is itemized as the third requirement to be addressed by the W3C XML Protocol working group.

There are many different strategies for generating application classes to process XML and a general acknowledgment that such flexibility is an essential part of application development. As component-based development frame-

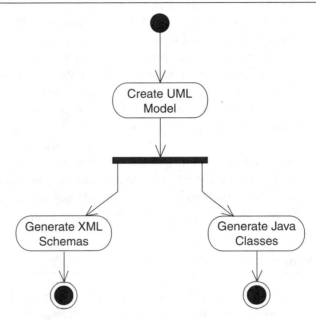

Figure 4-6 Activity diagram for integrated process

works like Enterprise JavaBeans (EJB) become part of mainstream development, these XML application classes may be integrated as another built-in persistence mechanism generated by the EJB framework tools. The companion Web site for this book lists several open source projects, commercial products, and emerging standard specifications that support this requirement.

Create Legacy Adapter

Using XML for e-business integration has become popular partly because of the difficulty in using application programming interfaces (APIs) to connect many different systems in a distributed B2B application. This difficulty is compounded by differences in operating systems and vendor product architectures that must be connected using the public Internet as a primary transport. Distributed object technology is readily available through use of CORBA, RMI, and DCOM, but integrating systems through Internet security firewalls is still a major obstacle to success.

B2B integration is usually implemented using asynchronous processes that may span seconds, hours, days, or even weeks between the start and end of the process. The adapters for legacy systems must accommodate the transaction length that is necessary for the processes in which it participates. It's most common for the legacy adapters and associated asynchronous messaging infrastructure to be implemented as part of an Enterprise Application Integration (EAI) product. These products are always bundled with a large set of adapters for common legacy systems and databases, and many of these adapters now include provisions for XML document interchange.

As shown in Figure 4-1, this use case diagram includes the use case named "Transform Message Content." As part of creating an adapter, the adapter's XML document output may need to be transformed into a shared vocabulary for use by other systems in the marketplace. Conversely, inbound documents represented in the shared vocabulary must be transformed to the proprietary document schema understood by the adapter. By including this other use case, we reflect the common requirements in our system specification.

Chapter Summary

- The Catalog Exchange Service and Catalog Markup Language were introduced. CatML is the primary application example used in this book.

- A use case diagram described the primary requirements when developing integrated e-business applications using XML. An overview was provided for each use case, but the details must be specialized for your application.

- Agreement on a shared XML vocabulary is necessary for e-business integration, but it is not sufficient for coordinating business activities.

- A business process model defined using a UML activity diagram specifies the coordination of activities among business partners.

- XML schemas (both DTD and XML Schema) were created from the vocabulary defined in UML class diagrams. The generated schema was used for validation and transformation of XML documents.

- Application integration is best driven from a common UML class model that generates both XML schemas and application class libraries, for example, in the Java programming language.

Steps for Success

1. Refine and specialize the Figure 4-1 use case diagram for your development organization and application requirements. Begin by reviewing the actor roles and possibly dividing them among more specialized positions.

2. Have you selected a vendor product platform for deployment of your application? If so, then review these use cases for alignment with that product's architecture and tools. If not, then apply these use cases as criteria for evaluating product features.

3. Which UML modeling tools are used in your organization? Do they support XML metadata interchange (XMI) import and export format for the model definition? Do they support DTD and/or XML Schema generation? Use this book's Web site as a guideline for available tools and features. Schema generation from UML is analyzed in Chapter 9.

4. Process definition and workflow modeling tools vary greatly among vendor product offerings. Some are tightly coupled with XML vocabulary transformation and application integration, while others are more modular development toolkits. Specialize these use cases accordingly, while paying particular attention to dependencies. Create a UML activity diagram describing the process development activities.

5. Application integration is dependent on your organization's development languages, middleware platform and adapter architecture, legacy systems and databases, and many other criteria. These use cases are described for a development process that is guided by UML models and the Unified Process, but each of these final two use cases must be specialized for your environment.

Chapter 5

Building Portals with XML

Most of us take the Web for granted, and we are rapidly becoming dependent on it as a source of both business and personal information. The growth and change of the Web continue at an exponential pace. But the Web is neither limited to Microsoft's Internet Explorer and Netscape's Mozilla browser nor to the typical capabilities provided by these client applications. The Web is a globally distributed information network and a massive, heterogeneous database. The dominant HTML representation for Web content has limited our ability to manipulate and repurpose this information for new uses, but the adoption of XML will enable the Web to enter a new dimension of use and usefulness.

XML enables communication of information *content* without limiting the choice of its *presentation*. The previous chapter introduced the possibility for e-business integration by defining shared business vocabularies and exchanging XML-encoded messages as part of interorganizational business processes. The Web applications introduced in this chapter recombine the XML information content with a presentation that is appropriate for the viewing device and the user's requirements. These Web applications have several significant responsibilities.

- Aggregating multiple XML sources into a unified view
- Disaggregating a large XML document into its parts
- Filtering a document's content to a subset required by a user in a particular context
- Reordering or restructuring the content for an application's user

- Formatting the content for presentation appropriate to the user's viewing device
- Managing navigation of links within and between the aggregated information content

All of these features are commonly brought together in a *portal* application. A portal provides a view into these information sources that is tailored to the requirements of a particular user. In the context of a B2B e-commerce application, this portal is generally focused on the information required in a single vertical market segment, yielding the common term *vortal* that describes these vertical portals. The use case descriptions included in this chapter summarize the requirements for designing a portal application.

But a portal is not necessarily viewed from a PC desktop nor rendered from HTML. A portal provides a view into the World Wide Web of distributed information content, and it presents that content and navigation in the most appropriate way for the current user device. In the last section of this chapter we'll look through a wide-angle lens at the emerging landscape of wireless Web applications and their convergence with more conventional wired desktop application. As you read through the following use cases, keep your mind's eye on this vision of global content accessed from many devices.

Use Case Analysis

Two primary components of the Web applications are discussed in this book: content management and portal design. These components are illustrated in the UML use case diagram in Figure 5-1. This diagram represents the next level of detail for two use cases introduced in Figure 1-1.

The use cases for content management, illustrated with gray shading, describe the requirements for business analysts and content developers, the two stakeholders responsible for defining the business vocabularies that determine the structure of XML documents created as an application's content. In addition, many Web applications depend greatly on the metadata assigned to content that will personalize the portal presentation. Personalization rules evaluate the relevance of content by matching its metadata with the profile attributes of the current user.

The use cases shown for portal design are not exhaustive, but they illustrate the principal requirements, including the dependencies on content management. The sub-panes of a portal application interface are often called *portlets* (an obvious outgrowth of applets and servlets used in Web application design). A portlet often includes a template for its presentation and an XSLT

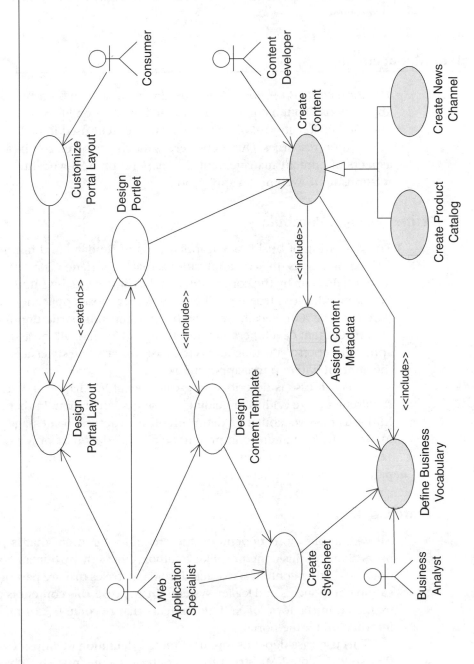

Figure 5-1 Web design use case diagram

73

stylesheet to format the underlying XML data. Most portal applications also allow users to customize the portal layout and portlet selection in their personalized view.

Content Management

The term *content management* is used very broadly in both Web and non-Web applications. It often encompasses the full production lifecycle for editing, storing, and version control of text and binary content used in on-line and printed information resources. Our focus here is much narrower, emphasizing only the aspects of content management that depend on XML vocabularies and their relationship to Web portal applications.

Define Business Vocabulary

The definition of business vocabularies is of fundamental importance to all XML applications. In Web applications, that importance is emphasized in the use case diagram by the convergence of dependency arrows upon the use case. This dependence is true regardless of whether those applications are wired or wireless. The XML vocabulary, which determines the structure of content created by content developers, defines the metadata that will be assigned to guide application personalization and is the basis for creating stylesheets that present the content within portal applications.

This use case is described in greater detail in Chapter 4, where the same requirements are critical in guiding e-business integration. In that situation, the XML business vocabularies determine the structure of message content and identify the document components exchanged as part of a workflow. That same content may be extracted from B2B messages and presented to users as part of a vertical market portal.

Create Content

All Web applications depend on the creation of content that is presented to users. Some of this content is likely authored directly by human content developers and other content is extracted from databases that are part of other application components and legacy systems. In any case, this content is produced or extracted in the form of XML documents that become the primary source of information for the portal.

This use case depends foremost on the definition of a business vocabulary that specifies the XML structure of content documents. This chapter's examples focus on creating product catalog documents using the CatML vocabulary, although a complete application architecture would likely include several such vocabularies specifying other components in addition to the catalog content. The RSS vocabulary described in previous chapters is likely to be incorporated into portal content management. When legacy system integration is involved, their business vocabularies define the structure of XML documents extracted from those systems' database queries or transaction messages.

As shown in Figure 5-1, the Create Content use case is further specialized by two additional use cases; the hollow-headed arrow indicates a generalization relationship. UML class diagrams use generalization to represent inheritance of attributes and operations by subclasses; in a use case diagram the same type of relationship indicates that one use case specializes the behavior of another, more general use case. Create Content is specialized by use cases that describe the requirements for Create Product Catalog and Create News Channel.

Create Product Catalog

In our example application, the product catalog is created as an XML document based on the CatML vocabulary. This vocabulary may be used in many different ways as a guide to catalog creation. The most straightforward approach is to use an authoring tool such as XMetaL from SoftQuad that enables a word-processing interface for any XML DTD. The sample screen shot of XMetaL in Figure 5-2 illustrates a "normal view" of a product catalog. Alternatively, it supports viewing and editing XML documents in text-mode where all of the underlying XML tags are exposed.

XMetaL applies a CSS stylesheet to the XML document in order to produce the formatted view. An author can add new products or edit existing products using this word-processing like interface. The dialog panes on the right are created from the CatML DTD and are used by an author either to pick new types from a list of valid XML elements or to change attribute values for the current element being edited.

XMetaL was used to author the following XML definition of a CatML Product.

```
<Product xmi.id="sku-Z505JE">
  <CatalogItem.name>Sony VAIO Z505</CatalogItem.name>
  <CatalogItem.description>
     The small size and weight of the Sony VAIO Z505 ...
  </CatalogItem.description>
  <CatalogItem.listPrice>
    <Money currency="USD">
      <Money.amount>2499</Money.amount>
    </Money>
  </CatalogItem.listPrice>
  <CatalogItem.sku>Z505JE</CatalogItem.sku>
  <Product.photoURL>/examples/images/SonyZ505.jpg
  </Product.photoURL>
```

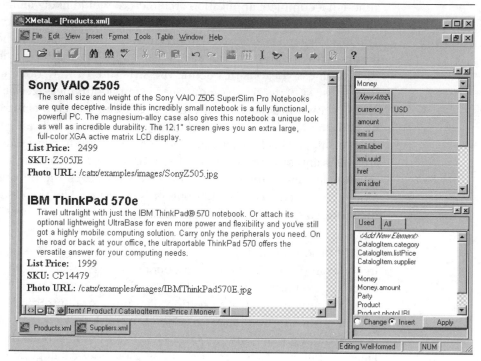

Figure 5-2 Editing a product catalog in XMetaL

```
<CatalogItem.category>
  <Category href="Taxonomy.xml#Laptop_Computer_System"
            xmi.label="Laptop Compter System"/>
</CatalogItem.category>
<CatalogItem.detail>
  <Resource href="http://www.ita.sel.sony.com/jump/z505/"
            xmi.label="Product Specifications"/>
</CatalogItem.detail>
<CatalogItem.supplier>
  <Party href="Suppliers.xml#Sony" xmi.label="Sony""/>
</CatalogItem.supplier>
</Product>
```

This CatML example, along with its vocabulary definition, DTD, and XML Schema, are described in great detail throughout the remainder of this book.

Create News Channel

News headline summaries are becoming ubiquitous in Web portals. In many cases, these news channels are focused on general headlines from sources such as the *New York Times* or CNN, though the same techniques can be applied to create customized news feeds for any topic. Vertical market specialized news-feeds are especially relevant in B2B vortals. The information used to produce many of these headline listings is communicated using the Rich Site Summary (RSS) vocabulary.

Because RSS is simply another XML vocabulary, we can easily transform our CatML catalog information into the RSS structure. If we produce an RSS head-line document that represents special promotional offers from our product cat-alog, then this "news channel" could be immediately and easily used by any of the consumer portals available today. Each promotional item listed in the RSS document would include a hyperlink pointing back to the relevant page of our catalog portal, thereby allowing the consumer to get additional information or to purchase the product. This use of RSS is illustrated in a detailed example in Chapter 11, in the section "A Portlet for Promotional Discounts."

Assign Content Metadata

After the content documents have been created, it is often necessary to assign additional metadata attributes that describe the type of content contained within each document. These metadata might include general attributes such as title, subject, and language, or application-specific attributes such as target audience demographics, product category, and price range. In either case, the metadata are used either to enable more precise searching of the Web site or to write personalization rules that match content with user profile characteristics.

The use case diagram in Figure 5-1 specifies that Create Content includes Assign Content Metadata, which in turn includes Define Business Vocabulary. Thus, the metadata assignment depends on the definition of one or more vocab-ularies, although those vocabularies may be drawn from one of the shared pub-lic repositories. For example, an application could use a standard set of metadata attributes defined by the Dublin Core[1] or combine them with other standard or customized metadata vocabularies specific to e-commerce.

Portal Design

The most important functions of a Web portal are to aggregate content from several sources and to personalize the presentation for each user or user role. Our example portal for the catalog exchange service is called MyCat. This por-tal allows users to personalize their selection from a variety of content sources,

---

1. The Dublin Core is a metadata vocabulary intended to facilitate discovery of electronic resources—see *http://purl.org/DC/*.

including a category browser, product search, current promotional discounts, and so on. Each user can choose which sources to display, where to display them on the screen, and what colors to use for text and background.

A Web page as viewed in a browser is often the result of combining the output from several server-side components. Each component, or portlet, is responsible for producing a part of that page and is dedicated to one of the aggregated content sources. In the simplest architecture, one component might be responsible for the heading and menus, another for the footer, and a third for the main body of the page content. A page, however, can be decomposed into any number of regions, and a component can be assigned to produce the content within each region. A portal server provides a framework for configuring (and reconfiguring) the regions, including their size, relative location, presentation style (often called "skin"), and assignment of a component that will produce each region's content.

This architecture and terminology is used by the open source Apache portal server named Jetspeed.[2] The Jetspeed server is used in Chapter 11 to illustrate portal design and especially to describe XML to HTML transformation using XSLT. A sample screen shot of Jetspeed used to present our demonstration MyCat portal is shown in Figure 5-3.

The Jetspeed portal framework controls the overall screen configuration in this example. Each sub-pane is produced by a separate portlet, and each portlet draws its content from one or more XML documents, which are combined and formatted by an XSLT stylesheet. The requirements for each of these functions is summarized by the following use case descriptions.

Design Portlet

A portlet's design determines the content and appearance of one region within the portal screen. The following design questions must be answered.

- What is the source of content data (for example, file name, URL, database)?
- How frequently will the data be refreshed?
- What is the source data format (for example, XML, HTML, comma-delimited text)?
- If the source is XML, what vocabulary schema defines its structure?
- What kind of filtering is required to personalize content for the current user?

---

2. Information on the Apache Jetspeed project can be found at *http://java.apache.org/jetspeed*.

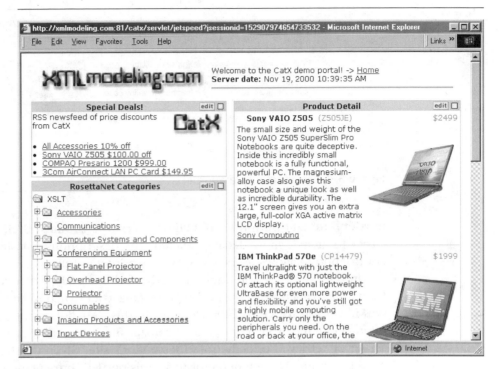

Figure 5-3 MyCat portal screen in CatX application

- What content language is required for the current user?
- How will the data be presented? What is the layout structure, color, font, and style?
- How much space is required for its presentation?
- What interactive controls are required (for example, edit, search, submit)?

Let's narrow our focus to one of the portlets shown in the MyCat portal. Figure 5-4 shows the product display portlet that presents the details about one product selected from the catalog. As shown previously, the XML document used to produce this portlet was authored in XMetaL.

A portlet is not required to include the title bar and control buttons as shown in this example; these design decisions were made as part of this use case. This portlet could also be displayed with a plain border or with no border or title at all. These simple configuration choices are available in the Jetspeed portal framework and in most other portal server products.

As you'll see in later chapters, the CatML catalog vocabulary includes links to other product detail resources in addition to the description shown in this

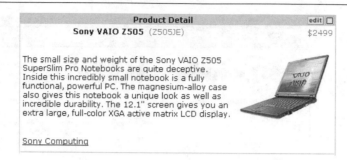

Figure 5-4   Product display portlet

portlet. The Edit button should allow users to customize their presentation either to include more detail or exclude the description as desired. The other control button allows users to display this portlet as full screen.

In the prototype application underlying this portal, portlet content is read from a file named `Products.xml` that contains data structured according to the CatML vocabulary. One of the elements in this XML document contains a URL reference to the product image, so the image file may be co-located on the same server or retrieved directly from the vendor's site. Given this information we need to design the content template for this portlet's presentation and select an approach for transforming the XML data into HTML. These decisions are the result of the next two use cases. You can trace these dependencies in Figure 5-1 where the Design Portlet use case includes Design Content Template.

Design Content Template

A content template determines the structure of data presented in an individual portlet. In the spirit of proper use case specification, I make no assertions about *how* the content template is implemented; a use case only specifies the goal that must be achieved and a course of action that is followed when an actor invokes the use case. The primary goal in this case is to specify which product data items should be displayed and how those data should be positioned within the portlet. In the example shown in Figure 5-4, the CatML elements for product name, sku, list price, description, photo URL, and supplier are positioned within a simple two-column table structure for presentation.

There are many alternative choices available for implementing a content template, although some of these choices may be restricted or determined by your particular portal framework. Some portal server products are based on JavaServer Pages (JSP) and Enterprise JavaBeans (EJB) for their portlet implementation; others might depend on Active Server Pages (ASP). The Apache Jetspeed portal has a flexible architecture that could include the results of a JSP within the portlet content, or the content may be produced by a completely custom Java class implementation. However, for flexible rapid development, a Jetspeed portlet may use an XSLT stylesheet to both structure its content and to transform the XML data into that that structure. The next use case is optional but may be included to implement the content template and/or specify the XML data mapping.

Create Stylesheet

The stylesheet accepts XML data as input, then filters, reorders, summarizes, and presents the data as required to populate the content template. But the final presentation style applied to that data is partly determined by the user's device that displays this portlet. You could extend the use case diagram shown in Figure 5-1 to include several specializations of the Create Stylesheet use case. Similar to the way that Create Content has two sub-use cases that describe requirements for specialized types of content, you could define additional use cases for Create HTML Stylesheet, Create WML Stylesheet, and so on. Each would address the unique requirements of those presentation formats.

A portlet is not necessarily limited to a single stylesheet. Rather, a portlet is often designed with a set of alternative stylesheets, where each is specialized to a particular client application, such as Microsoft Internet Explorer or Netscape Mozilla, or to a type of device, such as a desktop PC, mobile phone, or PDA. The portal server dynamically selects an appropriate stylesheet for each portlet when a user's browser requests the portal Web page to be displayed.

The UML activity diagram shown in Figure 5-5 illustrates the decisions required to select a stylesheet for a user's device. The first decision uses information provided in the HTTP header to determine the user agent type and version, then the flow branches one of three ways. The HTTP header information also declares which MIME types are accepted by that user agent, thus determining whether a mobile device can accept advanced stylesheets using WML Script. The Wireless Markup Language (WML) has been standardized as part of the Wireless Application Protocol (WAP).[3] WML documents are similar to HTML documents, but the markup language is specialized for the requirements of small Web browsers in mobile devices.

Web browsers contained in mobile devices are similar in concept to the familiar desktop browsers, but their capabilities are much more restricted. The most important point to remember from this use case summary is that a common

---

3. For more information on WML and WAP, see *http://www.wapforum.org*.

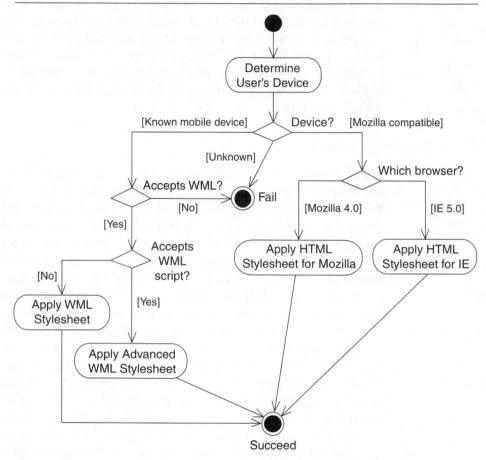

Figure 5-5 Activity flow for selecting a stylesheet

XML document can be transformed into alternative presentation markup languages applicable to each of these device types and capabilities.

XSLT is a powerful transformation and presentation language that can fulfill many of the portal requirements listed in the introduction to this chapter. One XSLT stylesheet may aggregate the data from several XML source documents, where the specific source documents and elements from those documents are selected by the stylesheet rules at the time of presentation. Conversely, a stylesheet may disaggregate a large XML document by filtering its content based on stylesheet parameters. The stylesheet can also create HTML or WML hyperlinks in the presented portlet content based on a variety of advanced linking elements included in the source XML documents. However, the processing overhead of XSLT requires careful attention to caching of results in order to assure a scalable portal server. All of these XSLT features are described in greater detail in Chapters 10 and 11, along with examples of transforming CatML into HTML.

Design Portal Layout

Review Figure 5-1 to reestablish your context for this next use case. Assume that a Web application specialist has designed several portlets that pull their data from a variety of different sources. Each portlet design has made its own choices for structure and presentation of its data; the portal itself is not concerned with these decisions. However, the overall portal framework contributes configuration control and layout algorithms that are applied to the current set of portlets selected for display.

The portal layout may differ radically when viewed from alternative client devices. For example, a mobile phone cannot display all portlets simultaneously positioned within a large screen. Instead, a mobile phone treats each portlet as a card in a stack, and the layout must include navigational controls that enable a user to select the current portlet from a structured menu. In this situation, the portal layout is focused on *navigational* rather than positional layout within a screen, although both are equally important in their own contexts.

The specific details of how these layout algorithms work and how a designer applies them are not critical to this discussion. Each portal server vendor has made its own unique choices for how this is done, based in part on the underlying software platform used for the portal server implementation. Some additional details of portal layout are provided in Chapter 11 where I describe Jetspeed's Portal Site Markup Language (PSML) applied to the design of our CatX portal implementation. But first we must continue to focus on how such a markup language is designed.

Customize Portal Layout

One of the ubiquitous features of Web portals is the ability for each user to personalize the portal content and presentation style. In most cases, an end-user cannot create substantially different portlets but can pick from a set (maybe a very large set) of predefined portlets designed by the portal Web specialists. Figure 5-1 shows a Consumer interacting with the Customize Portal Layout use case; that use case includes the results of the portal layout design produced by the Web specialist.

The most radical customization allowed by portals is for a user to add or remove portlets from his or her current display. This permits the user to alter substantively the information aggregation provided by his or her personalized view. The second most significant customization is for the portlet designer to include an "Edit" control on the portlet title bar that gives a user control over the content of an individual portlet. The design of such a customization is very specific to each portlet's implementation. A good example of this feature is the stock ticker portlet available on most mass-market Internet portals. In this case, the Edit button allows, at minimum, customization of a user's preferred stock portfolio.

The third type of customization allows a user to control the skin applied either to individual portlets or to the portal as a whole. The term *skin* is frequently used in consumer-focused Web applications. Its implementation and capabilities vary. In the simplest case, a skin defines the background color, text color, and font applied to the display; in more advanced designs, a skin defines a collective theme of styles, button images, background wallpaper, and so on. Most business-oriented portals support skins that customize fonts and colors.

When the portal is viewed from small devices such as mobile phones, the customization should allow users to control order and hierarchy of navigational menus, in addition to the other customizations described above. The specifics of mobile device Web applications are beyond the scope of this book, but it's interesting to speculate about where they are headed.

Wired and Wireless Convergence

We're entering an era where small mobile devices are becoming an integral part of the Web's global information network—wherever you go, there they are. In the future, mobile applications will work best in situations where they can capitalize on the core virtues of wireless networks: convenience, personalization, and location. Such thinking is driven by the idea that putting the Internet in the palms of our hands will give both business professionals and consumers ever-increasing access to data and information, forcing e-business strategists to rethink and redesign their technical architectures and e-business processes. The job of organizing, managing, and targeting Web content for delivery to wireless devices—in addition to traditional wired access—has become much more challenging.

Oracle Corporation is working toward a mobile Web architecture similar to what I have described in this chapter.[4] Figure 5-6 illustrates Oracle's Portal-To-Go architecture. Oracle has implemented a Java servlet toolkit for producing XML from database queries and other Web content and then transforming that XML to a range of browsing devices. I'm not highlighting this particular design as a recommendation, but their diagram is a good illustration of products being

---

4. See the Oracle Corporation white paper on *Customizing Data Presentation* at *http://technet.oracle.com/tech/xml*.

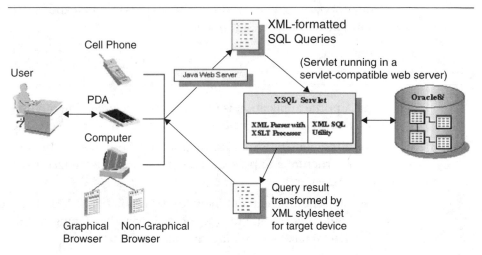

Figure 5-6 Oracle's Portal-To-Go architecture

created by most major enterprise software vendors.

The consumer-oriented wireless applications deployed to date have emphasized some rather bland uses, such as purchasing books via mobile phones, or services like real-time airline schedule information and reservations that offer significant value and convenience. Mobile entertainment applications and games have been a big hit in Japan, although these areas have had little penetration in the United States. The European market has moved very aggressively into new services that offer location-specific convenience, such as paying for parking by keying a parking location code into your mobile phone.

The B2B market holds the potential for many new, high-value uses of wireless technology. Most e-marketplaces or exchanges depend on a portal interface that is an integral part of supply chain or procurement operations. Some of the information sources displayed within these portals would benefit from convenient, remote access. For example, as auctions and bidding become commonplace features of these exchanges, it may be critical for the bidder to be in continuous contact with the status of an auction for a large commodity purchase. In addition, the buyer may need to monitor the status of several commodity markets to determine if or when to place a bid. A mobile phone or wireless PDA is an ideal access device for this requirement.

If this auction data were made available using an XML vocabulary, then all of the concepts described in this chapter could be applied. This data is only one of many aggregated sources that buyers would want on their desktop computers in a more comprehensive portal. But several of these portlets would be redirected and appropriately styled for presentation on the mobile portal. I look forward to seeing more of these kinds of applications that offer significant value, in addition to convenience.

Chapter Summary

- A portal application is responsible for aggregating multiple sources of information content, customized for each user's needs and context.
- If the content is in XML, then XSLT stylesheets can be used to filter, restructure, and present the same source customized for each user or device.
- Content management includes definition of the XML vocabulary, creating content according to that vocabulary, and assigning additional metadata that facilitates searching and personalization.
- Portal design includes specification of the portlets, content templates, and stylesheets required to present content within the portal.
- A portal often allows each user to select and reposition portlets within the overall presentation format.
- A portal is not necessarily displayed on a desktop PC, but the same general concepts apply when designing wireless applications using XML content.

Steps for Success

1. Customize the Web design use case diagram for you situation, especially in the areas of Create Content and Create Stylesheet. You may also wish to specialize the use case for Design Content Templates based on your selected portal platform. Add or remove actors as appropriate to your organizational structure. For example, you may wish to add a Graphic Designer as a new stakeholder and expand on the use cases for interface design.

2. Write a description for each use case in the diagram that explains how its goal will be achieved for your portal platform and content types.

3. Apply these use cases as requirement guidelines and evaluation criteria when selecting a portal platform for your business.

4. Emphasize flexibility in your choice of a portal platform. Future applications will likely require convergence of wired and wireless connectivity—PCs, mobile, and interactive television devices—and ever-expanding sources of information.

5. Choose your content vocabularies carefully and look for common vocabularies shared by your business partners. If necessary, select authoring tools that support the chosen vocabulary.

PART II

XML Vocabularies

Chapter 6
Modeling XML Vocabularies

Part I of this book focused on the business models and architectures for e-business applications. The business models for our CatX catalog exchange service are specified in accordance with the Unified Process (that is, they are use case–driven and architecture centric). The use cases for e-business integration and portal development were further specified through realizations as activity workflow processes in Chapters 4 and 5. We are now able to plunge into the methods for developing the vocabularies that enable distributed agents to communicate with one another.

The CatX vocabulary definitions are specified using UML static structure diagrams. It is important to understand that there is *always* a model—either explicit or implicit—underlying each vocabulary. In addition, a model is usually interpreted relative to a context or perspective. The stakeholder groups described in Part I provide the context perspectives for our analysis. In other words, we are supplying vocabularies that enable our stakeholders to communicate in a B2B e-commerce application.

What Is a Vocabulary?

Asking "What is a vocabulary?" is a lot like asking "What is e-business?" There are many opinions on both subjects. Fundamentally, a vocabulary is the list of terms used in communication; but a basic vocabulary does not define its semantics. The semantics specify constraints about how each term can or cannot be used in combination with other terms. The semantics also specify a taxonomy or classification structure for abstract concepts and specialization of terms. For example, a basic vocabulary might define this list of terms, sorted alphabetically: airplane, automobile, car, engine, vehicle, and wheel. But is an automobile the same thing as a car? How is a car related to a vehicle? To an airplane? What is a well-formed automobile with respect to the number of wheels that it can have? Can an automobile have four engines as does an airplane? I have seen an airplane fly, so can a car fly also? All of these questions should be answered by a complete definition for this vocabulary's semantics.

Most current XML vocabularies answer such questions incompletely; some are merely lists of terms. There is, however, a wealth of research and literature directly related to this issue. Ontology, which examines our understanding of the conceptual structure of the world,[1] has long been a part of knowledge representation in the field of artificial intelligence. The growing importance of ontology in e-business was recently evidenced by VerticalNet's appointment of a Director of Ontological Engineering.

Although grammar and taxonomy contribute to the semantics of terms in a vocabulary, ontologies include richer relationships and constraints among those terms. Ontology is more than a taxonomy or classification of terms. Ontological engineering therefore provides a conceptual basis for representing and communicating knowledge about a topic as well as a set of relationships and properties that hold for the entities denoted by that vocabulary.

Ontology can also serve as a guide to evaluating proposed industry standard XML vocabularies. Some vocabularies are limited to lists of XML tags having few relationships other than a shallow containment hierarchy. Such vocabularies carry little meaning in communication among distributed e-business agents. The intended meaning of terms must be embedded within the application programs that process these documents, leading to very inflexible designs. On the other hand, some vocabularies have much more richness in their definitions, but these definitions are often provided as text documents that describe a complete semantic specification for human readers and are not for direct use by e-business systems. We need a vocabulary representation that supports both presentation to humans and processing by applications. For our purposes "vocabulary" will have a meaning closer to that of ontology.

UML models can capture the semantics for an application domain model, and the definitions can be directly processed by e-business systems. The UML also standardizes the graphical notation for use by human readers. The four chapters in Part II, beginning with this one, step through the concepts and stan-

---

1. For addition background on use of ontologies in e-commerce and distributed systems, see the Web site *http://www.ontology.org* or the Foundation for Intelligent Physical Agents (FIPA) at *http://www.fipa.org*.

dards for translating UML class and object models into XML vocabularies and documents. Chapters 6 and 7 concentrate on defining a vocabulary's structure and relationships and focus on the decomposition of UML object instance diagrams into XML documents. Chapter 8 reviews the current standards for defining schemas used to validate XML documents, and Chapter 9 reviews the process for automatic generation of XML DTDs and Schemas from UML class models.

We begin this journey with a more complete description of the vocabulary requirements for our CatX service, first in words, then as a UML model.

CatML Vocabulary

The Catalog Markup Language (CatML) is used to author, store, process, and exchange product catalog data in B2B e-commerce applications. It is also used to deliver catalog content to a personalized Web portal, where the final selection and presentation are determined by the portal's personalization rules and stylesheets. The UML model, as a specification of the CatML vocabulary, describes the business objects required for businesses to communicate about catalog content. CatML is not an industry standard but was created for the purpose of examples in this book. It is, however, quite realistic for illustrating what might be designed and serves as a launching point for new projects.

CatML vocabulary must enable a product marketing manager to create any number of different catalogs for offering products to targeted groups of customers. For example, there might be a comprehensive annual catalog, plus new monthly and seasonal catalogs that both update the offering with new products and highlight subsets of the total product line; also, the catalog must include both products and services. No doubt the marketing manager would also like a flexible model for creating product bundles that provide special pricing on combinations of existing products. You'd be in line for a big raise if the catalog could be easily extended with new undefined catalog items in a long-term plan!

This catalog must support businesses serving as intermediary distributors, where the catalog offers products aggregated from many different suppliers. Also, because this is an international business, its product prices must be represented in different national currencies, and the catalog must include product documentation in the appropriate language for each nationality.

Finally, there are many different categorization schemes used for organizing the catalog content. The sales manager should be able to assemble a special promotion catalog directed to resellers, where the products are categorized by industry standard product codes. Alternatively, the on-line Web catalog is personalized with products whose features match the browser's user profile and are categorized by support for national language. Of course, any other categorization scheme dreamed up by the sales manager must be quickly implemented in future catalogs.

Given these vocabulary requirements, how do we employ UML to model their structures, and how are these UML models mapped into XML documents and schemas? These subjects are the focus of Part II.

Simplified Product Catalog Model

Although the textual description of a business vocabulary is useful as a general definition for human readers, it lacks the precision required by a formal specification for an industry standard and is not machine readable. A UML static class structure model satisfies both of these requirements. In the UML, a structure diagram typically documents a view of related class definitions that may be divided into several packages or namespaces.

An XML document could be defined by a set of simple class definitions that specify all of the basic terms required by an application's vocabulary. However, most vocabularies also require additional grammar rules specifying how these basic elements are assembled into composite structures. The UML includes a rich set of relationships that may be defined between classes or between other kinds of model elements. I'll start with a small subset of basic UML associations in this chapter, then in Chapter 7 we'll see how more complex UML structures can be modeled and mapped into XML hyperlinks within and between documents.

The simplified CatML vocabulary model includes eight classes representing the catalog, its items and suppliers, internationalized pricing, and the units for measuring quantities of those items. This model is shown in Figure 6-1.

A catalog is composed of zero or more catalog items, and each catalog item is associated with exactly one supplier organization. However, a catalog item is a general entity for representing the more specific types of products and services; other subtypes, such as a Warranty or a ProductBundle, could be added.

An independent class named Money is defined so that the prices of catalog items may be internationalized for multiple currencies. The Money class includes an attribute containing the amount value and an attribute specifying which currency is used to measure that amount (for example, USD for U.S. dollars). This class definition for Money is generic and may be reused in other vocabularies. The Money class is used as the data type for the CatalogItem listPrice attribute. In the UML class diagram shown in Figure 6-1, this class attribute is specified as having the type Money.

Finally, the model includes two classes named UnitOfMeasure and UnitOfTime, which are annotated with an <<enumeration>> stereotype. We want to limit the selection of measurement units in the CatML to one of a predetermined list, so by UML convention, attributes are added to the enumeration

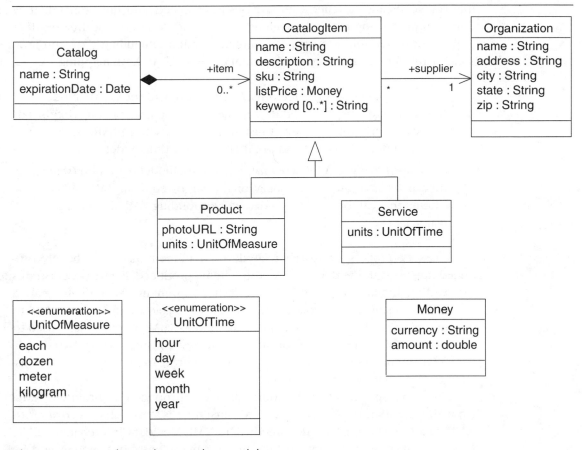

Figure 6-1 Simple product catalog model

class to define the list of possible value tokens. No attribute types are necessary for these enumeration list values. In Figure 6-1, the UnitOfMeasure class defines the enumerated list: each, dozen, meter, and kilogram. In CatML vocabulary, the units attribute of a Product must have a value taken from this list.

Mapping UML to XML

How do we translate this UML model into an XML vocabulary? There are several alternative solutions. There have been a number of proposals and implementations for generating XML documents from Java objects and XML DTDs and Schemas from Java class definitions. These approaches, however, assume that you've already designed your Java business objects, and, unfortunately, they don't support a language-independent analysis and design of vocabularies that will be translated into a number of implementations, including XML and Java. We can, though, explore two fundamental dimensions to XML mapping.

1. *Object instances to XML documents.* An instance of the CatML model (that is, a set of specific product, service, and supplier objects) is exported to one or more XML document instances. Conversely, an XML document may be imported to create an instance of the CatML model.

2. *Class definitions to XML schemas.* The CatML model definition (that is, the classes, attributes, and associations) is exported to an XML DTD or Schema that can be used to validate corresponding XML document instances.

These two topics are closely related: the document instances that are produced must be valid with respect to the schema produced. Figure 6-2 illustrates the relationship among these UML and XML components. When you create a UML model using your favorite UML design tool, you are in fact creating an instance of the UML metamodel. This UML model, CatML in our case, is used to produce an XML schema (DTD or one of its newer cousins) that is used to validate XML document instances. Instances of the CatML model can then be translated to and from the XML documents.

Figure 6-2 specifies that the XML schema is "produced according to XMI" from the CatML model. Also, the CatML instance is "translated according to XMI" to and from the XML document. The XML Metadata Interchange (XMI) specification provides a standard method for mapping object models and in-

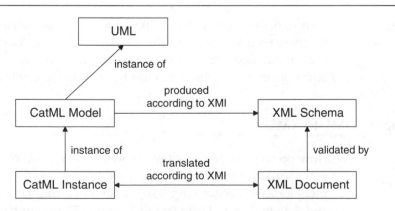

Figure 6-2   Mapping UML models to XML schemas and documents

stances to XML. Our focus on UML models is only one specific subset of how XMI can be applied.

XML Metadata Interchange

The XML Metadata Interchange specification[2] defines a rigorous approach for generating an XML DTD from a metamodel definition and generating XML documents from models that are instances of that metamodel. The generation rules in the XMI specification are based on use of the Meta Object Facility (MOF) specification;[3] the metamodel definition that is to be mapped to XML must be compliant with a MOF-specified metamodel. Fortunately, it's not necessary for you to understand this metalevel analysis to benefit from the mapping of UML to XML.

Simply stated, the MOF is the language used to define the UML language itself. Because the CatML model is defined using the UML and the UML is defined using the MOF, the XMI production rules can be applied to mapping CatML schemas and instances to XML. I will mostly ignore these higher levels of metamodeling and emphasize the practical use of XMI rules for exchanging application models designed using the UML. To quote the XMI specification:

> This submission does not actually require an implementation to make use of the MOF, the MOF-defined Reflective interfaces, or even have metamodels represented as instances of the MOF model. The implementation must, however, conform to the generation rules. These rules are based on the metamodels defined via the MOF and the use of the operations in the Reflective interfaces.[4]

The XMI specification also focuses on the exchange of metamodels and models, whereas the emphasis in this book is placed on the exchange of e-business data represented in XML. This use is acknowledged within the XMI specification, albeit only in one paragraph.

> While the typical use of the MOF involves a four layer metadata architecture, there are situations in which only three layers are required. In such cases, the meta-layers are shifted and MOF Model effectively becomes the metamodel for operational data. XMI can then be used as a data interchange medium. Note that this is only appropriate when the MOF Model is suitable for modeling operational data.[5]

---

2. XML Metadata Interchange version 1.1 specification is at *ftp://ftp.omg.org/pub/docs/ad/99-10-02.pdf*.

3. Meta Object Facility version 1.3 is at *ftp://ftp.omg.org/pub/docs/formal/00-04-03.pdf*.

4. XMI version 1.1 specification, p. 8-192.

5. XMI version 1.1 specification, p. 4-43.

When operational models such as CatML are based on the UML, it is relatively easy to assure compliance with the suitability of MOF, thus validating our use of XMI production rules. The remaining chapters of this book describe XMI production rules from the perspective of the UML; however, the result of the XML generation is equivalent to having used models based on the MOF. The rules contained here are less formal than those contained in the specification, but the end result is the same. That's all that is required for compliance with the specification.

The Object Management Group (OMG) adopted XMI version 1.0 in early 1999. XMI version 1.1 was adopted in early 2000 as a revision based on feedback from vendor implementations. Additional detail and references to the XMI and MOF specifications are provided in Chapter 9 and in Appendix B. The summary descriptions in the sidebar below are based on the version 1.1 specification.

Many people believe that XMI is limited to exchanging UML models between alternative UML modeling tools from different vendors—this was the original motivation behind creation of the XMI specification. For example, a model may be exported from Rational Rose and imported into TogetherJ, and vice versa. Also, system designers believe that XMI is limited to the more general case of exchanging models between software development tools or between tools and metadata repositories. In fact, XMI has wider applicability for producing XML vocabularies that enable integration of many e-business applications.

■ Principal XMI Assumptions

The translation is automated. The UML model definitions and instances may be translated to XML schemas and documents using a fully automated processor; the translation will not be handcrafted by a human designer.

The translation is repeatable. Any XMI compliant processor will produce the same XML document schema or instance from a given UML model or model instance.

Multiplicity is not enforced. XMI (version 1.1) does not constrain the element order or multiplicity in the generated DTD or document. All multiplicity information in the UML model is lost in translation. This has minimal impact on automated data exchange applications but has significant implications for docu-ments edited by humans. Due to limitations of DTDs, enforcing multiplicity often requires unnecessary fixed element ordering. Future versions of the XMI specification will undoubtedly improve this situation through use of the new W3C XML Schema.

Focus on data interchange. The XMI specification emphasizes applications using XML for data exchange rather than human-edited documents.

Low priority on compactness. Many handcrafted XML schemas and documents can be made more compact and more human-readable (but not more machine-readable) than those produced by an XMI processor. This is not, however, a goal of XMI.

This chapter covers the mapping from UML object instances to XML documents; the mapping from UML models to XML schemas is postponed until Chapters 8 and 9. Although this order may seem backwards to some readers, I have good reasons for selecting this sequence. First, I want to include a thorough coverage of the concepts associated with mapping UML to XML, and these concepts are most easily explained through the use of specific instance examples. Second, there is not one standard for XML schemas; several approaches are in common use, and there are significant differences in their representation and capabilities. (Actually, the differences among schemas are much less significant at the level of document instances; in principle, a single document instance can be validated with any type of schema.)

This mapping from UML to XML is not an exact science. In fact, modeling in general is far from an exact science. There will always be trade-offs between the model structure and design of the application(s) that process that model. I present a set of prescriptive mapping rules in the following sections that have been standardized by the XMI specification, but it is also essential that you understand the design decisions, assumptions, and trade-offs inherent in that mapping.

Disassembling UML Objects into XML

The next several sections delve into the details of mapping UML object instances to XML document instances, with emphasis on examining the underlying concepts and trade-offs. I'll disassemble the UML model for CatML in the following order: classes, class inheritance, attributes, enumerated attribute values, compositions, and associations. The diagram in Figure 6-3 illustrates the mapping of these UML structures to XML and serves as a road map for these specifications.

This diagram illustrates a subset of the product catalog model shown in Figure 6-1. Each of the major UML model constructs is mapped to a simple XML document fragment that represents an instance of that class, attribute, or association end role. For each of these topics, a UML object instance diagram is presented, followed by an XML example that demonstrates how those objects would be mapped. In several cases, there is more than one way to implement the mapping from objects to documents.

UML Classes to XML Elements

A UML class is a container of structural and behavioral features, but only the structural features are relevant when defining an XML vocabulary. The struc-

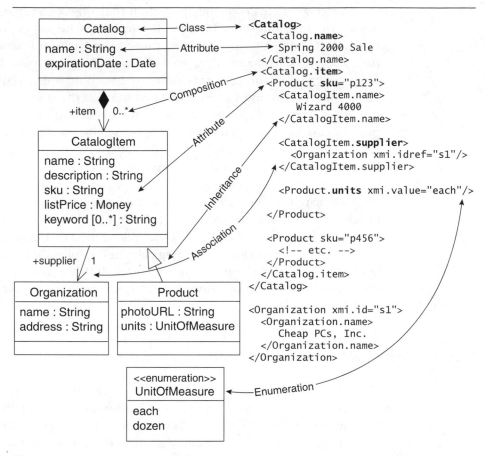

Figure 6-3 Mapping UML to XML

tural features consist of attributes, association end references with role names, and compositions. To be precise, the associations and compositions are not part of the class definition itself but are defined as independent association objects in the UML. The association ends refer to their anchoring classes, but I'll treat the association ends as being contained by the class because they appear that way in the resulting XML documents.

The mapping to XML is quite straightforward in that each instance of a UML class produces one XML element. In XML, an element serves as a container for attributes and child elements. So, as in UML, the XML element (the class instance) serves as a container for attributes and association roles. An XML element for a `Product` instance is represented as follows:

```
<Product>
</Product>
```

The XML tag name is the same as the UML class name, although XML imposes some additional constraints on valid names. The tag name cannot contain spaces, is limited to alpha or numeric characters, but allows the special characters '.', '-' and '_'. A tag name must begin with either a letter or a '_', but a name may not begin with the letters XML in any case or mixture of cases. Remember—don't begin your UML class or package names with the letters XML if the model will be used to produce XML documents.

The XMI version 1.1 specification allows but does not require use of XML namespaces as part of a tag name. For example, the `Product` element may begin with a namespace prefix that associates it with the CatML vocabulary. The prefixed tag might look like this:

```
<cml:Product xmlns:cml="http://xmlmodeling.com/schemas/CatML/1.0">
```

The prefix serves to distinguish this `Product` element from an element of the same name that originates in a different vocabulary. The `xmlns` attribute associates the `cml:` prefix with a unique Uniform Resource Identifier (URI) that identifies the CatML vocabulary namespace. Additional discussion of the benefits and limitations of XML namespaces is included at the end of this chapter, where XML namespaces are described in relationship to UML packages.

Inheritance

The use of inheritance is a fundamental characteristic in object-oriented modeling and is essential for representing abstract concepts and a classification of terms in a vocabulary. In Figure 6-1, inheritance is used to define first the attributes and associations that are common to all catalog items and second the specialized features that are unique to Products and Services. Inheritance indicates that a product is a kind of catalog item; thus, anything you can do to a catalog item can also be done to a product.

The current XML standards do not have a built-in mechanism for representing inheritance. A DTD cannot represent inheritance among element definitions; it can only represent the aggregation structure of elements contained in other elements. As a result of this limitation, XMI specifies use of copy-down inheritance for attributes, association references, and compositions. This simply

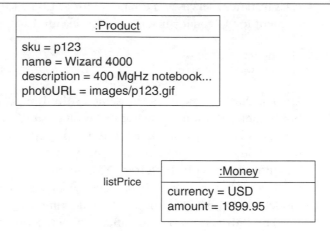

Figure 6-4 One product with its attribute values

means that these definitions from all superclasses (and recursively to their superclasses) are copied down to the class being translated into XML. Copy-down inheritance will be illustrated in the following sections and applied to attributes and associations.

UML Attributes to XML Elements

Given an instance of a UML class, begin by mapping each of its attributes into XML. It is common practice to define each data value as a separate child element when designing XML vocabularies. Consider the following example of a Product and its attributes, including those inherited from CatalogItem. This example is illustrated as a UML object instance diagram in Figure 6-4 followed by the corresponding XML document. If you review the class diagram in Figure 6-1, you'll notice that a Product includes the inherited listPrice attribute, which contains a value of type Money. In the object diagram, this attribute value is shown using a link from the Product instance to a Money instance.

```
<Product>
  <CatalogItem.name>Wizard 4000</CatalogItem.name>
  <CatalogItem.sku>p123</CatalogItem.sku>
  <CatalogItem.description>
    400 MgHz notebook computer with Windows 98
  </CatalogItem.description>
  <CatalogItem.listPrice>
    <Money>
      <Money.currency>USD</Money.currency>
      <Money.amount>1899.95</Money.amount>
```

```
      </Money>
    </CatalogItem.listPrice>
    <Product.photoURL>images/p123.gif</Product.photoURL>
  </Product>
```

Because this document's schema is generated automatically from the UML model by applying the rules of XMI, the element name for each UML attribute is made unique by pre-pending the class name onto each attribute name. For example, in Figure 6-1 the classes `Catalog`, `CatalogItem`, and `Organization` all have an attribute named `name`. In the XML document, these attributes would become `Catalog.name`, `CatalogItem.name`, and `Organization.name`. The XMI rule for copy-down inheritance results in all attributes from `CatalogItem` appearing in the `Product` element. Because all superclass attributes are prepended with their owner's class name, we use `CatalogItem.name` instead of `Product.name` in this case.

This `listPrice` attribute of the `CatalogItem` class in Figure 6-1 specifies another class, `Money`, as its attribute type. In this situation a new child element must be inserted to represent this attribute value in the XML document. The `CatalogItem.listPrice` element contains a child element representing the `Money` object. The two attributes of `Money` are produced in the same way as the attributes of `Product`. These mapping rules are applied recursively to each UML class encountered when generating an XML document.

UML Attributes to XML Attributes

When either a primitive data type (including String) or an enumeration, UML attributes may be represented as an XML attribute in the resulting document. Consider this revision to the last example, also based on the object diagram in Figure 6-4.

```
<Product sku="p123" photoURL="images/p123.gif">
  <CatalogItem.name>Wizard 4000</CatalogItem.name>
  <CatalogItem.description>
    400 MgHz notebook computer with Windows 98
  </CatalogItem.description>
  <CatalogItem.listPrice>
    <Money currency="USD" amount="1899.95" />
  </CatalogItem.listPrice>
</Product>
```

The `sku` and `photoURL` UML attributes are now mapped as XML attributes of the `Product` element in this document (`sku` was inherited from `CatalogItem`), and `currency` and `amount` are XML attributes of the `Money` element. Following the same rule, `name` and `description` could have been attributes of

`Product`, not child elements. So why did I leave them as elements? The answer is that it's important to consider the nature of data that will be assigned to the UML attribute value when deciding whether to use XML elements or attributes. If the UML attribute contains a string value, then XMI allows either elements or attributes. However, the value of an XML attribute is always whitespace normalized, meaning that the XML parser removes all extra whitespace characters, such as tabs, linefeeds, carriage returns, and multiple spaces. XML attributes also may not be appropriate for large string values. These are the reasons for leaving the product name and description as XML elements in the example.

XML allows shorthand syntax for empty elements that have no child elements, although empty elements may have attributes. The `Money` element is empty in this example, so it omits the end tag and terminates the tag with '`/>`'. However, the `Money` element does contain the two UML class attributes represented as XML attributes.

Also notice in the above example of `Product` that it is not necessary to prefix the XML attribute names with the class name, as was done when producing XML elements from UML attributes. You are allowed to simply use `sku` instead of `CatalogItem.sku`. This is because an XML element provides a separate namespace for its attributes, whereas an element name must be unique throughout the entire document DTD.[6]

The following is also a valid document fragment using XML attributes (where `Catalog.item` represents a UML association role that is explained in a later section):

```
<Catalog name="Spring Specials">
  <Catalog.item>
    <Product name="Wizard 4000"/>
  </Catalog.item>
</Catalog>
```

But, when using elements, you need to qualify names like this:

```
<Catalog>
  <Catalog.name>Spring Specials</Catalog.name>
  <Catalog.item>
    <Product>
      <Product.name>Wizard 4000</Product.name>
```

---

6. Note that the new XML Schema specification removes this requirement for global element name uniqueness. In an XML Schema definition, element names must be unique only within the scope of their containing element. But this significant difference in schema validity rules creates problems when an XML document instance must be validated using either a DTD or a Schema. These trade-offs are examined in great detail in Chapters 8 and 9.

```
    </Product>
  </Catalog.item>
</Catalog>
```

One additional complication arises if a class attribute is specified as multi-valued. This is shown in a UML model by including a multiplicity declaration for an attribute. In the catalog vocabulary UML diagram, the `CatalogItem` class includes a `keyword` attribute that may contain zero or more values, specified as

```
keyword [0..*] : String
```

There is no representation for multivalued attributes in XML, so these attributes must be translated to XML elements. A `Product` with multiple keyword values, shown as an object instance in Figure 6-5, would produce the following XML:

```
<Product sku="p123" photoURL="images/p123.gif">
  <CatalogItem.name>Wizard 4000</CatalogItem.name>
  <CatalogItem.description>
    400 MgHz notebook computer with Windows 98
  </CatalogItem.description>
  <CatalogItem.keyword>Personal Computer</CatalogItem.keyword>
  <CatalogItem.keyword>Windows 98</CatalogItem.keyword>
  <CatalogItem.keyword>Notebook</CatalogItem.keyword>
</Product>
```

XML attributes are unordered, so there is no way to enforce the `sku` attribute to be first among the list for a particular element. All attribute values must be quoted, and an attribute name must not be included more than once. Other than these restrictions inherent in XML, the XMI version 1.1 specification allows XML documents to freely interchange between representing UML attributes as XML elements or attributes. The XMI specification offers no guidelines for choosing whether to use XML elements or attributes when representing UML attribute

```
                    :Product
  ┌──────────────────────────────────────────┐
  │ sku = p123                                 │
  │ name = Wizard 4000                         │
  │ description = 400 MgHz notebook...         │
  │ photoURL = images/p123.gif                 │
  │ keyword = ['Personal Computer',            │
  │            'Windows 98',                    │
  │            'Notebook' ]                     │
  └──────────────────────────────────────────┘
```

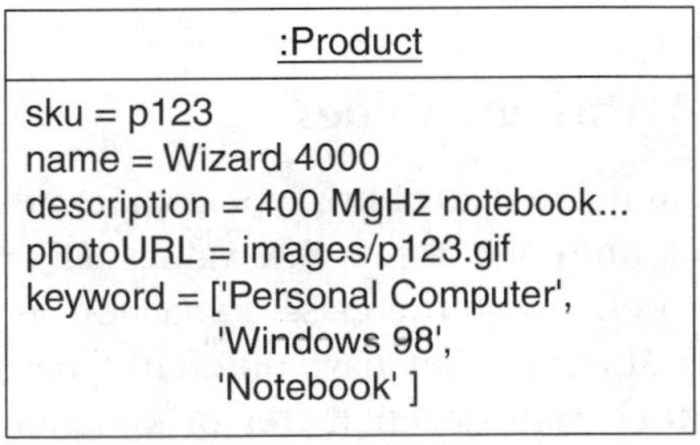

Figure 6-5   A product with multivalued keyword attribute

values. This choice is one of the most frequently asked questions among new-comers to XML—and the answers by XML experts don't always agree. In fact, this decision is heavily dependent on knowledge of the applications that will process the XML documents.

Elements versus Attributes

The distinction between elements and attributes may be unimportant when the vocabulary is used primarily for data interchange. In such a case, the vocabulary's purpose is to encode data for transfer from one application to another, and cus-tomized applications or XSLT transformations can be easily written to process either attributes or elements. However, if an XML application is unpredictable in its use of elements versus attributes, then a processor must do much more work when interpreting the documents. In particular, it's much more difficult to write understandable and maintainable XSLT stylesheets when they must handle an unpredictable combination of elements and attributes. The bottom line: be con-sistent in your use of XML elements and attributes for a given vocabulary!

When a human user is one of the processors of this application (for exam-ple, editing the catalog content), then the human factors for usability and ease of interpretation by that user must also be considered. Some XML editing tools allow the documents to be viewed in a text mode, similar to what's seen with a word processor. However, when using these editors the XML attributes are often hidden from view and must be selectively edited through use of pop-up dialog boxes. This application tool behavior may help you choose whether to represent information using XML element content or attributes. The element content appears in-line as part of the document text within the editor, whereas the attribute values are edited as out-of-line metadata.

Finally, when using an XML DTD or Schema with the document, the schema may define default values for any of the XML attributes. The ability to define defaults is especially important for enumerated attribute values. There is, however, no way to specify defaults for element text content when using a DTD. I'll expand on these issues related to use of DTDs and Schemas in Chap-ters 8 and 9.

Enumerated Attribute Values

An enumerated attribute type requires the UML attribute value to be assigned from a finite list of possible values. Figure 6-1 includes two enumerated attri-butes defined on the classes Product and Service. Both attributes are named units, although they have different types. For example, a product's units would be either each, dozen, meter, or kilogram; whereas a service's units would be either hour, day, week, month, or year.

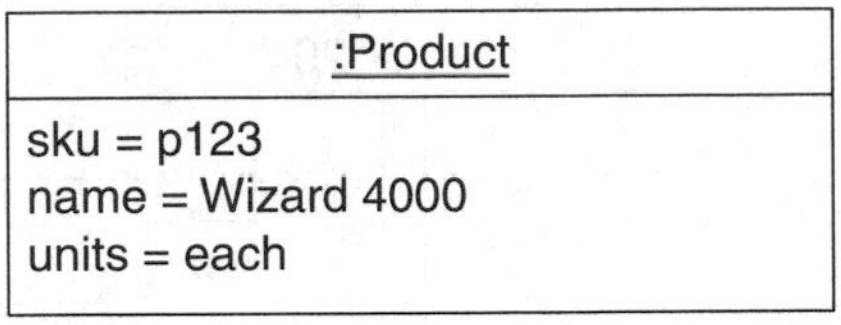

```
                          :Product
        sku = p123
        name = Wizard 4000
        units = each
```

Figure 6-6   Enumerated attribute value for product units

XMI specifies two alternatives for mapping enumerated values from UML to an XML document. These alternatives correspond to the use of either an XML element or attribute, similar to the previous descriptions, but there is a new twist added that enables an XML DTD to check for a valid enumeration value. The XML attribute is simplest, so I'll start there. Each of the two alternative XML representations is based on the UML object diagram shown in Figure 6-6.

The following example represents a `Product`'s `units` using an XML attribute.

```
<Product sku="p123" units="each">
  <CatalogItem.name>Wizard 4000</CatalogItem.name>
</Product>
```

The attribute appears no different than other nonenumerated attributes, but the DTD limits the attribute's valid value to one of the enumerated list. The next example is somewhat different when representing an enumerated attribute using an XML element.

```
<Product sku="p123">
  <CatalogItem.name>Wizard 4000</CatalogItem.name>
  <Product.units xmi.value="each"/>
</Product>
```

Unlike nonenumerated UML attributes, the element for an enumerated attribute always includes an XML attribute named `xmi.value` whose value is constrained by the DTD. An element such as `Product.units` that represents an enumerated UML attribute value is always empty (that is, it has no child elements between its start and end tags).

Mapping UML Compositions

A UML composition is shown in Figure 6-1, linking `Catalog` with `CatalogItem`. Compositions are always shown in UML diagrams using a solid diamond on the association end, indicating that the related objects are owned by value, not by reference. In a similar way, an XML element owns its child elements by value. In

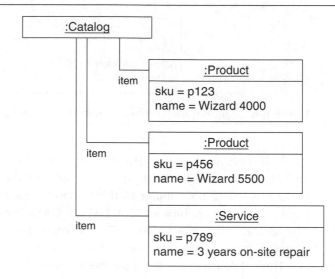

Figure 6-7   Composition of catalog items

either case, if the owner is deleted, then all of the owned objects/elements are deleted as well. Consider this example of a catalog that is composed of three catalog items. Figure 6-7 shows one Catalog object linked to three Product objects using the item role name.

These four objects are represented in XML as a Catalog element containing the three items, as follows:

```
<Catalog>
 <Catalog.item>
  <Product sku="p123">
    <CatalogItem.name>Wizard 4000</CatalogItem.name>
  </Product>
  <Product sku="p456">
    <CatalogItem.name>Wizard 5500</CatalogItem.name>
  </Product>
  <Service sku="p789">
    <CatalogItem.name>3 years on-site repair</CatalogItem.name>
  </Service>
 </Catalog.item>
</Catalog>
```

The role name on a UML association end is mapped onto an XML element analogous to the way that UML attributes are mapped to elements. In this example, the item role is mapped to the qualified name Catalog.item; this role element serves as a container for the linked objects. This example also illustrates an interesting use of inheritance in the UML model. Because `Catalog` is composed of any `CatalogItem` objects, and `CatalogItem` is the superclass of `Product` and `Service`, then a catalog may contain either of these objects. Thus, the `Catalog.item` container holds a mix of products and services.

This is a very typical XML document. We might tentatively conclude that UML compositions are very common when modeling XML document structures. However, as we'll see in Chapter 7, this approach to composition constrains the parent and child elements to being contained in the same physical XML document. It is often more flexible to distribute elements across several physical documents or database repositories, similar to the way that HTML pages are hyperlinked in the Web.

Mapping UML Associations

The CatML model does not use composition for the supplier relationship between `CatalogItem` and `Organization`. This is because a single organization object is created, and then associated with many catalog item objects. Consider the following example, where an `Organization` element is associated with two different `Product` elements. The example is shown first as a UML object diagram in Figure 6-8, then as the corresponding XML document.

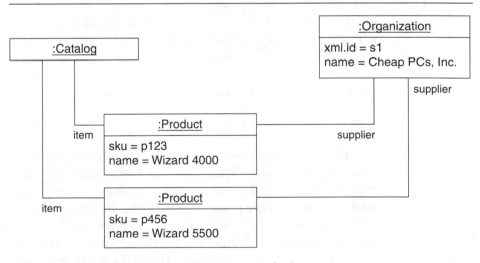

Figure 6-8 Association of products to a supplier

```
<Catalog>
  <Catalog.item>
   <Product sku="p123">
     <CatalogItem.name>Wizard 4000</CatalogItem.name>
     <CatalogItem.supplier>
       <Organization xmi.idref="s1" xmi.label="Wizard PCs, Inc."/>
     </CatalogItem.supplier>
   </Product>
   <Product sku="p456" supplier="s1">
     <CatalogItem.name>Wizard 5500</CatalogItem.name>
   </Product>
  </Catalog.item>
</Catalog>

<Organization xmi.id="s1">
  <Organization.name>Wizard PCs, Inc.</Organization.name>
</Organization>
```

This example introduces several additional features of the XMI specification required when representing UML associations in XML. First, notice that the Organization element includes an attribute named xmi.id. Any element in the document may include this attribute as an identifier for that element within the document. However, the id *must* be unique within the scope of the document, regardless of the element tag name. The xmi.id attribute enables creation of associations between elements in the document.

Given this Organization element, we can now link to it from the two Product elements. XMI defines two approaches for including association references, based on using either an XML element or attribute. The first Product element includes a child element named CatalogItem.supplier. The UML association role is used to create the element name, analogous to the way element names were created for UML attributes. However, instead of including a complete Organization element definition as its child (as was done for UML composition), a *proxy element* is included that refers to the complete definition for the Organization. The most basic proxy element looks like this:

```
<Organization xmi.idref = "s1"/>
```

The XML attribute xmi.idref represents a reference to an xmi.id contained elsewhere in the *same document*. The XMI specification also defines another attribute, xmi.label, that may be included in a proxy element to contain a title or brief description of the linked element. Using this label, an application could present the subject of the link to a user without retrieving the actual element. During processing, an application would recognize the xmi.idref attribute and link to the Organization element containing the equivalent xmi.id to obtain the remaining attributes and associations for that organization object.

The second `Product` element in this example uses an XML attribute, named `supplier`, to contain the reference to a supplier `Organization`. Instead of including an `Organization.supplier` child element, the association role name is used as an XML attribute, and the attribute value is set to the associated `Organization` element's `xmi.id` value.

Both of these approaches for representing association roles are valid and equivalent, according to the XMI specification. However, the `xmi.id` and `xmi.idref` attributes can be used for associations only when both elements are contained in the same physical XML document. This is too limiting in many distributed application designs. A more complete description of the mapping of UML relationships to XML links is sufficiently complex to warrant a dedicated chapter. Chapter 7 introduces additional XML XLink hyperlink standards for representing intra- and interdocument associations in XML.

Roots and Broken Branches

How would you go about reassembling all of the document fragments created in the last several sections? A UML model does not necessarily have one class that is the root of a composition hierarchy for all other classes. Yet, this is exactly the configuration that must exist in a valid XML document. An XML document must contain exactly one root document element. In addition, e-business applications often require one or more document fragments to be exchanged, for example, in response to a catalog query. These broken branches of a larger catalog structure need some type of container to hold them.

The XMI specification defines an <XMI> element that serves this purpose; it also includes additional metadata about the document's contents and supports exchange of incremental model fragments and differences. The following template illustrates the XMI root element structure:

```
<XMI xmi.version = '1.1' timestamp = 'Mon May 22 14:54:39 MDT 2000'>
  <XMI.header>
    <XMI.documentation>
      <XMI.contact>Wizard PCs Inc.</XMI.contact>
      <XMI.shortDescription>Spring Catalog</XMI.shortDescription>
    </XMI.documentation>
    <XMI.metamodel xmi.name = 'CatML' xmi.version = '1.0'/>
    <XMI.model xmi.name = 'eCatalog' xmi.version = '1.5'
            href = 'http://www.Wizard-PCs.com/Spring2000.xml'/>
  </XMI.header>
  <XMI.content>
    <!-- contains model content being transferred -->
  </XMI.content>
  <XMI.difference>
```

```
   <!-- contains changes to an existing model -->
   <XMI.add> </XMI.add>
   <XMI.delete> </XMI.delete>
   <XMI.replace> </XMI.replace>
  </XMI.difference>
  <XMI.extensions>
   <!-- contains elements that are an extension to the metamodel -->
  </XMI.extensions>
</XMI>
```

The `<XMI.header>` includes a number of optional elements, such as documentation about the document sender, contact name, short and long descriptions, and the name and version of the software tool used to export this document. It also refers to the metamodel that defines valid element structures to be included in the `<XMI.content>` element. In our case, the CatML model defines the metamodel for catalog content. A receiving application may choose to use this information for performing additional semantic validation of the document content, beyond the scope of what can be done using XML DTDs or Schemas.

What if I want to transmit only one product rather than a complete catalog? Using this XMI document structure, I can include any valid CatML elements in the document content, even a single `Product` element. Note that the CatML model prohibits an `Organization` element as a child of a `Catalog` element; it's not part of the catalog. Both of these element types can be included within the `<XMI.content>` container element, as shown in this example.

```
<XMI.content >
  <Organization xmi.id="s1">
    <Organization.name>Wizard PCs, Inc.</Organization.name>
  </Organization>
  <Organization xmi.id="s2">
    <Organization.name>Wizard Networks</Organization.name>
  </Organization>
  <Product sku="p123">
    <CatalogItem.name>Wizard 4000</CatalogItem.name>
    <Catalog.supplier>
      <Organization xmi.idref="s1"/>
    </Catalog.supplier>
  </Product>
  <Product sku="p456">
    <CatalogItem.name>Wizard 5500</CatalogItem.name>
    <Catalog.supplier>
      <Organization xmi.idref="s2"/>
    </Catalog.supplier>
  </Product>
</XMI.content>
```

There are also situations where you need to send incremental updates to an existing product catalog. The <XMI.difference> element includes sub-elements for adding, deleting, and replacing elements from a base model. The base model location would need to be identified using a <XMI.model> element included in the header. The incremental catalog updates must refer to specific element positions in the base catalog identifying where the differences are inserted. These positions are specified using XML's XPointer locators, which are explained in the next chapter.

B2B communication requires more than the exchange of isolated e-business documents and data elements. The necessary conversation-level architecture was described in Part I within the discussion of B2B business models. The XMI specification does not address the B2B communication protocol but does provide for the metadata required to describe a document's content. Additional conversation-oriented document wrapper elements are presented as part of deployment frameworks in Chapter 12.

Packaging Vocabularies

How many different application systems have been created that use the terms "Catalog" and "Product"? Probably thousands. If a successful global e-business infrastructure is to be established, it is essential that we define generalized, reusable XML vocabularies. Many articles have been written about the threat of "balkanization" in the proliferation of XML vocabularies; but if each business develops its own XML vocabularies, the Semantic Web will either fail or struggle under a burden of vocabulary translation.

If we hope to exchange information between applications, or more significantly, reuse parts of these applications in a new design, we must distinguish one vocabulary from another. This problem is not unique to XML; it's a universal issue in the design of global information systems. As a conclusion to this chapter, I'll first describe a broader vision for CatX that includes the use of several different vocabularies. Next, I'll introduce the packaging constructs in UML and compare this with the corresponding XML namespace standard. Finally, I'll discuss how the UML packages used in CatX are mapped into XML namespaces.

The CatX service is described by four vocabularies that are further decomposed into a total of six subvocabulary packages. The four primary vocabularies are named CatML, FpML, PSML, and ProML. Many e-business problems require the combination of several domain vocabularies, each with its own definition that may be reused in other applications. These vocabularies may be independent from one another or interdependent through relationships or specialization (see summary in the sidebar on page 114).

■ **The Four Primary Vocabularies**

CatML—The Catalog Markup Language represents the core catalog content, categorization taxonomies, and promotional discounts.

FpML—The Financial Products Markup Language[7] illustrates reuse of a major XML vocabulary developed by an independent industry organization for use in financial service e-business.

PSML—The Portal Site Markup Language was designed as part of the Apache Jetspeed portal project.[8] It represents the layout, skin, and parameters of portlets that are composed into a Web site portal.

ProML—The Procurement Markup Language (a fictitious example vocabulary) defines a standard vocabulary for purchasing and order processing.

Given this example scenario, how do we make choices about the packaging of generalized, reusable vocabularies? The age-old system design principles of cohesion and coupling are useful guidelines in the design and integration of XML vocabularies. There should be well-defined cohesion and integration of concepts within a vocabulary but relatively loose coupling of relationships between vocabulary packages. I'll start with a high-level overview of the FpML vocabulary before probing the details of UML and XML packaging applied to the CatML and FpML vocabulary models.

FpML Vocabulary

The Financial Products Markup Language (FpML) is an information exchange standard for Internet-based electronic dealing and processing of financial instruments, initially focusing on interest rate and foreign exchange derivative products. FpML enables Internet-based integration of a range of services, from electronic trading and trade confirmations to risk and sensitivity analysis of trade portfolios. A more detailed description of FpML and its mapping to UML is provided in Appendix A.

FpML was designed with a modular, extensible, object-oriented structure that is well aligned with the design principles used in the development of our CatX service. FpML was not, however, designed using the UML. The final FpML 1.0 recommendation is limited to a single namespace in one DTD, primarily due to the lack of namespace support in several of the current XML parsers (as of early 2001). However, the previous FpML beta 2 draft written in 1999 was de-

---

7. For more information on FpML, see *http://www.FpML.org*.

8. For more information on Apache Jetspeed, including a complete definition of PSML, see *http://java.apache.org/jetspeed*.

fined with several shared vocabulary modules that communicate general business information. The final FpML recommendation has a more limited scope, but a description of the beta specification is included because it's more illustrative of the design principles described in this book. A small subset of these modules include these items.

- *Contact*—a person's street address, phone number, e-mail address, and so on.
- *Trading Party*—contains information about one of the parties involved in a trade. This module contains more detail than our catalog needs in the beginning, but it would be useful to include the entire Trading Party vocabulary in our CatX service.
- *Money*—internationalized currency amounts and notional streams of scheduled amounts. For now, we'll reuse only the basic internationalized currency elements.
- *Date*—dates, time periods, and schedules for specifying financial transactions. Some of these elements have useful general application, while others are specific to financial transactions. Although this module is interesting, we'll skip it for now.

Based on an investigation of reusable vocabularies and the proposed FpML standard, parts of the Contact, Trading Party, and Money packages are integrated into our CatX service vocabulary. In particular, class specifications for `Party` and `Money` are reused without change and linked into the CatML vocabulary definition.

UML Packages

UML is able to define a hierarchy of packages that specify *namespaces* for a model's elements. All model elements contained within a single namespace must have unique names, although two elements may have the same name if they are contained by two different packages. For example, we cannot have two classes named `Discount` within the CatML package, but we could have one in CatML and another very different class by the same name in the FpML package. UML packages serve as namespace separators within the model, but they also support code generation into other data and execution languages, including Java, C++, SQL DDL, and XML.

Figure 6-9 illustrates a UML package diagram of our CatX service, including the dependencies between those packages. Two of the packages (`ContactInfo` and `TradingParty`) are nested within another higher-level package named FpML beta 2. The containing package is noted parenthetically in the diagram (from FpML beta 2).

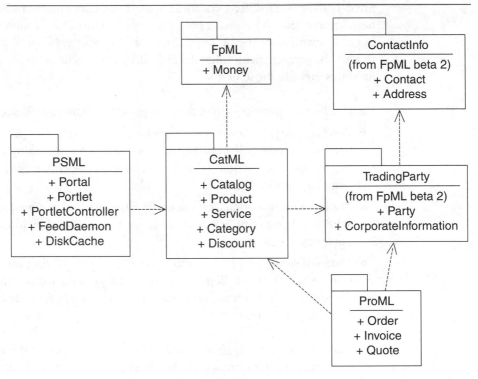

Figure 6-9   CatX vocabulary package dependencies

There are several levels of namespace hierarchy in the UML, in addition to the nested package definitions. Names contained within each namespace level must be unique. These are summarized as follows:

- Attribute names within a Class
- Class names within a Package
- Package names within a Package
- Package names within a Subsystem
- Package and Subsystem names within a Model

Now that you understand UML packages and namespace separation, I'll review the current standard for XML namespace definitions. XML namespaces have more modest goals, but we can map a subset of UML package definitions into XML namespace declarations.

XML Namespaces

The original XML specification did not include a way to combine elements and attributes from several vocabularies when composing a document. This capability is essential if we are to encourage the reuse of industry standard vocabularies rather than forcing each application to reinvent many of the same definitions. The Namespaces in XML[9] specification was written to address this requirement. This mechanism was intentionally kept simple; it is not a software engineering construct with the same general applicability as that defined in the UML.

Unlike UML, XML namespaces do not support a hierarchy of packages. An XML namespace is quite simply a prefix applied to a group of related XML elements and attributes. The namespace prefix differentiates an element or attribute from others that may originate in different vocabularies. By using the XML namespace prefix, you may integrate terms from several vocabularies within a single document. This is really the only goal of the current standard.

A namespace is declared using a special reserved attribute name in an XML element, and that declaration is valid until the element's matching end tag. For example, we could declare use of the CatML vocabulary namespace as follows:

```
<cml:Catalog xmlns:cml="http://xmlmodeling.com/schemas/CatML">
  <cml:Catalog.item>
    <cml:Product>
      <cml:CatalogItem.name>Wizard 4000</cml:CatalogItem.name>
    </cml:Product>
  </cml:Catalog.item>
</cml:Catalog>
```

The 'xmlns:' attribute prefix is reserved for use by the XML namespace specification—in fact, any prefix beginning with the letters 'xml' is reserved. The choice of our namespace prefix 'cml' is arbitrary and any other prefix could be chosen. The URI assigned to this prefix is *not* the location of a DTD or XML Schema document. It is simply a unique identifier and does not necessarily point to anything that you can retrieve. In this case, we declare that the 'cml' prefix is associated with this URI for CatML. This XML document fragment might be embedded within a larger document that uses a different namespace, or it may be part of an XHTML document.

The use of XML namespaces helps when exchanging business documents that combine several vocabularies, but in some cases we also need references

---

9. For more information on *Namespaces in XML*, 14 January 1999, see *http://www.w3.org/TR/REC-xml-names*.

to the schema documents that can be used to validate elements from each vocabulary. The XMI specification includes additional information in a reserved header element for this purpose. This XMI document declares the namespace prefixes as part of the root element, then also declares the metamodel(s) and their physical URL locations in the XMI.header element.

```
<XMI xmi.version = '1.1'
    xmlns:cml="http://xmlmodeling.com/schemas/CatML"
    xmlns:pty="http://xmlmodeling.com/schemas/TradingParty">
  <XMI.header>
    <XMI.documentation>
      <XMI.exporter>My XMI Tool</XMI.exporter>
    </XMI.documentation>
    <XMI.metamodel xmi.name = 'cml' xmi.version = '1.0'
        href="http://xmlmodeling.com/schemas/CatML.dtd"/>
    <XMI.metamodel xmi.name = 'pty' xmi.version = '1.0'
        href="http://xmlmodeling.com/schemas/TradingParty.dtd"/>
  </XMI.header>
  <XMI.content>
    <pty:Party href="http://www.Wizard-PCs.com/
                     catalog?supplier=WizardPCs"/>
    <cml:Catalog>
      <cml:Catalog.item>
        <cml:Product>
          <cml:CatalogItem.name>Wizard 4000</cml:CatalogItem.name>
        </cml:Product>
      </cml:Catalog.item>
    </cml:Catalog>
  </XMI.content>
</XMI>
```

Two namespaces were declared in this example, corresponding to the CatML and TradingParty vocabularies. The XMI.content element contains a Party element from the 'pty' vocabulary, and a Catalog element from the 'cml' vocabulary.

Some handcrafted XML schemas make extensive use of XML namespaces as a means to improve modularity and reusability. For example, the early FpML beta specification took this approach, although its designers were forced to simplify their DTD to a single namespace when confronted by limitations of current tools with respect to namespace support. We can duplicate this multi-namespace strategy using UML if each of the major packages in the model is generated into a separate DTD or XML Schema, each of which is assigned a unique XML namespace. This approach is examined in greater detail in Chapter 9 when I review the XMI standard and other extended techniques for automating the generation of DTDs and XML Schemas from UML.

Chapter Summary

- A complete vocabulary specification must define terms, generalization, relationships, and constraints. A UML class diagram enables vocabulary specification that is both human- and machine-readable.

- The Catalog Markup Language was created for use in this book, but its specification provides a helpful starting point for other catalog management projects. An initial simplified product catalog model is presented using a UML class diagram.

- The XML Metadata Interchange specification was created by the OMG as a standard for exchanging metamodels and models. The XMI production rules are used in this chapter to describe mapping from UML object diagrams to XML documents.

- UML object attributes may be mapped to either XML elements or XML attributes. All UML attribute names are prefixed with the class name in order to assure unique XML element names across the entire schema.

- UML inheritance is mapped using a "copy-down" strategy in which all attributes and association end roles are copied down from superclasses into each subclass definition.

- UML compositions are mapped into child elements within an XML document, but associations are mapped using proxy elements with `xmi.id` and `xmi.idref` linking.

- Both UML packages and XML namespaces define a scope for unique names within a model, but XML namespaces are much simpler in purpose and capability.

Steps for Success

1. Use UML class structure diagrams to clearly document the meaning and use of your vocabulary's elements, relationships, and constraints.

2. There are several equally valid alternatives for mapping UML objects and attributes to XML elements and attributes. Be consistent in your approach; otherwise you may experience a higher cost of development and maintenance.

3. Define modular, reusable vocabularies similar to the way that you create reusable packages and components in your software design. Your vocabularies should have these characteristics:

   - Strong cohesion of elements and attributes within a vocabulary
   - Loose coupling between vocabularies, documented using UML package diagrams

4. Establish a plan for creating and maintaining XML namespace URIs assigned to your organization's vocabulary definitions.

5. Plan a configuration management and version control strategy for your XML vocabularies with attention equal to that of other non-XML application components.

6. Plan your strategy for exchanging XML document fragments that represent subsets of vocabulary models. XMI provides a document wrapper for this purpose.

Chapter 7
From Relationships to Hyperlinks

As previously noted, the Web is a massively distributed, loosely coupled information network that is tolerant of incomplete and contradictory information. These are some of the key characteristics that have enabled the Web to grow faster than even the most optimistic projections. However, because the current Web is largely based on HTML documents, only human readers can interpret the implied meaning of its hyperlinks. XML, however, is able to put machine-interpretable meaning into the Web. This next generation Web, commonly referred to as the *Semantic Web*, includes hyperlinks and resource metadata that are based on well-defined concepts, relationships, and constraints defined in the underlying vocabulary.

The Semantic Web builds on the concept of XML vocabularies that was introduced in Chapter 6. Much of the vision behind it is attributable to Tim Berners-Lee, who is also the original inventor of the current World Wide Web. Tim concisely summarizes the Web as "a universe of network-accessible information."[1] He then describes the Semantic Web this way:

> The Web was designed as an information space, with the goal that it should be useful not only for human–human communication, but also that machines would be able to participate and help. One of the major obstacles to this has been the fact that most information on the Web is designed for human

---

1. Tim Berners-Lee, "Web Architecture from 50,000 feet," *http://www.w3.org/DesignIssues/Architecture.html*.

consumption, and even if it was derived from a database with well defined meanings (in at least some terms) for its columns, that the structure of the data is not evident to a robot browsing the web. Leaving aside the artificial intelligence problem of training machines to behave like people, the Semantic Web approach instead develops languages for expressing information in a machine processable form. . . . The Semantic Web is a web of data, in some ways like a global database.[2]

The Web is composed of resources that are each addressable by a Uniform Resource Identifier (URI) and assembled with interconnecting hyperlinks. In the Semantic Web, these links are not limited to the simple, unidirectional HTML hyperlinks but also include much more flexible, powerful linking mechanisms enabled by XML. The XLink specification was only recently adopted as a candidate recommendation by the W3C, but it holds great promise for enabling the global database of the Semantic Web.[3] Effective use of relationship modeling in UML is an important prerequisite for adding machine interpretable meaning to XML vocabularies used in B2B applications. These UML relationships are mapped into XML hyperlinks that become the foundation for a globally distributed information network.

B2B integration leverages the power of the Web infrastructure to create an adaptable global marketplace that crosses enterprise boundaries. A B2B supply chain or marketplace will remain a fragmented information landscape if each document stands alone or if the elements within those documents are isolated bits of data. B2B integration must become better aligned with Web-like connectivity and distribution that is not based on exchange of isolated data transactions. These adaptable B2B systems are not coupled by relational databases or by APIs that are shared across enterprise boundaries. Instead, they are integrated via shared vocabularies that are used to compose documents exchanged using existing Internet protocols.

Expanded CatML Vocabulary

A distributed catalog and its related resources are not contained in one document but are widely distributed in a continuously evolving infrastructure. It's this dynamic nature that makes the current World Wide Web a living, organic me-

---

2. Tim Berners-Lee, "Semantic Web Road Map," at *http://www.w3.org/DesignIssues/ Semantic.html*.

3. The vision for the Semantic Web is also based on the Resource Description Framework (RDF); however, its description is beyond the scope of this book. For additional information, see *http://www.w3.org/TR/REC-rdf-syntax/*.

■ The Six Enhancements to the Simplified CatML Model

1. Taxonomy of product categories and features that may be used to group and describe catalog items.

2. Negotiated price lists that are specific to each major customer. The negotiated price may be a discount from the catalog list price or an alternative price for an item.

3. Promotional coupons that offer discounts to specific catalog items or to entire categories of products.

4. Product bundles that group catalog items into new, aggregate products sold and priced together. This is a common practice used to offer a discounted promotion on a bundle.

5. Product detail documents that may be associated with any catalog item. These are especially useful when producing interactive catalogs on Web portals.

6. Reuse two preexisting FpML packages for `Money` and `TradingParty` and integrate these with the CatML vocabulary. The `Money` class used in Chapter 6 should be explicitly linked to its definition in FpML, and the `Party` class from FpML should replace the previous `Organization` class.

dium. Our CatX service will be more successful if its design is aligned with the Web's strengths. I'll make the CatX service and its requirements more tangible with a specific example. The catalog for Cheap PCs, Inc. (a completely fictitious company) represents the product line for a distributor of PCs and their associated software and peripherals. Cheap PCs issues a monthly update that supplements their annual baseline catalog with new items and special promotions.

The six CatML vocabulary enhancements (see sidebar above) are added to the model described in Chapter 6, resulting in an expanded UML class diagram shown in Figure 7-1. This diagram may appear a bit overwhelming at first glance, but we'll work through all of the classes and associations with detailed examples in this chapter. For now, review the model's general layout to get familiar with the class names. I'll begin by describing a set of components that group these classes into clusters of related functionality. Then, after describing more advanced linking mechanisms available for XML, I'll analyze new alternatives for distributing objects and documents from this model across a Semantic Web.

Because the focus of this chapter is on hyperlinking the elements of a distributed catalog, it's helpful to consider an approach for clustering these classes into components. Each of these components should have relatively tight cohesion of functionality among the classes that are assigned to it, and there should be relatively loose coupling between components so that they can be distributed across the network. As we analyze the XML linking techniques available for design, some are better suited for use within components and others are better for linking across components.

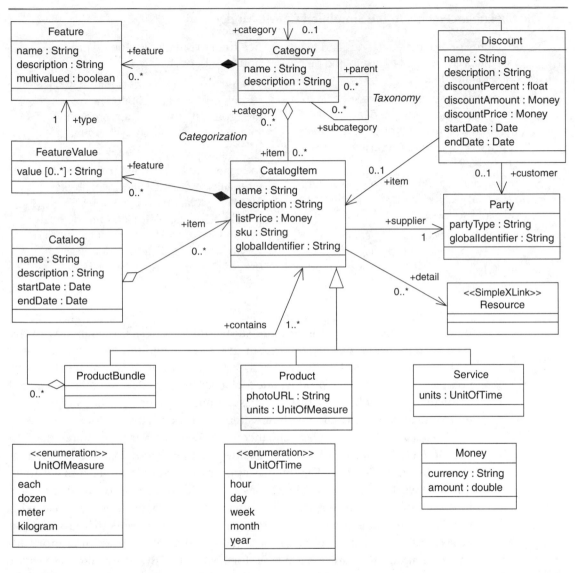

Figure 7-1 Product catalog model

In our Cheap PCs, Inc. example, each component corresponds to an XML document that contains a set of XML elements representing that component's objects. Table 7-1 defines the mapping of UML classes to components. Notice that a class might be deployed in more than one component. In addition, two named associations in Figure 7-1, Taxonomy and Categorization, are also assigned to components. These last two components are used in the extended XLink representations.

Table 7-1 Realization of components by classes

Component	Classes	Associations
Catalog	Catalog, Product, Service, ProductBundle	
Products	Product, Service, Feature	
Product Bundles	ProductBundle, Product, Service, Feature	
Price List	Discount	
Supplier	Party, Contact, Address	
Customer	Party, Contact, Address	
Product Detail	Resource	
Taxonomy	Category, Feature	Taxonomy
Categorization	CatalogItem, Category	Categorization

Most XML document fragments described in Chapter 6 used either parent/child element hierarchies or the XML ID and IDREF linking mechanism to represent UML associations. Although this approach works reasonably well when all XML elements are contained in the same document, it does not provide the capabilities needed when building a globally distributed Semantic Web. The next section provides an introduction to more advanced linking mechanisms enabled by XML. In the following section, these new capabilities for hyperlinking XML are applied to detailed examples using the expanded CatML vocabulary model.

XML Standards for Linking

Hyperlinks are what make the Web what it is: a *web* of linked resources. The power of these simple links—when multiplied by millions of instances—enable the Web to become a worldwide database of information and enable search engines to crawl the Web while scanning for new information references. When a link's URL refers to a script or Java servlet that creates dynamic content, the Web's reach approaches infinite size. However, the Web's original linking mechanism, based on HTML, has limits.

- HTML links can point only to a single resource. They cannot represent the equivalent of a "0..*" multiplicity on a UML association, except by creating a list of separate links.
- Links are one-way, not bidirectional. To create a bidirectional link, you must create two independent links, one contained in each document.

- Links must be contained in the referencing document. It would be beneficial in some situations, especially for bidirectional links, to create a separate *linkbase* document that contains a list of links referring to other source and destination documents.

- Links can point to a single named location within the target document, but that location anchor must be defined within the text of the target document. You cannot point to a new location within a document unless you have permission to update that document.

All of these limitations are overcome by XML's linking language. *XLink* defines how one XML document links to others and how an extended linkbase may be created in a separate document or database. XLink is enhanced by the *XPointer* language, which defines how locations within other XML documents may be addressed by links. XPointer also depends on the *XPath* addressing specification for identifying locations in XML based on the document structure. Each of these parts of the linking language can optionally use, and extend, the XML ID mechanism already used to represent UML associations in XML documents.

XML ID and IDREF

The original XML 1.0 specification includes a basic linking mechanism that was inherited from its roots in SGML. Similar to use of HTML named anchors, an XML author may identify specific named locations within a document. But whereas HTML anchors can only be added using one predefined anchor element, any XML element may include an identifier (if it's properly declared in the DTD). A named anchor in HTML is written as follows:

```
<A name="p127">
<P>The Wizard 4000 desktop computer is . . .</P>
```

A document author might add this HTML <A> tag at the start of a product description for the Wizard 4000 desktop computer, assuming that this product is identified as "p127" in the inventory system. This HTML anchor would allow an HTML link to be written as follows:

```
<A href="#p127">Wizard 4000</A>
```

This HTML element defines a hyperlink, contained within the same document as the anchor, which links to that anchor location. In both HTML and XML, the '#' character and the following locator in an href attribute signifies a position within the target document, and the absence of a URL before the # means that the location is in the same document as the link.

In our CatML vocabulary, the equivalent information content might be written as follows:

```
<Product xmi.id="p127">
  <CatalogItem.description>
    The Wizard 4000 desktop computer is . . .
  </CatalogItem.description>
</Product>
```

Using this product description and identifier, we could add a link elsewhere in the same document, written as

```
<Product xmi.idref="p127" xmi.label="Wizard 4000"/>
```

Or, alternatively, using the XMI href attribute:

```
<Product href="#p127" xmi.label="Wizard 4000"/>
```

Notice that in the descriptions for both HTML and XML, both the anchor location and link definition must be contained in the same document. HTML links can, of course, span two documents simply by adding a URL location before the '#' character in the link href location. However, XML adds an ID reference mechanism that is separate from interdocument hyperlinks and is limited to the scope of a single document. These are the IDs that we have been applying in Chapter 6. The HTML link is limited to intradocument anchors in this example so that it is comparable to use of the xmi.idref attribute in XML. As we'll see in the next sections, XLink and XPointer define XML's interdocument linking mechanism.

It's important to dispel a possible misconception about the use of ID and IDREF link attributes in XML documents. Simply using the id and idref characters in the attribute names does *not* cause them to become ID and IDREF attribute types in XML. It's also not by accident that I always capitalize the terms ID and IDREF. These terms are reserved data types for use when declaring linking attributes in an XML DTD. In order for an attribute to be of type ID or IDREF, it *must* be declared as such in the DTD or Schema.

The declaration of these XMI linking attributes in a DTD is explained in Chapter 8, but they are introduced here to distinguish the alternative approaches that are available when linking XML documents. The XMI version 1.1 specification defines five XML attributes that are included in every element of the vocabulary and may be used as the basis for linking elements within and between XMI-compliant documents. These standard declarations are listed in Table 7-2. The attribute type CDATA specifies that the value may contain any character data.

Table 7-2 Standard XMI attributes for linking

Attribute Name	Type	Description of Use
xmi.id	ID	Defines an identifier for the element containing this attribute. The identifier must be unique across the entire document.
xmi.idref	IDREF	This attribute value must be equal to an xmi.id value assigned to another element within the same document.
xmi.uuid	CDATA	Provides a globally unique identifier for this element. This value may be used, for example, with XPointer links or as an identifier when exchanging data with remote systems.
xmi.label	CDATA	Provides a string label for this element.
href	CDATA	Contains an XPointer link that may identify an element within this document or any other document.

Although XML's ID and IDREF mechanism have some advantages over HTML's anchors and hyperlinks for intradocument links, both approaches have significant limitations as the foundation for a global B2B information infrastructure. First, neither is able to reference arbitrary locations within other XML documents without modifying those documents to include identifier attributes. XPath overcomes this limitation for XML. Second, we need to create hyperlink references that address those locations using XPath, which is the subject of XPointer. Finally, we would like any XML element to participate as a link origin, either directly through its attributes or indirectly via external linking elements. XLink defines this linking language. Let's unravel this alphabet soup of acronyms.

XPath

XPath is a language for addressing parts of an XML document, with or without the presence of an ID attribute. XPath is a powerful, abstract language that operates on the tree structure of any XML document.[4] The name "XPath" was chosen because the language syntax resembles a file path in an operating system or a Web URL. This similarity was intentional on the part of XPath's designers, partly to help speed its adoption by current Web developers. The path syntax also facilitates embedding XPath expressions in URI strings, for example, in XPointer URIs.

---

4. World Wide Web Consortium. XML Path Language (XPath) 1.0, W3C Recommendation, 16 November 1999—see *http://www.w3.org/TR/1999/REC-xpath*.

A complete coverage of XPath would fill several chapters of a book. The goal of its coverage here is to introduce the role of XPath in expressing addresses for content elements of XML documents. XPath is not particularly useful *by itself*; it is a general-purpose addressing and pattern-matching language intended to be used by other XML applications. Two such applications currently exist: XSLT and XPointer. Other developers are evaluating the use of XPath as part of XML query languages. The description in this section is not a programmer's reference guide but an introduction to the capabilities of XPath [Kay, 2000].

Consider the following simple XPath expression:

```
/Catalog/Catalog.item/Product
```

Similar to a file system directory path, this XPath is an absolute location reference. The initial '/' character means that the Catalog element must be at the document's root level, the Catalog.item element must be directly contained as a child of Catalog, and Product is directly contained by Catalog.item. This XPath expression will return a set of all product elements that match these criteria. However, it's usually not very helpful to return all products from a catalog. Instead, we would like to filter this set of products to a more manageable subset, which is accomplished by this revision:

```
/Catalog/Catalog.item/Product[CatalogItem.name = 'Wizard 4000']
```

This expression will return zero or more references to Product elements whose CatalogItem.name child element has content equal to 'Wizard 4000'. The XPath expression contained in square brackets is called a predicate. It must contain a boolean expression that selects which Product elements to return (that is, it filters the Product elements in this branch of the document tree to return a subset that meet the filter criteria). XPath defines a set of functions that may be used within these filters. For example, if we want to return all products whose name starts with "Wizard," the XPath expression could be rewritten as follows:

```
/Catalog/Catalog.item/Product[starts-with(CatalogItem.name, 'Wizard')]
```

Review the UML class diagram shown in Figure 7-1, and trace this path through the classes, associations, and attributes. Although XPath's designers did not plan for its application to UML, the same path language is quite useful for expressing trace paths through the instances of a class model. I have found that a UML class diagram is my best reference guide when writing XPath expressions for a complex XML vocabulary.

For a more complex use of XPath, recall our example of the category taxonomy in the CatML vocabulary model, where a recursive association in the UML model allows Category elements to be contained as subcategories of other categories. XPath supports many additional path expressions for more complex selections such as this one. The following expression will return all matching Category elements whose name contains 'Software':

```
//Category[contains(Category.name, 'Software')]
```

This XPath statement begins with a double-slash, which selects *all* Category elements that are descendants of the document root, regardless of how many levels are nested in the document structure. (However, it may be very slow to execute for large documents.) This is useful for our product catalog because the recursive Category structure allows arbitrary depth in the taxonomy of product categories. The filter expression introduces another XPath function, contains(), that is useful for testing whether one string value contains another.

These examples should give you a reasonable idea for what can be written using simple XPath expressions. But the real power of XPath is realized when you combine these basic expressions into more complex statements that select elements from an XML document. Before continuing with the next example, review the summary of XPath syntax listed in Table 7-3. Although this is not an exhaustive reference, it helps isolate the most important capabilities of XPath expressions. If two of these basic expressions are combined, then the results of the first expression provide the context for the second expression.

As preparation for the next example, review the following fragment of a catalog taxonomy document. Don't focus too much attention on the document

Table 7-3   Summary of XPath syntax

Expression	*Example*	*Meaning*
Context element	Product	All expressions are relative to a context element.
Root context	/	The root context contains all other elements.
Location path	Product/Product.name	Select Product.name if direct child of Product.
Descendent	Category//Product	Select Product from any descendent of Category.
Attribute	@xmi.id	Select the xmi.id attribute of the context element.
Filter	Money[@amount < 500]	Select all Money children of the context element, where the amount attribute of Money < 500.
Function	id('p17') or contains('Java')	There are many predefined functions in XPath that are most often used in filter expressions.

details at this time because we'll analyze a more complete taxonomy example in the next section of this chapter. For now, concentrate on understanding the XPath expression syntax based on this XML document.

```
<Category xmi.id="Software">
  <Category.name>Software</Category.name>
  <Category.item>
    <Product xmi.idref="p1"/>
  </Category.item>
</Category>

<Product xmi.id="p1">
  <CatalogItem.name>XML Portal Wizard</CatalogItem.name>
  <CatalogItem.sku>wiz-5543-92</CatalogItem.sku>
  <CatalogItem.listPrice>
    <Money currency="USD" amount="195.00"/>
  </CatalogItem.listPrice>
  <CatalogItem.category>
    <Category xmi.idref="Desktop_Computers"/>
    <Category xmi.idref="Turnkey_Systems"/>
  </CatalogItem.category>
</Product>
```

Assume that we wish to ask for the following information: "Find all software products whose price is less than $500." The use of proxy elements with xmi.idref links complicates the XPath expressions necessary to address this XML structure. The solution requires several steps.

1. For all software categories, select those having "Software" in their name.
2. For all product proxy elements in those categories, select a subset.
3. Lookup the Product element whose ID is equal to the proxy xmi.idref.
4. Find the Money element that represents its listPrice.
5. Test if the amount attribute is less than 500.

Trace this example through the class diagram. Recall that the Category-item-CatalogItem association may contain Product objects because Product is a subclass of CatalogItem. This selection is expressed in XPath as follows (this is one XPath expression, but it is split across three lines for layout).

```
//Category[contains(Category.name, 'Software')]
  /Category.item/Product
    [id(@xmi.idref)/CatalogItem.listPrice/Money/@amount < 500]
```

There are two predicate expressions enclosed by square brackets in this example. Think of this as a two-stage filter that extracts a subset of the elements associated with each test. The first predicate filters the categories, and the second predicate filters products within the selected categories. There is also a new complication in the predicate expression: `id(@xmi.idref)`. The @ sign means that `xmi.idref` is an attribute of the current XML element rather than of a child element. The XPath function `id( )` looks up the document element having this ID. So together they return either the full Product element in the XML document that matches the `xmi.idref` value of the proxy or they return no elements if the ID is not found.

XPath is not used in isolation but instead is used as a common language for writing expressions that address or select XML elements and attributes as part of other applications. XPointer uses XPath expressions for XML linking, and the XSLT transformation language uses it for matching elements in a document. Other XML search and query facilities are under development that may use the XPath language as part of their syntax.[5] Unlike SQL database query languages that are optimized for relational set structures, XPath and a future XML query language (XQL) are optimized for the XML information set structure.

Let's put this detail back into focus. Our goal is to construct a Semantic Web of information using vocabularies that are based on UML models. The Semantic Web requires a richly structured vocabulary that captures the relationships, constraints, and ultimately the meaning of a large distributed information network. XPath is one tool in our toolkit for selecting objects from this Web. It's not the best choice in every situation, but it is a standard language that will become widely used when you need to traverse structured XML content. As we'll see in Chapters 10 and 11, XPath is an essential part of using XSLT to transform and present XML documents in e-business applications.

XPath is needed as a solution for removing the limitations of HTML and its unidirectional, one-to-one hyperlinks. We need multidirectional, one-to-many and many-to-many hyperlinks as building blocks to assemble our Semantic Web. XPointer enables us to create one-to-many hyperlinks that point into the structure of XML documents, using XPath as the language for selecting the target locations.

XPointer

XPointer enables hyperlinks to locate specific internal structures of XML documents.[6] It overcomes several of the HTML hyperlink limitations that were summarized at the beginning of this section. XPointer supports one-to-many links,

---

5. World Wide Web Consortium. XML Query Requirements, W3C Working Draft, 15 August 2000—see *http://www.w3.org/TR/xmlquery-req*.

6. World Wide Web Consortium. XML Pointer Language (XPointer), W3C Candidate Recommendation, 7 June 2000—see *http://www.w3.org/TR/xptr*.

and the links do not need to predefine named locations in the target document. The XPointer language uses XPath as a sublanguage for traversing the document tree and selecting locations based on element types, attribute values, and relative positions. An XPointer address is intended to be used as the fragment identifier in a URI reference that locates XML-based Internet resources.

Uniform Resource Identifiers[7] are a superset of Internet resource identifiers that include the more familiar URL. A URI may represent a globally unique resource name that is resolved via a directory service, whereas a URL typically refers to a particular file or data location. However, for our purposes, URIs are similar or identical to the URLs that you use daily. I'll use the term URI because it is now the standard term used throughout W3C specifications.

A URI reference may be absolute or relative and may have additional information attached in the form of a fragment identifier. The fragment identifier is the portion of the URI that follows the '#' character. XPointer specifies syntax and semantics of the fragment identifier. To keep things simple, my examples use relative URIs that are essentially file names for XML resources. The simplest XPointer-compliant URI appears identical to HTML hyperlink references. For example, the following URI identifies the XML element having an ID attribute equal to 's38' within the `Suppliers.xml` document.

```
Suppliers.xml#s38
```

There is no guarantee that this URI will point to any particular type of XML element—it points to whatever element has the indicated ID. This XPointer shortcut was allowed in part to provide backward compatibility with HTML links but also to encourage use of IDs as a robust form of linking. An equivalent complete XPointer locator is written as follows:

```
Suppliers.xml#xpointer(id('s38'))
```

Notice that this fragment identifier uses an XPath expression within the `xpointer()` scheme. The XPointer specification intends for schemes other than `xpointer()` to be provided in future standards, for example, to support addresses into non-XML resource types. But recall that the XPath `id()` function will work only if the XML document is parsed using a DTD (or other XML schema) that declares one or more of its attributes to be of type ID. An XML document is not required to be accompanied by a DTD, even if one is available. So there is no guarantee that this ID locator will find the intended element.

---

7. RFC 2396: Uniform Resource Identifiers. Internet Engineering Task Force, 1995—see *http://www.ietf.org/rfc/rfc2396.txt*.

XPointer defines an alternative syntax of providing multiple parts to the locator, as in this example:

```
Suppliers.xml#xpointer(id('s38'))xpointer(//*[@xmi.id='s38'])
```

If the first `xpointer()` part fails, then the second part is evaluated. The first part would use an efficient lookup of the requested ID value, whereas the second part would perform a very inefficient exhaustive search of all elements in the resource, testing each for the required attribute value. The second part has no dependence on presence of a DTD and, in fact, would work for any non-ID attribute value as well.

Beyond ID retrieval, XPointer locators enable one-to-many hyperlinks based on any valid XPath expression. The following URI points to all products within the June 2000 sale catalog whose list price is less than $500. Note that, unlike the previous XPath example, this example assumes that the Product elements are not proxy elements, so ID lookup is not required. Also note that this pointer may require substantial execution time for large documents. Depending on the XPointer engine implementation, it would probably execute a linear search of all products, testing each for its list price value. Finally, note that this hyperlink addresses a set of product elements that are not necessarily adjacent in the catalog document. The URI does not identify a physical location within a document, but its address is based on the document's logical structure.

```
http://www.wizardPCs.com/Catalog-June2000.xml
    #xpointer(//Product[CatalogItem.listPrice/Money/@amount < 500])
```

Consider one final example that might be useful when developing our CatX catalog portal. This URI locates the first ten products contained in the `'Notebooks'` category. The first ten products are determined by the order in which the products appear in the source XML document. The XPath expression is similar to one presented in the previous section, except that this one uses a new function `position()` that returns the sequence of a Product within the `Category.item` parent element.

```
Categorization.xml#xpointer(//Category[Category.name='Notebooks']
    /Category.item/Product[position() <= 10])
```

XLink

A restricted set of hyperlink tags was predefined in HTML. The `<A>` tag allows linking to other documents and the `<IMG>` tag was specialized for linking to image files. No other hyperlink tags are defined or allowed. XML is an extensible metalanguage; how will XML applications determine which elements to treat as links? XLink does not standardize the element names; those names are determined by your domain vocabulary. XLink specifies a standard set of XML attributes that determine which containing elements are recognized as links and partial information about how those links should behave in an application.[8]

Unlike HTML hyperlinks, XLinks may not be intended for human use in browsers. An XLink element represents an association in a UML class structure model, and that association may be optionally transformed into a hyperlink for human use in a Web application. However, many of the most obvious behavioral characteristics of HTML hyperlinks are not covered by the XLink specification. An HTML hyperlink's effect on windows, frames, go-back lists, stylesheets in use, and so on is determined by user agents (for example, browser applications) and not by the hyperlink itself. For example, traversal of <A> links normally replaces the current view, perhaps with a user option to open a new window. Similar to the way that XML vocabularies define the structure of an information model without specifying its presentation, XLink attributes define associations within and between documents without specifying their behavior.

The XLink specification is a W3C Candidate Recommendation as this book goes to press, so minor changes to the specification are possible. Some of the details described in these examples may be changed as the specification is completed, but it appears that those changes will be minor.

Some of these XML linking concepts go beyond the standards defined by the version 1.1 XMI specification. XLink was not yet adopted at that time, so the XMI committee avoided its use. I am anticipating (and recommending) the following use of XLink as a supplement for the deployment of UML models in XML vocabularies. Because XLink is intended to be easily integrated into any XML vocabulary, it is also easily integrated into an XMI-based vocabulary. With the exception to two redundant attributes that pose a minor challenge, we can merge XLink into the CatML vocabulary developed in the last two chapters. Use of the XMI attributes href and xmi.label are replaced by two analogous attributes from XLink, which are xlink:href and xlink:title.

I explained in Chapter 6 how XML namespaces are used as a means for packaging and integrating XML vocabularies without causing a collision of duplicate names. This is exactly the approach used by XLink. Any XML element can become a link by declaring the XLink namespace, as follows:

```
<MyElement xmlns:xlink="http://www.w3.org/1999/xlink">
  . . .
</MyElement>
```

---

8. World Wide Web Consortium. XML Linking Language (XLink) Version 1.0, W3C Candidate Recommendation, 3 July 2000—see *http://www.w3.org/TR/xlink*.

This declaration allows any of the XLink attributes to be used within <MyElement> or its child elements, as long as those attributes are prefixed with the xlink: namespace. The Resource CatML class and its corresponding <Resource> XML element are used to link product detail documents into a catalog. Using the standard XMI attributes, a resource element may be written as follows:

```
<CatalogItem.detail>
  <Resource href="/docs/WizardDataSheet.xml"
            xmi.label="Technical specifications for the Wizard PC"/>
<CatalogItem.detail>
```

This example becomes a simple XLink when rewritten with several new attributes.

```
<CatalogItem.detail>
  <Resource xmlns:xlink="http://www.w3.org/1999/xlink"
            xlink:type="simple"
            xlink:href="/docs/WizardDataSheet.xml"
            xlink:title="Technical specifications for the Wizard PC"/>
<CatalogItem.detail>
```

By converting the detail document link into a standard simple XLink, this CatML document can now be processed by a generic XLink application that either recognizes such links and renders them as hyperlinks in a browser or extracts these links as part of an indexed search engine.

Declaring the XLink namespace in the Resource element allows use of the XLink attributes without compromising the validity of our existing CatML document. Three new attributes were added, replacing use of the XMI attributes xmi.label and href. The complete set of valid XLink attributes is listed in Table 7-4. However, you may not arbitrarily choose and combine these attributes in any element.

An application that supports XLink would detect presence of the namespace declaration, then analyze the contained attributes to determine what linking behavior is required. I'll describe two uses of the XLink attributes for adding hyperlinks to XML vocabularies such as CatML. A *simple XLink* may be used as an implementation of unidirectional UML associations, and an *extended XLink* provides a more flexible implementation of bidirectional associations. These examples are provided as part of more detailed descriptions of the CatML vocabulary.

A Hyperlinked CatML Vocabulary

Four detailed examples in this section describe the enhancements made to our CatML vocabulary in Figure 7-1. Two goals guide the way these examples were

Table 7-4 XLink attributes

Attribute Name	Type	Description of Use
xlink:type	enumerated	This attribute dictates the constraints such an element must follow and the behavior of XLink-conforming applications on encountering the element. One of: (simple | extended | locator | resource | arc | title | none).
xlink:href	CDATA	Contains a URI, with an optional XPointer locator that identifies an element within the target document.
xlink:role	CDATA	Describes the meaning of the link's remote resource.
xlink:arcrole	CDATA	Describes the meaning of the link's remote resource in the context of a particular arc.
xlink:title	CDATA	Contains the title of the destination document or element.
xlink:label	CDATA	Identifies use of a locator or resource when participating in an arc.
xlink:from	CDATA	Resource label from which traversal can be initiated.
xlink:to	CDATA	Resource label that can be traversed to.
xlink:show	enumerated	Indicates desired display of target resource upon traversal of this link. Must be one of: (new | replace | embed | other | none).
xlink:actuate	enumerated	Indicates the desired timing of the link traversal. Must be one of: (onLoad | onRequest | other | none).

constructed. First, the examples explain the design rationale supporting the new vocabulary features and show how those features are realized in XML documents. Second, the examples illustrate the advanced linking capabilities that are possible in XML and demonstrate a small beginning for a distributed Semantic Web. The following four linking mechanisms are highlighted in these examples.

- `xmi.id` and `xmi.idref` attributes used for links within a document.
- `href` attributes, with and without XPointer locators, for linking between documents.
- Simple XLink used for unidirectional one-to-one and one-to-many links.
- Extended XLink for bidirectional links, possibly stored external to the linked documents.

Negotiated Price Lists

A product distributor often maintains a separate negotiated price list for each of its major customers. The `Discount` class in the expanded model enables the

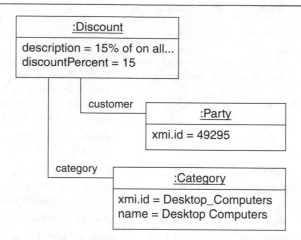

Figure 7-2 Customer discounts

creation of these price lists. In addition, this same Discount class may be used to represent promotional coupons that are valid for a limited period of time for a specific CatalogItem or an entire Category of items. The XML representation of these price lists and promotional coupons is managed in a separate Discounts document that includes links to the Products, Taxonomy, and Supplier documents, as listed in the Table 7-1 component definitions. This example thus illustrates linking between four components.

The following XML document and the object diagram in Figure 7-2 represent a Discount object that is linked to a particular customer Party object. This discount allows 15 percent off the list price for any product in the Desktop Computers category. This discount is available only to the customer whose id equals 49295.

This example illustrates the following XML linking concepts:

- href link attributes using an ID fragment and a dynamic URI.

```
<Discount>
  <Discount.discountPercent>
    15
  </Discount.discountPercent>
  <Discount.description>
    15% off on all desktop computers, good until canceled
  </Discount.description>
  <Discount.category>
    <Category href = "Taxonomy.xml#Desktop_Computers"/>
  </Discount.category>
```

```
<Discount.customer>
 <Party href = "/servlet/Customers?id=49295"/>
</Discount.customer>
</Discount>
```

The `Category` element represents a proxy object with reference to the full category definition in another document. In this case, the `href` attribute value references an external XML document and the URI includes an XPointer locator of the destination element's ID. Similarly, the Party element includes an `href` attribute for the remote element. But in this case the value is a dynamic URI that could be implemented as a Java servlet, which accepts one parameter named `id`. Although the document definition doesn't constrain the result, this dynamic URI should return an XML document fragment containing a valid `Party`, as specified in the FpML vocabulary.

In a deployed system, many similar XML elements would be collected into a document that defines the price list for a customer. We could create a separate XML document for each customer, plus an additional document containing special, time-limited promotional coupons. If we omit the customer link in the `Discount` element, and if we include the `startDate` and `endDate` attributes, then this element defines a coupon for a sales promotion that is valid for the indicated period of time. We could also add values for the `name` and `description` fields, and then use this discount coupon definition as part of an e-commerce portal implementation. In fact, we'll do just that in Chapter 11.

The UML diagram in Figure 7-1 does not show several constraints that are included in the model; these are summarized as follows:

- A `Discount` object may be linked to either a `Category` or a `CatalogItem` object, but not to both objects. In other words, we either specify a discount for a category of products or for one specific product.

- A `Discount` object may include a value for only one of the following attributes: `discountPercent`, `discountAmount`, or `discountPrice`. These are mutually exclusive approaches for specifying a discount.

- The `endDate` attribute value must fall after the `startDate` value.

The UML allows a constraint expression to be specified for any model element, so this list of constraints could be added to semantics of the `Discount` class definition. All UML-compliant modeling tools include a dialog box for a class definition (or other model elements) where these constraints can be documented. However, I am not aware of any commercially available UML tools that execute or enforce these constraint expressions. When the generation of XML schemas from UML models is analyzed in Chapters 8 and 9, you'll see that XML is especially lax at enforcing these types of semantic constraints in vocabulary definitions.

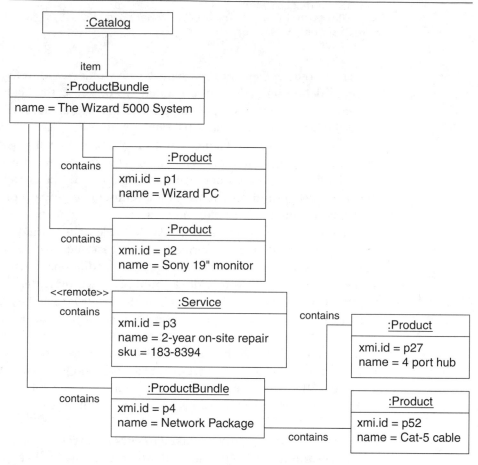

Figure 7-3 ProductBundle object diagram

Product Bundles

The expanded CatML model adds a ProductBundle class that enables a marketing manager to define combinations of products and/or services that are sold together, with a single price. Because a ProductBundle is a subclass of CatalogItem, it inherits all attributes and associations of its superclass. A ProductBundle can be contained in a Catalog, associated with a Category, or the subject of a Discount.

A ProductBundle must contain one or more CatalogItems. This is an interesting structure that has very powerful, generalized implications for the resulting XML documents. Because a ProductBundle is a subclass of CatalogItem, a ProductBundle may contain other ProductBundles. Consider the following example, which is presented first as a UML object diagram in Figure 7-3, then as an XML document instance. (Many of the child elements have been omitted for simplicity; for example, each catalog item must have a supplier.)

This example illustrates the following XML linking concepts:

- ID/IDREF linking within the `ProductBundle` definition document
- `href` link attribute to a remote `Service` item definition, plus a `Service` proxy element within the `ProductBundle` document

```
<Catalog>
 <Catalog.item>
  <ProductBundle>
    <CatalogItem.name>The Wizard 5000 System</CatalogItem.name>
    <ProductBundle.contains>
      <Product xmi.idref="p1"/>
      <Product xmi.idref="p2"/>
      <Service xmi.idref="p3"/>
      <ProductBundle xmi.idref="p4"/>
    </ProductBundle.contains>
  </ProductBundle>

  <Product xmi.id="p1">
    <CatalogItem.name>Wizard PC</CatalogItem.name>
  </Product>
  <Product xmi.id="p2">
    <CatalogItem.name>Sony 19" monitor</CatalogItem.name>
  </Product>
  <Service xmi.id="p3"
           xmi.label="2-year on-site repair"
           href="/servlet/Catalog?sku=183-8394"/>
  <ProductBundle xmi.id="p4">
    <CatalogItem.name>Network Package</CatalogItem.name>
    <ProductBundle.contains>
      <Product xmi.idref="p27"/>
      <Product xmi.idref="p52"/>
    </ProductBundle.contains>
  </ProductBundle>
 </Catalog.item>
</Catalog>
```

Why is it necessary to use ID/IDREF linking between the `Product` proxy elements within the `ProductBundle` and the `Product` elements contained later in the same document? The UML association between a `ProductBundle` and its contained `CatalogItem` objects is an *aggregation*, not a composition. So a `ProductBundle` owns its members by reference, not by value. Also, it is very likely that we will wish to include the same `Product` in more than one bundle. If all of these products and bundles are stored in the same XML document, then the ID/IDREF linking provides an efficient implementation.

This example introduces another new possibility for linking within and between XML documents. The document includes two `Service` elements, shown in boldface font. The first `Service` element is a proxy to the second `Service` element *within* the document. But the second occurrence is also a proxy element for the complete service definition *outside* of this document. This approach is common practice in XMI document generation. The idea here is that there may be many references to this service for two-year on-site repair, so we use an efficient ID/IDREF mechanism to link from all of these references to a single instance of a `Service` element (the second one in our example). The `xmi.label` attribute provides a description of this reference to the human reader.

This primary `Service` element is also a proxy, but it uses an `href` link attribute instead of a `xmi.idref` link. The `href` attribute value contains a hyperlink to an external document resource using a dynamic URI. Because only this one `Service` element needs to contain the URI reference, this design makes the catalog document easier to maintain. All other references to this same service simply refer to this primary proxy element. This two-stage proxy structure also facilitates better caching strategies in the XML applications that process this document. After the primary proxy element link is retrieved from the remote resource, all other links within the document gain access to this cached element.

Product Details

A `CatalogItem`, or any of its subclasses, may be associated with additional remote resources that provide detailed documentation. On most vendors' Web sites, a product will have links to an overview, a PDF datasheet, press releases, evaluation downloads, and so on. This is a straightforward addition to the model in Figure 7-1, where an association is included from `CatalogItem` to `Resource`. The `Resource` class in the CatML model represents any remotely accessible Web resource and is reusable in many other situations. In this model context, its use is identified by the role name `detail`. The `Resource` class is defined with a `<<SimpleXLink>>` stereotype indicating that the generated schema should include the required XLink attributes for simple links.

There are two different examples of these product detail links. The first example uses the standard XMI linking attributes, `href` and `xmi.label`, to define the links. The second example replaces these attributes to use simple XLink attributes. The first example, shown in Figure 7-4, contains three remote `Resource` objects linked to a `Product`.

This example illustrates the following XML linking concepts:

- `href` link attribute referencing a remote non-XML document containing HTML

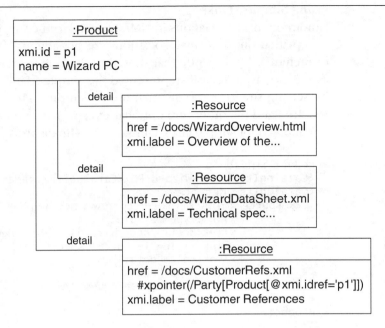

Figure 7-4   Product details

■ href link attribute using an XPointer locator to reference multiple elements within a remote XML document

```
<Product xmi.id="p1">
  <CatalogItem.name>Wizard PC</CatalogItem.name>
  <CatalogItem.detail>
    <Resource href="/docs/WizardOverview.html"
              xmi.label="Overview of the Wizard PC"/>
    <Resource href="/docs/WizardDataSheet.xml"
              xmi.label="Technical specifications for the Wizard PC"/>
    <Resource href="/docs/CustomerRefs.xml
                    #xpointer(/Party[Product[@xmi.idref='p1']])"/>
              xmi.label="Customer References"/>
  </CatalogItem.detail>
</Product>
```

Each Resource element includes the attributes href and xmi.label. These attributes are allowed for every element in an XMI 1.1-compliant document, thus enabling any element to be a proxy for a remote definition. But XLink provides significant additional capabilities and flexibility for XML linking.

Using Simple XLinks

Unidirectional associations in UML are similar in concept to HTML hyperlinks, except that one-to-many associations are possible in UML and it's often useful to include a label or title that describes the remote resource. A unidirectional association is most easily represented as a simple XLink. A simple link is created by setting the `xlink:type` attribute to 'simple'. The `xlink:href` attribute is required and the others are optional, except that `xlink:from` and `xlink:to` are not allowed for simple links. Our `Resource` link is thus expanded as follows:

```
<Product xmi.id="p1">
  <CatalogItem.name>Wizard PC</CatalogItem.name>
  <CatalogItem.detail>
    <Resource xmlns:xlink="http://www.w3.org/1999/xlink"
              xlink:type="simple"
              xlink:href="/docs/WizardDataSheet.xml"
              xlink:title="Technical specifications for the Wizard PC"
              xlink:role="detail"
              xlink:show="new"
              xlink:actuate="onRequest"/>
  </CatalogItem.detail>
</Product>
```

If a one-to-many link is required, simply add an XPointer locator to the end of the `xlink:href` URI value. The `show` and `actuate` attributes indicate that a new window should be created by the user agent, but the link should be traversed only on request. The actual behavior produced by these two attributes is subject to implementation and relevance by the user agent browser or device. If a mobile phone user traverses this link, it's unlikely that a new window will be produced.

Taxonomy of Categories

This last example is quite lengthy, so grab a cup of coffee, take a deep breath, and dive in! It is, however, a very worthwhile journey that illustrates the most significant benefits of XML linking and shows how those capabilities are used to create a more modular, distributed design for catalog applications.

It's common for products to be classified into categories within a catalog. Each category is defined as having a name and a description, and it may have zero or more descriptive features that provide assistance when searching the catalog for matching products. Each category is associated with zero or more `CatalogItem` instances. Of course, any subclass of `CatalogItem` may also be associated with a category.

Unlike the previous relationships that we've seen, this is a bidirectional association from `Category` to `CatalogItem`, so it must include role names and

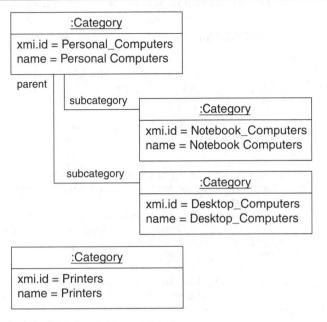

Figure 7-5   Taxonomy of product categories

multiplicity constraints on each end of the association. The association name is also new; this association is named `Categorization`. This is the name of the entire association, which is distinguished from the role name assigned to each association end. It is not necessary to name bidirectional associations, but it is sometimes useful to assist code-generation tools used with the UML modeling tools. In this case, the association name will be used to generate extended XLink elements that allow the categorization associations to be stored in an XML document separated from the `Category` and `CategoryItem` elements.

The product categories may be organized into a taxonomic hierarchy, where each category has zero or more sub-categories and zero or more optional parent categories. This hierarchy is modeled as a recursive association in the class diagram shown in Figure 7-1 (that is, both ends of the association are linked to a `Category` instance). Similar to the categorization association, this association is named `Taxonomy` to assist in mapping its instances to extended XLinks. These associations will be stored as extended XLink elements in a separate `Taxonomy.xml` document.

The example in Figure 7-5 defines four categories that are organized into a simple taxonomy with two parent elements. The example is shown as a UML object instance diagram, then as an XML document fragment.

This example illustrates the following XML linking concept:

- ID/IDREF linking within the Category definition document.

The XML representation in the following document uses the XML ID and IDREF linking mechanism that is limited to the scope of one document. Note that the ID values assigned are almost the same as the category names, except that the ID values replace all space characters with an underscore. Spaces are invalid in XML ID values.

```
<Category xmi.id="Personal_Computers">
  <Category.name>Personal Computers</Category.name>
  <Category.subcategory>
    <Category xmi.idref="Notebook_Computers"/>
    <Category xmi.idref="Desktop_Computers"/>
  </Category.subcategory>
</Category>

<Category xmi.id="Notebook_Computers">
  <Category.name>Notebook Computers</Category.name>
  <Category.parent>
    <Category xmi.idref="Personal_Computers"/>
  </Category.parent>
</Category>

<Category xmi.id="Desktop_Computers">
  <Category.name>Desktop Computers</Category.name>
  <Category.parent>
    <Category xmi.idref="Personal_Computers"/>
  </Category.parent>
</Category>

<Category xmi.id="Printers">
  <Category.name>Printers</Category.name>
</Category>
```

The CatML model allows zero or more Feature objects to be associated with each Category, plus zero or more FeatureValue objects to be associated with each CatalogItem. A FeatureValue is always associated with one Feature. In other words, a category defines a set of features and a catalog item optionally defines values for its category features. Notice the use of a solid diamond on these association ends, unlike the open diamonds on other associations in the model. As described in Chapter 3, a solid diamond designates a composition in the UML, and an open diamond indicates an aggregation association.

The difference between composition and aggregation has important significance in the mapping of UML to XML. A UML composition creates nested child elements in the resulting XML document instances, whereas an aggregation

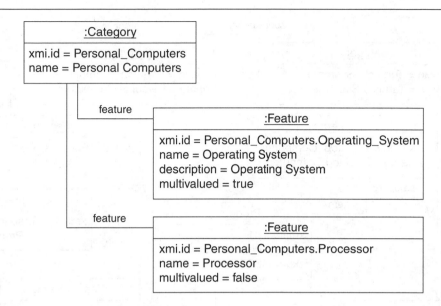

Figure 7-6   Category to Feature composition

may be represented as either a nested child element or a proxy element linked to its remote element definition. The `Category` to `Feature` composition is represented in Figure 7-6 as UML objects, then as an XML document.

This example illustrates the following XML linking concept:

■ Basic composition hierarchy of elements in an XML document.

```
<Category xmi.id="Personal_Computers">
  <Category.name>Personal Computers</Category.name>
  <Category.feature>
    <Feature xmi.id="Personal_Computers.Operating_System">
      <Feature.name>Operating System</Feature.name>
      <Feature.description>Operating System</Feature.description>
      <Feature.multivalued xmi.value="true">
    </Feature>
    <Feature xmi.id="Personal_Computers.Processor">
      <Feature.name>Processor</Feature.name>
      <Feature.multivalued xmi.value="false">
    </Feature>
  </Category.feature>
</Category>
```

On the other hand, aggregation associations are treated in XML the same as unadorned association ends. By default, an XMI-generated document produces a

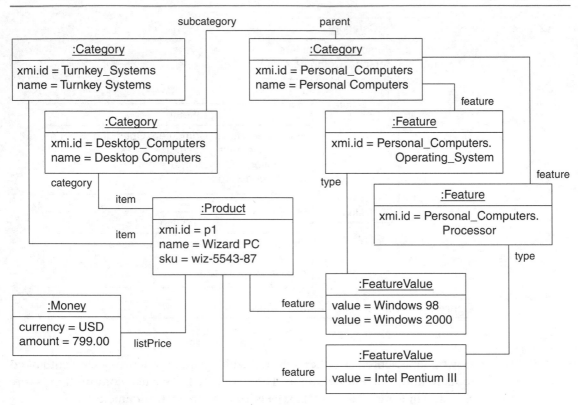

Figure 7-7 Category to CategoryItem aggregation

proxy element as a child contained in the aggregate, with a reference link to the remote element definition. The `Category` to `CategoryItem` aggregation is represented in Figure 7-7 as UML objects, followed by an equivalent XML document.

This example illustrates the following XML linking concepts:

- ID/IDREF linking between `Category` and `Product` elements
- Composition hierarchy of `FeatureValue` elements within `Product`

```
<Category xmi.id="Desktop_Computers">
  <Category.name>Desktop Computers</Category.name>
  <Category.item>
    <Product xmi.idref="p1"/>
    <Product xmi.idref="p22"/>
  </Category.item>
</Category>
```

```
<Product xmi.id="p1">
  <CatalogItem.name>Wizard PC</CatalogItem.name>
  <CatalogItem.sku>wiz-5543-87</CatalogItem.sku>
  <CatalogItem.listPrice>
    <Money currency="USD" amount="799.00"/>
  </CatalogItem.listPrice>
  <CatalogItem.category>
    <Category xmi.idref="Desktop_Computers"/>
    <Category xmi.idref="Turnkey_Systems"/>
  </CatalogItem.category>
  <CatalogItem.feature>
    <FeatureValue type="Personal_Computers.Operating_System">
      <FeatureValue.value>Windows 98</FeatureValue.value>
      <FeatureValue.value>Windows 2000</FeatureValue.value>
    </FeatureValue>
    <FeatureValue type="Personal_Computers.Processor">
      <FeatureValue.value>Intel Pentium III</FeatureValue.value>
    </FeatureValue>
  </CatalogItem.feature>
</Product>
```

In summary, the CatML category taxonomies were described in three parts. First, the recursive association produced a hierarchy of Category objects, where the ID/IDREF mechanism was used to construct the links within this document. Second, a straightforward addition was made to include Feature objects as child elements within each Category. Third, the categories were linked with Product objects, and FeatureValue objects were added to the Product description. All of these categorization links were made using ID/IDREF references. But this approach to linking creates a very limited application design because all elements must be included in the same document. This problem is solved by using XLinks.

Using Extended XLinks

Refer back to Figure 7-1 where a bidirectional association connects Category with CatalogItem. This association represents a many-to-many association; for example, a product might be assigned to several categories within the catalog taxonomy and, of course, a category will likely contain many products. That association is also named Categorization for reasons that will now become apparent.

In the previous examples of the taxonomy, the Product references were explicitly included as child elements of the Category definitions. In the same way, the Category references were included as child elements of the Product definitions. This works reasonably well for small examples but is problematic for large numbers of products. Also, we may wish to categorize a product within two or more totally independent taxonomies. A product might be categorized within the RosettaNet taxonomy and also within a proprietary taxonomy developed by Cheap PCs. This will become a common requirement when companies begin to participate in several trading exchanges that have not agreed on a single taxonomy definition.

To solve this problem, we would like to separate the assignment of products to categories into one or more separate components. Using this design, an independent categorization component could be created for each taxonomy deployed in the multimarketplace scenario. This design can be realized through the use of XLink.

We'll begin by stripping out the linking elements from the previous product and taxonomy definitions. The XML documents are also reorganized to fit the distributed component architecture. The Taxonomy.xml component is simplified and focused strictly on defining the category hierarchy and the features of those categories. This is a much cleaner design and enables the creation of several such components that represent alternative taxonomies. Although this example is limited to one Category element that has one Feature, the complete taxonomy would probably include more than one hundred categories, each with several features. This example also omits the subcategory hierarchy structure among the category definitions.

Taxonomy.xml
```
<Category xmi.id="Desktop_Computers">
  <Category.name>Desktop Computers</Category.name>
  <Category.feature>
    <Feature xmi.id="Personal_Computers.Operating_System">
      <Feature.name>Operating System</Feature.name>
      <Feature.description>Operating System</Feature.description>
      <Feature.multivalued xmi.value="true">
    </Feature>
  </Category.feature>
</Category>
```

Notice that the Category element includes an xmi.id attribute, which must be unique among all elements within this document. As we'll see in Chapter 8, this attribute is declared as an ID so that it may be used for indexed linking between elements in a document. The Products.xml component is similarly streamlined to include only Product descriptions, omitting the Category associations that were part of the earlier example. This component would include many such products, services, and product bundles, each with a unique value for the xmi.id attribute.

Products.xml
```
<Product xmi.id="p1">
  <CatalogItem.name>Wizard PC</CatalogItem.name>
  <CatalogItem.sku>wiz-5543-87</CatalogItem.sku>
</Product>
```

```
<Product xmi.id="p2">
  <CatalogItem.name>Wizard Network Hub</CatalogItem.name>
  <CatalogItem.sku>wiz-7792-35</CatalogItem.sku>
</Product>
```

We are now in a position to create an extended XLink element that associates products and categories. A simple XLink was used for unidirectional associations (that is, the xlink:type attribute was assign a value of 'simple'). Extended XLink elements are much more powerful but also more complex to apply. I only introduce a partial description of their use, but this example does touch on many of the key features.

Whereas the simple unidirectional XLink attributes were added to an existing CatML element, we define a new element for the extended bidirectional link. This element is assigned a name equal to the UML association name shown in Figure 7-1, Categorization. In UML, this name refers to the entire association and is distinct from the two association end roles that are also specified; because the XLink element captures the entire bidirectional association, this name is a natural fit for the new association element. As with the Taxonomy and Products components, this Categorization component is defined separately, and the example shows one of many such elements in the document.

Categorization.xml

```
<Categorization xmlns:xlink="http://www.w3.org/1999/xlink"
                xlink:type="extended">
  <CatalogItem xlink:type="locator"
               xlink:label="item"
               xlink:href="Products.xml#p1
               xlink:title="Wizard PC"/>
  <Category xlink:type="locator"
            xlink:label="category"
            xlink:href="Taxonomy.xml#Desktop_Computers"/>
  <Category xlink:type="locator"
            xlink:label="category"
            xlink:href="Taxonomy.xml#Office_Equipment"/>
  <Categorization.item.category xlink:type="arc"
            xlink:from="item"
            xlink:to="category"/>
  <Categorization.category.item xlink:type="arc"
            xlink:from="category"
            xlink:to="item"/>
</Categorization>
```

The version 1.1 XMI specification does not include XLink definitions such as this one, but I expect that something similar will be added to a future version after the XLink specification is voted as a recommendation by the W3C. Meanwhile, this XLink element poses no conflicts with the remainder of our CatML vocabulary and is added as a new component. I'll step through the XML elements in this example at a high level of review; please consult the XLink specification for additional explanation.

First, as with the simple XLink, the namespace must be declared for the scope of this element and its children. The `Categorization` element then includes the `xlink:type` attribute with the value 'extended'. Unlike a simple XLink, an extended XLink does not need to be directly part of the link origin, but it indirectly relates two or more other elements. The URI references to these other elements are included in child elements of the extended link. Three such elements are included in this example: one `CatalogItem` and two `Category` elements. XLink requires that these remote element references have an `xlink:type` value equal to 'locator'. In other words, these are locator elements that the extended XLink uses to find the link ends. Each of these locators must include an `xlink:href` attribute containing the URI reference and may optionally include an `xlink:title` attribute containing a human-readable title for the remote resource. The locator element also has an optional `xlink:label` attribute, but as we'll see, this attribute is critical to the link definition.

Until this point, we've said nothing about which of these locators are origins or destinations of the link. That is where `arc` elements come in. As the name suggests, an `arc` joins two resources to form a link. However, in this example, an `arc` does not specify a link between two specific resources, such as `Product` 'p1' with `Category` 'Desktop_Computers', but it creates a general declaration for arcs between two labels. The example includes two `arc` declarations, one from label 'item' to label 'category' and the second from 'category' to 'item'. Each `arc` declaration is an element with the `xlink:type` value equal to 'arc'. The element names for these arcs are not critical; it's just important that their declarations be present within the parent extended XLink element.

So, what do these arcs do? When an XLink aware application reads this document, it effectively creates four links: two links associating the product with the categories, and two associating the categories with the product. You could simply insert additional locator elements as children of this `Categorization` element and define their label as either 'item' or 'category', and then the application would create arcs for their associations.

Now imagine n-ary associations with greater than two participating classes, and you can quickly see how the extended XLink enables a very generalized linking model. A generic XLink processor would scan any XML document for the presence of XLink attributes and interpret the containing elements according to the `xlink:type` attribute value. A database or other cross-reference table of link information could be created with functionality similar to Web search engines but specialized for interpreting the labels and arcs of extended links.

Chapter Summary

A Semantic Web is not limited to the links within one XML document nor even to XML as the sole information source. The Semantic Web is a massively distributed information network containing both human- and machine-interpretable meaning. Flexible linking mechanisms are a prerequisite for attaining this vision.

- The CatML vocabulary was expanded to enable more complex and complete catalog definitions. This expanded catalog also requires better linking mechanisms.
- The XML ID and IDREF linking is defined as part of the XML 1.0 specification but is limited to links between elements within a single document.
- The href attribute defined as part of XMI 1.1 enables basic interdocument linking.
- Use of XPath and XPointer expand the usefulness of URIs included in href links but is still limited to one-to-many linking within and between documents.
- Simple XLink definitions are also limited to one-to-many links, but the link semantics are expanded through a set of standard link attributes that are recognized by any XLink-enabled application.
- Extended XLink enables a very flexible, although somewhat more complex, linking mechanism useful for many-to-many and bidirectional links.
- Use of extended XLink allows the links to be extracted from the origin and destination documents and stored within an external linkbase document or database.
- Although the examples in this chapter focus on B2B applications, the same principles may be applied to internal system integration and to vocabularies intended for Web-based presentation.

Steps for Success

1. Work toward the vision of a Semantic Web that connects a universe of network-accessible information.

2. Plan your application integration as a set of addressable resources, where each resource becomes a URI in the Semantic Web. XPointer locators enable URI addresses to select one or more elements within a large XML resource.

3. Plan your linking strategy to support a loosely coupled, distributed application architecture. A complex vocabulary will include many relationships among its elements, including elements from other vocabularies. These relationships may be contained within one XML document or between many documents and virtual URIs distributed over the public Internet.

4. Assign the classes of your vocabulary to components that define clusters of related information. There should be relatively tight cohesion within a component to allow efficient indexed linking among its elements. There should be relatively loose coupling between components so that flexible XLink mechanisms may be used to link elements across components.

Chapter 8

XML DTDs and Schemas

The previous two chapters described how UML class diagrams are used to model XML document vocabularies. The UML model is independent of the implementation language(s) used to represent a vocabulary's concepts, relationships, and constraints; it focuses attention on the requirements for successful interagent communication, whether those agents are human or machine. The mapping of UML model elements to XML was accomplished by applying the XML Metadata Interchange (XMI) standard. The examples mapped *instances* of the UML classes (the Wizard 4000 PC product) to instances of XML document elements and attributes. But this still begs the question of how the UML model definitions can be used to produce the equivalent document schema definitions used by XML applications.

The XML community has developed a number of schema languages for representing document models. The Document Type Definition (DTD) is the original XML schema language included in the XML 1.0 specification. However, many individuals have recognized the limitations of this DTD standard for supporting data interchange in global e-business applications. The new schema proposals extend the capabilities for validating documents and exchanging information with other non-XML system components. The role of XML schemas is analogous to the way that relational database systems use the SQL data definition language to create schemas for a particular set of database tables, attributes, attribute datatypes, and referential integrity constraints. XML schemas must support compatibility with database system schemas, but not lose sight of using XML to present information content to users in many other media, such as Web browsers, printed documents, Braille, voice synthesis, mobile phones, and PDAs.

After a brief introduction to the role of XML schemas, I first summarize the DTD standard and the XML Schema Candidate Recommendation under development by the W3C. Next, I describe the use of these two schema languages for validating the content of XML documents. In Chapter 9, I describe XMI as a standard for automatically generating these XML DTDs and Schemas from the UML model definitions.

The Role of an XML Schema

Do you really *need* a schema? As you know, XML is unique among data interchange formats in that schemas are optional. The XML element tags make a document self-describing and easily parsed using generic tools. In fact, the XML specification explicitly defines the use of schema-less XML processing. And since all XML documents must be well formed according to a relatively simple set of rules governing element and attribute composition, they can be parsed without a schema. But there remain some compelling reasons for creating an XML schema to accompany your application (see sidebar).

These schema roles apply regardless of which XML schema variant you are following. As discussed previously, the term *schema* can be confusing at times. It may refer to the official W3C XML Schema Recommendation, but the term is also widely used as a general descriptor for other XML document definitions, including DTDs. To review: I consistently use schema when describing general use and Schema when referring to the official W3C XML Schema.

All schemas provide some degree of definition and documentation for an XML vocabulary. The definitions are useful both to system integration specialists who are writing applications that process document instances of the

---

■ Reasons to Create XML Schema

- Defining and documenting the vocabulary for all users
- Validating documents when using XML parsers
- Providing structural guidance for content providers using XML authoring tools

- Providing default attribute values, enumerated lists, and identifier declarations
- Defining new application or domain-specific datatypes
- Generating application code, such as Java classes, database schemas, and XML schemas

vocabulary and to Web application specialists developing stylesheets for transforming and presenting the XML content. But the definitional aspects of the schema are often insufficient to communicate their purpose and recommended usage. This is particularly true for business analysts and content specialists who participate in the specification and use of a schema. Comments are generally placed within the text of the schema, and supplementary text documentation is written to explain a schema's purpose and use. The UML's range of structural and behavioral models and diagrams make a significant contribution to this role of XML schemas.

When XML documents are created by application programmers (for instance, when the documents are exported as output from legacy systems) or manually authored using general-purpose editors, the document may be invalid with respect to the schema. (For example, an element may be inserted where it does not belong or omitted where it is required.) Although validation of a document's correctness is often the most significant use of XML schemas, alternative schema languages vary widely in their abilities to validate structural and semantic accuracy of the documents. Some schemas impose excessive or artificial structural constraints on documents in order to gain other types of validation benefits; this is especially true of DTDs. Most schemas provide little or no semantic validation but are limited to validating basic grammatical structure.

XML-enabled authoring tools may be used to create or modify documents; for example, content specialists would add new products to a catalog using our CatML vocabulary. These content specialists might use an XML authoring tool similar to SoftQuad's XMetaL[1] or Extensibility's XML Instance,[2] which guide an author in creating valid documents. Most similar authoring tools use an XML DTD to guide document creation and validation, but they are migrating now toward the newer, more capable schema languages. Extensibility's product supports both DTDs and XML Schemas.

Regardless of whether an XML document is used for data exchange or text-oriented content, there are situations where an XML authoring tool is helpful—for example, to list valid elements and attributes that may be inserted at each point in a document; to assist in copy-cut-paste of XML structured blocks; and to support easy authoring of XML tags having long names without a lot of typing (it generally does the latter well). These features are useful for any document type.

---

1. For information about the XMetaL authoring product, see *www.SoftQuad.com*.

2. For information about Extensibility's products, see *www.Extensibility.com*.

Authoring tools differ in their ability and emphasis on editing data-oriented or text-oriented documents. SoftQuad's XMetaL excels at creating a familiar word processor interface that is comfortable for nontechnical users. The editor interface is rendered using Cascading Style Sheets (CSS) applied to the XML document content, and the content is dynamically validated against any provided DTD.

Using a schema also provides benefits of attribute datatypes that are not available to schema-less well-formed XML documents. Very limited datatypes are available with DTDs and powerful, extensible datatypes are available with the new W3C XML Schema. The previous two chapters described use of ID and IDREF identifiers for linking, but none of these capabilities are available without a schema that declares which attributes are identifiers.

Using a schema, an XML vocabulary can also provide default attribute values and enumeration lists. For example, an Address element type may include a country code attribute that defaults to "US" if the value is not provided in a document instance. That same country code also may be restricted to an enumerated list of all valid values. The XML parser would validate the attribute value against this list and throw an error if an undefined value is used. The same enumerated list could populate a pull-down selection list in an authoring tool. But be cautious about depending on default attribute values in your XML application because some consumers of your documents may choose to process them without consulting the schema and will miss the defaults.

In sharp contrast, DTDs provide very limited datatype support for attribute values and no datatype support for the text content of elements. This limitation, which has been one of the most influential catalysts for creating a new standard schema specification, is discussed in detail for DTDs and W3C XML Schemas in the following two sections.

It has become common practice for developers to automatically generate Java class implementations and database schema definitions from XML schemas. The limitations of DTD expressiveness restrict the precision of this generated code, but this technique still saves considerable time that would ordinarily be required to manually produce programs that read and write the XML documents. Adoption of W3C XML Schemas will dramatically improve the quality of this generated code. However, this development process fragments the XML implementation from the other application components. The XML schema drives some components of the application design, the database model drives other components, and the non-XML business objects and user interface drive the remaining components. As argued in Part I of this book, the UML unifies this development process and improves communication among all stakeholders of the system. It makes sense for UML to be the primary driver for requirements analysis and design. Thus, the XML schemas, database schemas, and business objects are all generated from a common application model.

XML Document Type Definition

The purpose and syntax of Document Type Definitions (DTDs) have a long history, beginning many years before XML was specified. I won't belabor the description of the history, but it is important to know that it exists because XML's use of DTDs inherits this history, including its limitations. DTDs were originally adopted as the standard for the Standard Generalized Markup Language (SGML) document definitions. XML was adopted as a W3C Recommendation in February 1998, with a primary goal of simplifying SGML for use in distributed, on-line applications. XML creators attempted to capture 80 percent of SGML's benefits with 20 percent of its complexity. A majority subset of SGML's DTD specification was used in the XML specification, largely because its use was well understood and had been successful in prior use.

XML's creators probably could not have imagined the extremely wide range of use that XML applications would fulfill in current distributed system design. XML DTDs are helpful in the design of B2B applications but often are not sufficient. A complete description of DTD design principals would fill an entire book [Maler, 1996; St. Laurent, 1999]. My goal is to summarize its key features in order for you to appreciate the rules used to generate DTDs from UML models. Three features are presented: element declarations and content model, attribute declarations, and entity declarations. This summary also provides the basis for comparing DTDs to similar features of the W3C XML Schema specification.

DTD Element Declarations and Content Model

Declaring an element type is analogous to declaring a class in a UML model, although DTD element declarations are much more limited in their capabilities. An element type declaration defines its name, a composition of child elements as its content, plus optional attributes. Three elements are declared in the following simple example, where the first element has one attribute.

```
<!ELEMENT Book (title, publisher) >
<!ATTLIST Book price CDATA #IMPLIED >
<!ELEMENT title (#PCDATA) >
<!ELEMENT publisher (#PCDATA) >
```

This simple DTD would validate the following document instance:

```
<Book price="39.95">
  <title>101 ways to Groom Your Cat</title>
  <publisher>Cat Lover LLC</publisher>
</Book>
```

Table 8-1 Element content models

Content Model	Definition
EMPTY	No child elements or text are allowed.
ANY	Any declared element types may be used in this element content.
#PCDATA	Parsed character data other than elements is allowed (that is, free-form text).
Choice	One element from a list is included in the content: (x | y).
Sequence	A sequence of elements are included in the specified order: (x, y).
Group	A group of elements enclosed by "( )" may be nested: (x, (y | z)).
Mixed	Both elements and text are allowed: (#PCDATA | x | y)*.

Table 8-2 Element content multiplicity

Multiplicity	Definition
none	Exactly one element or group instance must be included.
?	Zero or one instances are required.
*	Zero or more instances are required.
+	One or more instances are required.

Unlike UML classes, however, an element may declare additional substructure within its content model. The alternatives for content model declaration are listed in Table 8-1. The element type declarations listed in Table 8-2 may also specify limited multiplicity constraints on its child elements.

Each of the element content models are used in the following example, except for EMPTY, which is used in a later description of enumeration. All four kinds of multiplicity are illustrated. These examples do not include any XML attribute declarations but are limited to element type declarations with a variety of content models.

```
<!ELEMENT Bibliography (Book | LibrarianNotes)* >
<!ELEMENT Book (Book.title, Book.author+, Book.abstract) >
<!ELEMENT Book.title (#PCDATA) >
<!ELEMENT Book.author (firstName, lastName, email?, website?,
            (officePhone | mobilePhone)* ) >
<!ELEMENT Book.abstract (#PCDATA | bold | italic | underline)* >
<!ELEMENT LibrarianNotes ANY>

<!ELEMENT firstName (#PCDATA) >
<!ELEMENT lastName (#PCDATA) >
<!ELEMENT email (#PCDATA) >
```

```
<!ELEMENT website (#PCDATA) >
<!ELEMENT officePhone (#PCDATA) >
<!ELEMENT mobilePhone (#PCDATA) >
<!ELEMENT bold (#PCDATA) >
<!ELEMENT italic (#PCDATA) >
<!ELEMENT underline (#PCDATA) >
```

This example defines a simple bibliography DTD. The `Bibliography` element declaration contains zero or more instances of the group, and the group specifies a choice of one of the two enclosed elements. The practical effect of this first declaration is that a `Bibliography` may contain any number of any of these elements, in any order.

The `<Book>` element declaration specifies a sequence that it must contain at least three child elements in the given order. It must contain exactly one `<Book.title>`, followed by one or more `<Book.author>` elements, followed by exactly one `<Book.abstract>`. The `<Book.author>` declaration includes a choice group nested within a sequence group. This element must have one first name, one last name, an optional e-mail address, an optional Web site URI, and zero or more phone numbers chosen from `<officePhone>` or `<mobilePhone>`.

It's relatively rare to declare an element using the ANY content model, as it requires no limit whatsoever on the child elements contained by that element. `LibrarianNotes` is included in this example to illustrate the ANY content model, but it is actually somewhat contrived and a bit unrealistic. In this example, `LibrarianNotes` could validly contain any of the other elements declared in this DTD.

The `<Book.abstract>` element is an example of mixed content, which means that the element may contain any combination of the specified elements intermingled with text. This is a typical declaration for text-oriented XML documents that are similar to HTML pages. In this example, an abstract is free-form text that allows some text to be highlighted as bold, italic, or underlined. It is, however, up to the XML application to render these highlighted elements appropriately in the document presentation. Again, this is identical to the way that HTML is processed by a browser.

Every element type must be declared in the DTD, so the last nine declarations specify simple elements that may contain text but may not contain child elements. Note that the DTD provides no way to specify that the `<website>` element must contain a URI to be valid; it can only specify #PCDATA content. Similarly, there is no way to restrict the content of the two phone number elements.

A document that complies with these DTD declarations is as follows. Notice that this DTD allows multiple `<officePhone>` elements for an author but requires neither an office nor mobile phone number. The document includes one author for this book but could include more. The DTD specified a multiplicity requiring that a Book must contain one or more authors (`Book.author+`).

```
<Bibliography>
 <Book>
  <Book.title>Modeling XML Applications with UML</Book.title>
  <Book.author>
    <firstName>David</firstName>
    <lastName>Carlson</lastName>
    <email>dcarlson@ontogenics.com</email>
    <officePhone>303-555-1212</officePhone>
    <officePhone>415-555-1212</officePhone>
  </Book.author>
  <Book.abstract>
    This book presents the <bold>benefits and concepts</bold>
    required for successful use of the <italic>Unified Modeling
    Language (UML)</italic> in XML application development.
  </Book.abstract>
 </Book>
</Bibliography>
```

The bibliography DTD is defined without the use of XML attributes, which is perfectly legitimate. Chapter 6 described some criteria for choosing between elements and attributes in the design of your XML vocabulary. You may want to use XML attributes to represent primitive datatype values that contain metadata about an element, or you *must* use attributes if you choose to define enumerated lists in your DTD. If you wish to include attributes in your documents, they must be declared in the DTD along with the element types.

DTD Attribute Declarations

DTD element type declarations do not support any restrictions on the character data included in elements having a #PCDATA content model. As an alternative, XML attribute declarations allow a very limited restriction of attribute value type and also enable enumerated value lists, default values, or fixed attribute values.

The primary XML attribute types relevant to UML modeling and XMI are listed in Table 8-3. Note that there is no attribute type corresponding to a conventional programming datatype, such as integer, float, or boolean. XML attribute values are either strings of characters or atomic string tokens without whitespace. There are several types of atomic values representing specific attribute usage in XML documents. In addition, there is no provision for arrays or other multivalued attribute types, except for simple space-delimited token lists in the case of IDREFS and NMTOKENS. These limitations are one of the primary motivators for replacing the DTD declarations with a more robust XML schema language. In addition to declaring the type of each XML attribute, the default value may be declared using one of the three forms listed in Table 8-4.

Table 8-3   XML 1.0 DTD attribute types

Attribute Type	*Definition*
CDATA	String character data
ID	A document-unique identifier
IDREF	A reference to a document-unique identifier
IDREFS	Multiple identifier references separated by whitespace
NMTOKEN	A name composed of CDATA characters but no whitespace
NMTOKENS	Multiple names composed of CDATA characters separated by whitespace

Each of these attribute types is illustrated in the following example, where six new attributes are added to the <Book> element declaration.

```
<!ELEMENT Book.author (firstName, lastName, email?, website?,
            (officePhone | mobilePhone)* ) >
<!ATTLIST Book
    pubDate    CDATA      #REQUIRED
    language (EN | FR | DE | other) "EN"
    xmi.id     ID         #IMPLIED
    xmi.idref  IDREF      #IMPLIED
    xlink:type CDATA      #FIXED    "locator"
    xlink:label NMTOKEN   #IMPLIED
>
```

A required attribute named pubDate is included to hold the value of the book publication date. Next, a language attribute is declared with an enumerated list of four possible values. One of these values may be optionally declared as the default value, which is 'EN' in this example. The #IMPLIED or #REQUIRED default type is not necessary for enumerated attributes if a default value is specified.

As described in Chapters 6 and 7, each element in an XMI-compliant document must allow attributes for xmi.id and xmi.idref; these are declared as type ID and IDREF, respectively.

Table 8-4   DTD attribute defaults

Default Type	*Definition*
#IMPLIED	An attribute value is optional.
#REQUIRED	An attribute value is required in each document instance.
#FIXED	An attribute value set in the DTD cannot be changed in document instances.

Finally, two XLink attributes are defined. The `xlink:type` attribute cannot be changed from its fixed default value "locator" and will cause a validating XML parser to throw an error if any other value is assigned within a document instance. The `xlink:label` attribute is defined with the value type NMTOKEN, as required by the XLink specification. Thus, this attribute value cannot contain any whitespace characters.

Consider the following document fragment that satisfies this DTD:

```
<Book
    pubDate = 'January 2000'
    xmi.id = '0-201-61577-0'
    xlink:label = 'book'
/>
```

When this document is read by an XML parser, it is assigned default values for `language` and `xlink:type`. If they are included, the remaining attributes are assigned values from the document instance. Because `xmi.idref` has no assigned value, it will remain null. If a document instance fails to assign a value to the `pubDate` attribute, the parser throws an error because this attribute is required by the DTD.

Because XML applications are not required to process the DTD, even if it's provided, there is a risk that the default values will not be assigned for `language` and `xlink:type`. If critical default values are included in the DTD, it is essential that your application design include the requirement for processing the DTD with each document instance.

There are often many redundant attribute declarations in a vocabulary DTD. For example, as described in Chapters 6 and 7, each element type must include several common attributes required by the XMI standard. In order to make DTDs more maintainable and to prevent accidental error of omission, a DTD may use entity declarations for these common definitions. These XMI attributes and their declarations are described in the next section.

DTD Entity Declarations

XML parameter entities are often used to ease the development and maintenance of DTDs. Parameter entities are similar to the macro string substitutions available in many software engineering tools, programming languages, or word processors. The XMI specification defines two parameter entities for common element and linking attributes. The following two parameter entities are defined near the beginning of an XMI-generated DTD and then are included in all following model elements.

```
<!ENTITY % XMI.element.att
 'xmi.id    ID    #IMPLIED
  xmi.label CDATA #IMPLIED
  xmi.uuid  CDATA #IMPLIED' >

<!ENTITY % XMI.link.att
 'href       CDATA #IMPLIED
  xmi.idref IDREF #IMPLIED' >
```

Each of these entities defines a fragment of attribute declarations, but neither entity value is a complete DTD declaration on its own. The entities are included as substitutions in other declarations. For example, we can replace the standard XMI attributes in the Book element declarations as follows:

```
<!ATTLIST Book
    pubDate   CDATA       #REQUIRED
    language (EN | FR | DE | other) "EN"
    xlink:type CDATA      #FIXED    "locator"
    xlink:label NMTOKEN   #IMPLIED
    %XMI.element.att;
    %XMI.link.att;
>
```

When this DTD is processed by an XML application, the entities are replaced by their values, resulting in the addition of five attributes to the Book element declaration.

Limitations of DTDs

Although the DTD syntax is relatively easy to learn and allows small, efficient validating parsers, it is too limited to describe the data-oriented vocabulary schemas used in B2B applications. The following are the primary limitations.

- Inadequate datatypes for attribute values and none for element text content
- Inadequate identifier definitions using ID and IDREF
- No constraints on the destination element type for links: any ID is acceptable
- Inadequate support for child element multiplicity constraints
- No support for element type inheritance
- Either one namespace for an entire DTD or a hard-wired namespace prefix
- No support for documentation, other than using general comment text

Given these limitations, it's not unusual for analysts or developers to ask, Why create a DTD when you need to write a document validation program anyway?

There are many examples of XML use where no DTD was ever created. In particular, DTDs lack the precision required for XML applications that emphasize complex data interchange and database import/export. This demand has accelerated the push for more robust schema languages and for the focus on a common next-generation schema standard.

W3C XML Schema

The charter of the W3C working group for schemas is to create a common framework for abstracting information, regardless of the form (narrative, normalized data, objects, or multimedia) and regardless of domain (literary, mathematical, financial, or e-commerce transactions). That's a tall order. The desire to satisfy so many diverse stakeholders has delayed completion of the specification and has added to its complexity. The long-awaited specification finally reached the W3C's Candidate Recommendation stage in October 2000, and there are several implementations that support many of the specification's features. There is great anticipation of the benefits that it will deliver for next-generation XML applications.

Although the essential features of DTDs were summarized in a few pages, a similar summary is not possible for XML Schema. The XML Schema specificatione[3,4] is 333 pages long, and the "easily readable description" contained in the primer for XML Schema[5] is 78 pages long. Instead, I summarize the key features that help to overcome the limitations of DTDs and emphasize those that are especially important for object-oriented analysis and modeling of vocabularies with UML. These are the key features.

- XML Schemas are XML document instances.
- Datatypes and datatype refinement.
- Extension of element types (inheritance).
- Locally scoped element declarations.
- Unordered content model.
- XML namespace support.

---

3. World Wide Web Consortium. XML Schema Part 1: Structures, W3C Candidate Recommendation, 24 October 2000—see *http://www.w3.org/TR/xmlschema-1*.

4. World Wide Web Consortium. XML Schema Part 2: Datatypes, W3C Candidate Recommendation, 24 October 2000—see *http://www.w3.org/TR/xmlschema-2*.

5. World Wide Web Consortium. XML Schema Part 0: Primer, W3C Candidate Recommendation, 24 October 2000—see *http://www.w3.org/TR/xmlschema-0*.

If schema definitions themselves could be saved as ordinary XML documents, then a single set of parsers, data structures, programming APIs, and authoring tools could be used to create the schemas. The fact that DTDs are written using a specialized syntax requires dedicated software tools for parsing the DTD documents; it also requires distinct data structures and APIs within programs to hold and manipulate those schema definitions. In addition, developers must learn a new syntax, and authoring software must include specialized support for editing the DTD structures. If you follow the recursive cycle, then an XML Schema can be written as a specification for XML Schema documents, thus enabling the current generation of authoring and development tools to be used for creating the next generation schemas. This is exactly what has been done with the XML Schema specification.

Even though we can easily create and parse these new XML Schemas, there remains the task of producing new validation and authoring tools that take advantage of the unique new features of these schemas. Adoption of the new schema language can occur in two phases. First, we can write new schemas that are able to validate the existing legacy document instances that were created using DTDs. Even with this conservative approach, we can begin to take advantage of new features that enable us to produce more modular schemas that have more restrictive validation capabilities.

As a second phase, we can begin to migrate to the new schema features that prohibit backward-compatible document instances. Many new B2B applications will jump straight to this second phase, but other applications such as XML-structured content for enterprise information portals may follow the more conservative migration path.

I'll begin with a summary of the most sought-after feature of XML Schema: datatypes and datatype refinement. The following section explores the first phase of schema deployment by describing schemas that are compatible with DTDs. This includes explanation of inheritance in schemas. The final section looks forward to the use of advanced Schema structures in the second phase of adoption. This includes description of the remaining XML Schema key features for locally scoped elements, unordered content models, and namespace support.

Datatypes and Datatype Refinement

Improved datatype support is of interest to many of the stakeholder groups introduced in Chapter 1. Business analysts are concerned with precisely defining the content and purpose of a vocabulary's elements and attributes; a DTD's datatypes of #PCDATA and CDATA just don't cut it. The datatypes must be defined in terms of specific ranges of valid integer values, money amounts, boolean values, string formats for social security numbers or telephone numbers, and so on. These datatypes are crucial to defining the vocabulary's proper usage.

System integration specialists have similar requirements but are also concerned with relational database datatype compatibility, legacy system data interchange, and Java object serialization and deserialization to XML. System integration often requires transformation of one vocabulary to another, and it is critical for datatype values to be converted as well. Web application and content specialists use the vocabulary definition as one input for determining proper authoring and presentation requirements. The semantics of the element and attribute names themselves are of primary importance, but the intended datatype of the values is also essential information. If an element content is defined to be positive integers with values less than 1000, that may determine presentation more than an element named `quantity`.

In response to requirements like these, the XML Schema Requirements document itemizes four datatype concerns that must be fulfilled by the specification.

1. Provide for primitive data typing, such as byte, data, integer, sequence, SQL, and Java primitive data types.

2. Define a type system, such as relational, object, or OLAP, that is adequate for import/export from database systems.

3. Distinguish requirements relating to lexical data representation versus those governing an underlying information set.

4. Allow creation of user-defined datatypes, such as datatypes that are derived from existing datatypes and which may constrain certain of its properties such as range, precision, length, format.

The first two requirements are self-explanatory. The current specification defines 43 simple datatypes that are built-in to XML Schema. The best summary of these built-in types is listed in the XML Schema Primer document. This list includes the usual suspects such as string, boolean, integer, float, and double. There are a wide array of date types including date and time, but also month, year, timePeriod, recurringDate, and timeDuration. All of the existing DTD datatypes, such as ID and IDREF, are also supported.

The third requirement is a bit abstract. A practical interpretation of the underlying information set is the primitive datatypes (for example, integer, float, or string) and subsets or enumerations of those primitives. The lexical representation determines the literal values that denote those primitive values. For example, a float primitive may be represented as either "100" or "1.0E2." These lexical specifications can also be used by the schema designer to derive user-defined datatypes from these primitives.

XML Schema includes a rich set of *facets* used to constrain the values of derived datatypes. Fourteen facets, including enumeration, length, minLength, maxLength, and pattern, are defined. A previous example showed how an enumerated attribute value could be represented in a DTD.

```
<!ATTLIST Product
    units (each | dozen | meter | kilogram) "each">
```

But there is no way in DTD definitions to declare that the content of an *element* must come from an enumerated list. Using XML Schema, you can define a new datatype and use it for both attributes and element content. The equivalent datatype would be defined as follows:

```
<xsd:simpleType name="UnitOfMeasure">
  <xsd:restriction base="xsd:string">
    <xsd:enumeration value="each"/>
    <xsd:enumeration value="dozen"/>
    <xsd:enumeration value="meter"/>
    <xsd:enumeration value="kilogram"/>
  </xsd:restriction>
</xsd:simpleType>
```

In XML Schema, the simpleType element is used to define new datatypes, usually by refining another existing datatype. In this example, the UnitOfMeasure datatype *restricts* a base datatype, xsd:string, whose definition is built in to XML Schema. In this case, the base string type is restricted to be one of four enumerated values.

Each of the elements used in the XML Schema language itself is prefixed with the namespace xsd: ('xsd' is an abbreviation for XML Schema Definition). Unlike DTDs, XML Schemas are specified with explicit integration of the XML Namespaces specification. When writing a schema, you are able to choose your own prefix; xsd: is just an example of what can be used.

This new datatype definition can be used to declare an attribute.

```
<xsd:attribute name="units" type="UnitOfMeasure"/>
```

Or, an element:

```
<xsd:element name="Product.units" type="UnitOfMeasure"/>
```

In a similar manner, other user-defined datatypes can be derived for application-specific vocabularies. The following datatype restricts an xsd:string to declare a social security number (SSN) that is required to match the pattern of three digits, followed by a hyphen, followed by two digits, a hyphen, and four digits. This pattern expression uses a small sample of the regular expression language that is part of the XML Schema specification.

```
<xsd:simpleType name="SSN">
  <xsd:restriction base="xsd:string">
    <xsd:pattern value="\d{3}-\d{2}-\d{4}"/>
  </xsd:restriction>
</xsd:simpleType>
```

These datatype definitions hold great potential both for improving the clarity and completeness of XML vocabularies and for better matching the attribute type declarations in UML class models. The remainder of the XML Schema specification includes features that match those available in DTDs as well as many others that reach far beyond what DTDs can capture. I'll start by redefining DTDs from the previous section and mapping them into XML Schema syntax (with a few new twists) and then conclude with a brief summary of more advanced features.

Schemas Compatible with DTDs

I like concrete examples that illustrate an idea, so let's launch right into it. To facilitate the comparison of an equivalent DTD and XML Schema, I've duplicated in Listing 8-1 the Bibliography example from the last section, presented first as a DTD then as an XML Schema. This example has been specifically crafted to illustrate many of the key schema concepts in relatively little space.

The DTD's root element is a `Bibliography`, which contains zero or more `Book` elements. I have added a `pubDate` attribute to the `Book` element and omitted the `LibrarianNotes` element; otherwise it's identical to the prior DTD example.

Listing 8-1   Bibliography.dtd

```
<!ELEMENT Bibliography (Book)* >
<!ELEMENT Book (Book.title, Book.author+, Book.abstract) >
<!ATTLIST Book pubDate CDATA #IMPLIED >

<!ELEMENT Book.title (#PCDATA) >
<!ELEMENT Book.author (firstName, lastName, email?, website?,
                       (officePhone | mobilePhone)* ) >
<!ELEMENT Book.abstract (#PCDATA | bold | italic | underline)* >

<!ELEMENT firstName (#PCDATA) >
<!ELEMENT lastName (#PCDATA) >
<!ELEMENT email (#PCDATA) >
<!ELEMENT website (#PCDATA) >
<!ELEMENT officePhone (#PCDATA) >
<!ELEMENT mobilePhone (#PCDATA) >
<!ELEMENT bold (#PCDATA) >
<!ELEMENT italic (#PCDATA) >
<!ELEMENT underline (#PCDATA) >
```

This DTD can be used to validate the XML document instance in Listing 8-2. The document includes a DOCTYPE declaration, which specifies that the document type is "Bibliography" and that the DTD is available at the system location "Bibliography.dtd." This declaration requires the single root element of this document to be `<Bibliography>`, which corresponds to the document type name. A validating XML parser would produce errors if this document either did not follow the grammatical rules specified by the DTD or if it had a different root element.

The same set of definitions from the DTD is provided in Listing 8-3, which depicts an XML Schema that can be used to validate the same document instance. Starting with a high-level overview, there are several things to observe. Like all XML documents (because the schema is now an XML document instance), the schema has exactly one root element: `<xsd:schema>`. This element declares the `xsd:` namespace used in the remainder of the schema (there are alternative approaches that make XMLSchema the default namespace, thus omitting the prefix, but I'll avoid those complications in this discussion). There are five `<xsd:complexType>` elements, each of which defines an element type in the schema. Any element that may contain attributes or child elements must be a defined using a `complexType`.

I have constructed this schema example such that it could be mapped to a UML class model, even though one has not been produced. Each of the complex type definitions would correspond to a class in the model. So what is this

Listing 8-2   Bibliography.xml

```
<?xml version="1.0" ?>
<!DOCTYPE Bibliography SYSTEM "Bibliography.dtd">
<Bibiliography>
 <Book pubDate = "2001-03-01">
  <Book.title>Modeling XML Applications with UML</Book.title>
  <Book.author>
    <firstName>David</firstName>
    <lastName>Carlson</lastName>
    <email>dcarlson@ontogenics.com</email>
    <website>http://www.XMLModeling.com</website>
    <officePhone>303-555-1212</officePhone>
    <officePhone>415-555-1212</officePhone>
  </Book.author>
  <Book.abstract>
    This book presents the <bold>benefits and concepts</bold>
    required for successful use of the <italic>Unified Modeling
    Language (UML)</italic> in XML application development.
  </Book.abstract>
 </Book>
</Bibliography>
```

Listing 8-3   Bibliography.xsd

```
<?xml version="1.0" ?>
<xsd:schema xmlns:xsd = "http://www.w3.org/2000/10/XMLSchema">

<xsd:element name="Bibliography" type="Bibliography"/>

  <xsd:complexType name="Bibliography">
    <xsd:sequence>
      <xsd:element name="Book" type="Book"
                   minOccurs="0" maxOccurs="unbounded"/>
    </xsd:sequence>
  </xsd:complexType>

  <xsd:complexType name="Book">
    <xsd:sequence>
      <xsd:element name="Book.title" type="xsd:string"/>
      <xsd:element name="Book.author" type="Author"
                   minOccurs="1" maxOccurs="unbounded"/>
      <xsd:element name="Book.abstract" type="Abstract"/>
    </xsd:sequence>
    <xsd:attribute name="pubDate" type="xsd:date"/>
  </xsd:complexType>

  <xsd:complexType name="Person">
    <xsd:sequence>
      <xsd:element name="firstName" type="xsd:string"/>
      <xsd:element name="lastName" type="xsd:string"/>
    </xsd:sequence>
  </xsd:complexType>

  <xsd:complexType name="Author">
    <xsd:complexContent>
      <xsd:extension base="Person">
        <xsd:sequence>
          <xsd:element name="email" type="xsd:string"
                       minOccurs="0" maxOccurs="1"/>
          <xsd:element name="website" type="xsd:uriReference"
                       minOccurs="0" maxOccurs="1"/>
          <xsd:choice minOccurs="0" maxOccurs="unbounded">
            <xsd:element name="officePhone" type="xsd:string"/>
            <xsd:element name="mobilePhone" type="xsd:string"/>
          </xsd:choice>
        </xsd:sequence>
      </xsd:extension>
    </xsd:complexContent>
  </xsd:complexType>

  <xsd:complexType name="Abstract" mixed="true">
    <xsd:choice minOccurs="0" maxOccurs="unbounded">
      <xsd:element name="bold" type="xsd:string"/>
      <xsd:element name="italic" type="xsd:string"/>
      <xsd:element name="underline" type="xsd:string"/>
    </xsd:choice>
  </xsd:complexType>
</xsd:schema>
```

<xsd:element> that occurs as the first element in the schema? The XML Schema specification makes a clear distinction between element *definitions* and element *declarations*. <xsd:element> is a declaration of an element that may appear in a valid document instance, but it does not define that element type. It declares that an element named "Bibliography" has the type "Bibliography" that is elsewhere defined in the schema. In fact, it declares the root element for valid document instances. It's not necessary for both the element declaration and the complexType definition to have the same name, but it's also acceptable if they do. I have found that this approach leads to a more intuitive mapping to the UML model.

Each of the <xsd:complexType> definitions includes child elements that define the content model and/or attributes for this element type. Both the child element definitions and the attribute definitions specify the type of their content. The type may be one of the built-in primitives from XML Schema (for example, Book.title is of type xsd:string), or the type may be one of the complex or simple types declared within this schema (for example, Book.author is of type Author). Also notice that the multiplicity can be specified more precisely than in DTDs by using the minOccurs and maxOccurs attributes in an element definition.

Each complexType must define the content model for its child elements. The content model for Bibliography, Book, Person, and Author is a *sequence*, which has identical properties to a sequence in DTDs. In the case of the Author definition, a *choice* group is nested within a *sequence* group, which has exactly the same semantics as in the previous DTD for this bibliography schema.

The greatest difference between the DTD and the XML Schema bibliography definitions is in the use of element type inheritance. The Author definition is a subtype of Person, and is derived by *extension*. This is specified as follows:

```
<xsd:complexType name="Author">
  <xsd:complexContent>
    <xsd:extension base="Person">
       . . .
    </xsd:extension>
  </xsd:complexContent>
</xsd:complexType>
```

As shown in the document instance example, an <Author> element extends the content model of Person by combining all element and attribute definitions. Because both Author and its parent type Person are defined with a sequence content model, the new elements defined for Author will be appended to the end of the sequence defined for Person. This capability of XML Schema enables schemas to be written in a much more object-oriented style than when using DTDs. The XML Schemas also map more directly onto UML class models than do DTD schemas.

One attribute and one element are defined with more precise datatypes than were possible in the DTD. The pubDate attribute is defined with type xsd:date, which will require that this attribute value contains a valid date when the document instance is validated against this schema. Similarly, the element website is defined with type xsd:uriReference, which will assure that the element content contains a valid URI string. This capability creates a very big advantage when using XML Schemas to validate documents exchanged between business partners in a B2B (or any other) application.

Finally, XML Schema includes a capability similar to parameter entities in DTDs. You can define named groups of elements or attributes then reference them for reuse in element definitions. In the DTD examples, we created a parameter entity named XMI.element.att that defined reusable definitions for the standard XMI attributes. The following XML Schema fragment defines an attributeGroup that is then included within the Book element definition.

```
<xsd:schema xmlns:xsd = "http://www.w3.org/2000/10/XMLSchema">
  <xsd:attributeGroup name="XMI.element.att">
    <xsd:attribute name="xmi.id" type="xsd:ID"/>
    <xsd:attribute name="xmi.label" type="xsd:string"/>
    <xsd:attribute name="xmi.uuid" type="xsd:string"/>
  </xsd:AttributeGroup>

  <xsd:complexType name="Book">
    <xsd:sequence>
      <xsd:element name="Book.title" type="xsd:string"/>
      . . .
    </xsd:sequence>
    <xsd:attribute name="pubDate" type="xsd:date"/>
    <xsd:attributeGroup ref="XMI.element.att"/>
  </xsd:complexType>
</xsd:schema>
```

XML Schema documents are typically named with the extension ".xsd". You can optionally include a reference to the associated schema in the root element of a document instance, as shown here. This replaces the DOCTYPE declaration with its reference to the document's DTD. In this example, the xsi: namespace prefix is used for attributes that are defined in a separate set of standardized definitions designated for use in XML document instances.

```
<?xml version="1.0" ?>
<Bibliography
    xmlns:xsi='http://www.w3.org/2000/10/XMLSchema-instance'
    xsi:noNamespaceSchemaLocation='Bibliography.xsd'>
  . . .
</Bibliography>
```

Let's review the highlights of what we gained using XML Schema, as compared to using a DTD.

- Schemas are represented in XML syntax and can be processed or edited using any existing XML programming tools, authoring tools, XML databases, and so on.
- Element type inheritance improves maintainability and avoids duplicate declarations (for example, Author inherits definitions from the Person type).
- Built-in and user-defined datatypes dramatically improve accuracy of document validation, eliminating the need to put this validation code in application programs.
- AttributeGroup definitions provide functionality that is equivalent to DTD parameter entities and enable reusable definitions within a schema.

Advanced Schema Structures

It is worthwhile to review three additional features of XML Schema because of their direct applicability to representing UML class models. None of these features are available with DTD definitions, so using them may prohibit the creation of document instances that can be validated with both a DTD and an XML Schema. However, after the XML Schema specification becomes an adopted W3C Recommendation, the benefits that these features provide when mapping UML models to schemas will likely justify their use.

Content Models with Unordered Elements

A DTD allows two alternative content models for child elements: sequence or choice. A sequence group requires elements in a document instance to be in the order specified in the DTD. A choice group allows one of the member types from a group. However, in many cases DTD designers use a choice group followed by a "*" multiplicity character as a way of declaring an unordered list of element types.

```
<!ELEMENT CatalogItem
        (CatalogItem.name | CatalogItem.description
        | CatalogItem.sku |CatalogItem.listPrice)* >
```

This declaration allows any number of these elements to appear in any order within a document. This approach is used throughout the XMI version 1.1 specification. The downside of this approach is that it is not possible to limit document instances to only one of each element type. A document author could include four `Catalog.sku` elements and the document would still be valid with respect to this DTD.

An XML Schema supplies a better alternative: the <all> content group. The DTD declaration may be redefined using XML Schema as follows:

```
<xsd:complexType name="CatalogItem">
  <xsd:all>
    <xsd:element name="CatalogItem.name" type="xsd:string"
                 minOccurs="0" maxOccurs="1"/>
    <xsd:element name="CatalogItem.description" type="xsd:string"
                 minOccurs="0" maxOccurs="1"/>
    <xsd:element name="CatalogItem.sku" type="xsd:string"
                 minOccurs="1" maxOccurs="1"/>
    <xsd:element name="CatalogItem.listPrice type="xsd:decimal"
                 minOccurs="0" maxOccurs="1"/>
  </xsd:all>
</xsd:complexType>
```

The <all> group in this definition specifies that the four elements within `CatalogItem` may appear in any order in a document instance. In addition, each of the element is optional (that is, minOccurs is 0 and maxOccurs is 1), except for `sku`, which is required. This definition is especially useful when mapping UML class definitions to schemas because the attributes in a UML class are not required to follow any particular order.

Locally Scoped Element Names

As described in Chapter 6, the attribute names of a UML class are always prefixed with the class name when mapping objects to XML elements. For example, the `Catalog` attribute `name` was mapped to the element <Catalog.name>. The reason for this requirement is that a DTD for this vocabulary has only one namespace, and all element names are in that one namespace. This naming convention assures that XML element types remain unique, even when several classes contain an attribute called `name`. I therefore have <Catalog.name>, <CatalogItem.name>, <Category.name>, and so on.

If we were to create this document schema using XML Schema instead of a DTD, then there is a provision for locally scoped element names that do not need to be unique across the entire schema. In fact, we can have two element declarations with the same name and different datatypes. I have modified our Bibliography schema such that the `Book` child elements are no longer prefixed with "Book.", and I have added a `title` element to the content model for `Person`. You'll notice that both `Book` and `Person` have a `title` element, and the `title` within `Person` is defined as an enumerated datatype.

```
<xsd:complexType name="Book">
  <xsd:sequence>
```

```
      <xsd:element name="title" type="xsd:string"/>
      <xsd:element name="author" type="Person"
                   minOccurs="1" maxOccurs="unbounded"/>
    <xsd:sequence>
  </xsd:complexType>

<xsd:complexType name="Person">
  <xsd:sequence>
    <xsd:element name="title" type="TitleEnum"/>
    <xsd:element name="firstName" type="xsd:string"/>
    <xsd:element name="lastName" type="xsd:string"/>
  </xsd:sequence>
</xsd:complexType>

<xsd:simpleType name="TitleEnum">
  <xsd:restriction base="xsd:string">
    <xsd:enumeration value="Mr."/>
    <xsd:enumeration value="Mrs."/>
    <xsd:enumeration value="Ms."/>
    <xsd:enumeration value="Dr."/>
  </xsd:restriction>
</xsd:simpleType>
```

This schema would successfully validate a document containing the following elements, whereas a DTD for this document would need to declare one generic global <title> element with string content.

```
<Book>
  <title>Modeling XML Applications with UML</title>
  <author>
    <title>Dr.</title>
    <firstName>David</firstName>
    <lastName>Carlson</lastName>
  </author>
</Book>
```

Target Namespaces

The topic of namespace support in XML Schema is complex, so this introduction is limited to a summary of benefits and an example. The XML Namespace specification was developed *after* XML 1.0 was standardized, so DTDs have no defined support for validating documents that combine vocabularies from several namespaces. There is, however, a growing need for XML document instances to combine several vocabularies that collectively define that document's content. This is especially true as industry standard schema repositories are developed for sharing vocabularies used in B2B e-commerce.

In Chapters 6 and 7, I introduced the FpML vocabulary along with our CatML vocabulary. The FpML beta specification was composed of several subvocabularies, each having its own namespace. The following example document instance declares CatML as the default namespace and includes two of the FpML vocabulary namespaces. The default namespace means that any element without a prefix belongs to the CatML vocabulary.

```
<Catalog xmlns = "http://xmlmodeling.com/schemas/CatML"
         xmlns:pty = "http://www.fpml.org/schemas/TradingParty"
         xmlns:m = "http://www.fpml.org/schemas/Money">
  <Product xmi.id="p1">
    <CatalogItem.name>Wizard PC</CatalogItem.name>
    <Product.price>
      <m:Money currency="USD">
        <m:Money.amount>799.00</m:Money.amount>
      </m:Money>
    </Product.price>
    <CatalogItem.supplier>
      <pty:Party href="/Suppliers?name=WizardPCs"/>
    </CatalogItem.supplier>
  </Product>
</Catalog>
```

Using XML Schema, one schema document is defined for each of the three vocabularies, and an XML parser combines all three schemas when validating the above document instance. The beginning of the CatML schema might look like this.

```
<xsd:schema xmlns:xsd = "http://www.w3.org/2000/10/XMLSchema"
            targetNamespace = "http://xmlmodeling.com/schemas/CatML"
            elementFormDefault = "qualified"
            attributeformDefault = "unqualified" >

  <xsd:element name="Catalog" type="Catalog"/>

  <xsd:complexType name="Catalog">
    . . .
</xsd:schema>
```

This schema declares its `targetNamespace`, which means that any document instance having this namespace URI can be validated by this schema. Notice that the previous document instance declared its default namespace with a value equal to this schema's target namespace. For additional information on the use of namespaces in document validation, refer to the *XML Schema Part 0: Primer*.[6]

---

6. World Wide Web Consortium. XML Schema Part 0: Primer, W3C Candidate Recommendation, 24 October 2000—see *http://www.w3.org/TR/xmlschema-0*.

Replacement or Coexistence?

Should we expect XML Schemas to completely replace DTDs after the specification is finalized by the W3C? That's unlikely, at least for the foreseeable future. XML Schema provides many compelling benefits for e-business applications and I expect rapid adoption, but there are several equally compelling reasons for DTDs to coexist.

1. DTDs are much simpler and allow small, efficient implementations. Full implementation of the XML Schema specification is likely to require larger, slower validation tools, which may not be required for all applications.
2. DTDs are still a good fit for many text-oriented applications.
3. There is a large, and rapidly growing, legacy-installed base of DTD vocabularies. These will not be immediately converted.
4. In cases where XML Schemas are developed first, it may be possible to create one-way transformation from XML Schemas to DTDs—one-way because a DTD is less expressive than an XML Schema.

So, assuming that DTDs and XML Schemas will coexist for some time as standards for vocabulary specification, how do we cope with this dual world? By using UML models as our primary vocabulary specification language, of course! It's a good approach because UML was designed as an expressive specification language that is independent of implementation language, whereas DTDs and XML Schemas are examples of implementation languages used by XML development tools.

The XMI standard has addressed the mapping of UML models to XML DTDs and will address a mapping to XML Schemas in the near future. The next chapter discusses principles of DTD and Schema generation from UML class models and gives detailed examples drawn from our CatML vocabulary.

Chapter Summary

-   A schema (either DTD or XML Schema) fulfills many different roles in an XML application, including documentation, validation, editing, and code generation. Although many developers omit schemas in their designs, there is good reason to give high priority to the analysis and use of an XML schema.
-   The XML DTD specification is mostly a subset of the preexisting SGML standard, including its limitations. DTDs cannot easily combine several

namespaces and have very restricted datatype capabilities. On the other hand, DTDs are easy to develop for small applications and are supported by many software tools.

- XML Schema includes a very rich datatype definition language that dramatically improves the precision of vocabulary definition and document validation. Both XML attribute values and element content can be validated by the same datatype definitions.

- XML Schema enables derivation of both simple and complex type definitions. This capability provides a better conceptual match to UML class inheritance than is possible with DTDs.

- Support for XML namespaces is built in to the XML Schema language and processing requirements.

Steps for Success

1. Clearly define the role (documentation, authoring, code generation, and so on) that either DTD schemas or XML Schema will serve in your XML application.

2. Determine whether you need a DTD for compatibility with older XML tools and applications, or if you can exclusively rely on XML Schema. If you are exchanging schemas with business partners, make sure that you know their requirements.

3. Will the schema be available when document instances are processed? If not, then don't plan to rely on default values defined in the schema.

4. How much validation is required beyond what is possible with schema definitions and constraints? XML Schema enables much more rigorous validation than is possible with DTDs.

Chapter 9

Generating XML Schemas from the UML

We have now completed the UML class structure model of our CatML vocabulary; we have also reviewed two options for representing this vocabulary as either an XML DTD or an XML Schema. So how can we automate the generation of a schema (DTD, XML Schema, or one of the other variants) from our UML model? This generation must be accomplished with a predictable set of rules that will produce semantically equivalent results for each schema, regardless of the implementation. This is precisely the subject of the OMG's XML Metadata Interchange (XMI) specification.

Because the current XMI version 1.1 specification was written prior to adoption of the XML Schema or XLink specifications (both are W3C Candidate Recommendations in early 2001), neither was incorporated into XMI. However, adoption is imminent for both XML Schema and XLink, so it is important to introduce a pre-standard prototype of what such a mapping would look like upon completion. You can begin using the mappings presented here and then modify the details that change when a final standard is adopted by the OMG. A prototype mapping for both XML Schema and XLink is included in this chapter.

The XMI production rules in the current specification create "relaxed," or loosely constrained, DTDs. This choice was made both to enable exchange of partial models and because of the limitations of DTD representation. There is, however, a possibility of producing somewhat stricter DTDs from the UML model and allowing designer discretion regarding which elements are constrained in what ways. UML stereotypes are used to allow this designer control. Because these strict DTDs are a subset of the standardized relaxed DTDs, any other party in a distributed B2B transaction could successfully use a relaxed schema to validate a document created according to a strict schema. In this chapter I describe the relaxed versus strict alternatives for both DTDs and XML Schemas.

These choices of DTD versus XML Schema and relaxed versus strict schema constraints create a two-by-two matrix of alternatives. In order to support your understanding and selection among these choices, I'll begin with a list of general principles for schema generation, then apply these principles to each of the four alternatives.

Principles of Schema Generation

There is a set of common principles that must be applied when generating XML schemas from UML class models. For each type of schema (DTD, XML Schema, or other) and for the choice of relaxed or strict validation, a decision must be made about how each of these criteria will be addressed. The nine criteria are summarized in the sidebar. None of these concepts are new. We encountered the first three criteria in Chapter 6; the last criterion on linking is in Chapter 7; and criteria 4 through 8 are introduced in Chapter 8.

■ Principles of XML Schema Generation

Namespace mapping—Should the entire UML model be mapped to one XML namespace or each UML package to a separate namespace?

Element name uniqueness—How are the generated XML element names assured to be unique, given the selected namespace mapping and target schema language?

Elements or attributes—Should UML attributes and association roles be mapped to XML elements or XML attributes?

Multiplicity constraints—If they can be mapped at all, how do we map UML attribute and association role multiplicity to XML schemas?

Inheritance—How does UML class inheritance map to XML schema definitions?

Content Model—What XML content model should be used to control the presence of elements and text (empty, textOnly, or elementOnly) and element group structure (sequence, choice, or all) in an XML element definition?

Element order—How do we map unordered UML attributes and association roles into XML element content models that may be ordered?

Datatypes—How do UML model datatypes map to XML element and attribute datatypes, which may be much more limited than in UML?

Linking—How are UML associations mapped to XML links within and between documents?

Although you may not have assembled this list in your own mind, you should have gained an understanding of the basic principles behind each item. This chapter begins by integrating these criteria by building the two-by-two matrix of schema strictness versus schema language. Each alternative in this matrix is specified by a set of responses to the list of nine criteria. The next two sections analyze the schema generation for DTDs and XML Schemas, where each schema language is described with rules for generating either relaxed or strict definitions. The final section describes how UML stereotypes provide the mechanism that allows designers to control the degree of strictness in a particular schema.

The mapping from UML model instances to XML document instances was described first, in Chapters 6 and 7, prior to introducing schema representations, because the document fragments presented in those chapters can be validated against *any of the four types of schemas* generated from the same UML model. In Chapter 8, we saw one XML document instance for a bibliography that was validated against both a DTD and an XML Schema. This chapter expands that choice into another dimension for strictness of the schema validation abilities, but the same document instance may still be validated against all four alternative schemas. The details of your business problem will dictate which schema language you use and how much validation is required in a particular application context. You may discover that two or more of these schema alternatives are applicable within different contexts of one XML application.

The XMI specification is more general than what is described here. XMI will produce a DTD for any metamodel that is compliant with the OMG's Meta Object Facility (MOF) and will produce an XML document instance for a model that instantiates that metamodel. To be specific, our UML model is interpreted as a MOF metamodel when applying the XMI rules for producing the DTDs and XML documents described in this book. If this metalevel description is unfamiliar to you, don't worry. If you are interested in more detail, Appendix B provides a bit more background on XMI and MOF and includes references for additional reading. I'll describe the production of DTDs and Schemas directly from the UML model rather than from the more abstract MOF metametamodel.

Generating DTDs

The XML DTD specification[1] was not created from an object-oriented design perspective. As a result, there is no direct one-to-one mapping of UML modeling

---

1. World Wide Web Consortium. Extensible Markup Language (XML) 1.0, W3C Recommendation, 10 February 1998—see *http://www.w3.org/TR/REC-xml*.

constructs to DTD definitions, and a common set of rules must be established that consistently maps a UML model into one or more XML DTDs. These rules must make the mapping assumptions explicit so that a designer of XML vocabularies understands the implications of choices made in the UML model. These mapping rules and assumptions are summarized for generation of both relaxed and strict DTDs, where a strict DTD defines document instances that are a subset of those possible when using a relaxed DTD.

Another problem in addition to the lack of object-oriented structures is that there is no standard way of validating XML documents that combine elements from several DTDs. A DTD contains only one namespace for all of the elements that it defines. As a workaround, specific element type prefixes (for example, `"pty:"`) are sometimes hard-coded into the DTD element declarations. The XML Namespaces specification[2] was adopted after XML 1.0 became a W3C Recommendation, thus creating this mismatch. A future version of the XML standard will likely combine these two specifications into a single, integrated document. A solution to this limited namespace support in DTDs must be incorporated into the mapping rules used to generate DTDs from UML models.

Relaxed DTDs

The XMI version 1.1 specification defines a standard set of rules for creating relaxed DTD definitions. The general characteristics of DTDs with *relaxed validation* may be summarized as follows:

- Unrestricted multiplicity allows exchange of model fragments
- Unordered content model imposes no restrictions on document generation
- Unrestricted choice of elements versus attributes when mapping UML to XML structure

A UML model defines all classes, attributes, and relationships required for an application vocabulary. However, it is sometimes necessary to exchange partial models or fragments of information that the document receiver will integrate into an existing model. This is roughly analogous to people exchanging e-mail containing individual paragraphs of a larger document, or even exchanging phrases of sentences. These text fragments are not complete in terms of an overall document stylesheet template or sentence grammar. Rather, it is the sender's responsibility to provide pointers to the required context (for example, which model or which

---

2. World Wide Web Consortium. Namespaces in XML, W3C Recommendation, 14 January 1999—see *http:// www.w3.org/TR/REC-xml-names*.

composition class within the model), and it is the receiver's responsibility to integrate these fragments into a complete, valid information model.

A relaxed DTD schema accommodates these exchanges of partial information both by removing the multiplicity specifications defined by the vocabulary model and by allowing child XML elements to appear in any order within the parent element. Another mechanism for relaxing the DTD validation is to allow each UML attribute and association role to appear as either an XML element or an XML attribute. As described in Chapter 6, design trade-off decisions must be made when producing XML documents using elements or attributes. The final choice is often at the discretion of a vocabulary's designer.

An illustration of the mapping from UML to relaxed DTDs in shown in Figure 9-1. A similar diagram was presented in Figure 6-3 as the road map for mapping UML model instances to XML document instances. This chapter describes how the same UML model definitions are used to generate a DTD schema that may in turn validate the document instances presented in Chapters 6 and 7.

We'll begin with a few high-level observations about this mapping. Each class in the UML model (with the exception of enumerations) produces an XML element whose content model includes all of the elements produced for that class's attributes and association roles. Because the rules of XMI 1.1 specify that both XML attributes and elements are produced for most UML attributes and association roles, these attribute and element definitions are generated following the class element. Each class includes two standard DTD parameter entities that define shared attribute groups, as described in Chapter 8. Finally, a UML class with an <<enumeration>> stereotype produces both an XML attribute and element that define this enumerated value list in the DTD.

The detailed mapping rules for generating relaxed DTDs from UML class models are listed in Table 9-1. This list is classified by the same nine criteria used to define the fundamental principles of schema generation at the beginning of this chapter. Most of these criteria rules should be understandable by referencing the examples from Chapters 6 and 7 and by relating the rules to the DTD feature summary in Chapter 8. Rather than describe additional details of these rules at an abstract level, I'll apply them to specific examples using the CatML vocabulary.

An XMI 1.1 compliant processor makes all of these criteria choices by default, without any designer control or choice of alternatives. Full compliance with these rules enables a predictable, reproducible generation of DTDs from any UML class model. As an illustration of these rules, I'll review the DTD declarations produced from two classes in the CatML model, plus element type declarations produced from the UML package definitions.

Refer to the package structure diagram shown in Figure 6-9. The CatML package contains two subpackages: CatalogContent and OrderMgmt. As a result, the DTD-generation rules produce one container element type named

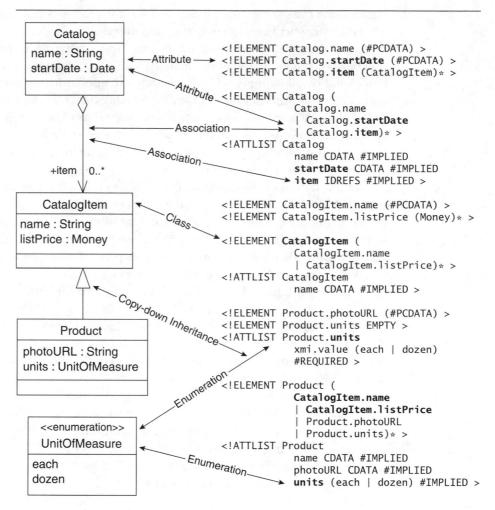

Figure 9-1 Relaxed DTD mapping

CatML, plus two additional element types for CatalogContent and OrderMgmt. Each package element contains the element names of its subpackages and/or classes. CatML and CatalogContent are produced as follows. (Boldface element names highlight those declarations included in this example.)

```
<!ELEMENT CatML (CatalogContent | OrderMgmt | XMI.extension)* >

<!ELEMENT CatalogContent (Catalog | CatalogItem |
                          Category | Feature | FeatureValue |
                          Product | Service | ProductBundle |
                          Resource | DiscountPrice |
                          XMI.extension)* >
```

Table 9-1   Criteria for relaxed DTD generation

Criterion	*Description*
Namespace mapping	An entire UML model is represented in a single DTD having no XML namespace or, optionally, one namespace prefix is hard-coded in all element type names.
	A simple XML container element is generated for each package that may contain that package's classes and subpackages as child elements.
Element name uniqueness	Prefix each UML attribute and association role with the class name followed by a '.' (for example, `Class1.role2`).
	If a prefixed name is not unique, add an additional prefix of the UML package name that contains the class (for example, `PackageA.Class1.role2`). If necessary, reapply this rule with additional package name prefixes until the resulting XML element name is globally unique.
Elements or attributes	Generate an XML element for each UML attribute and each association role.
	Generate an XML attribute for each UML attribute having a primitive datatype with maximum multiplicity equal to one.
	Generate an XML attribute for each association role that is not part of a composition association.
Multiplicity constraints	All element multiplicity is unbounded.
	All XML attributes representing association roles have an unbounded IDREFs datatype.
Inheritance	No support in DTDs; use copy-down inheritance to reproduce all superclass attributes and association roles in each subclass.
Content model	All content models are 'choice' groups.
Element order	All content models are unordered.
Datatypes	No support in DTDs; use CDATA attributes and #PCDATA elements.
Linking	Use ID and IDREF linking within a document.
	Use href attribute for linking to other resources.

All elements corresponding to a UML package or class also include a child element named XMI.extension. This is defined as part of the XMI specification, and its element type declaration is as follows:

```
<!ELEMENT XMI.extension ANY >
```

The ANY content model imposes no constraints on the XML element(s) that may appear as its children. The purpose of including this element in XMI is to allow applications to extend the document with additional elements that are not defined by the metamodel, CatML in this case. The purpose of these nonstandard model extensions would need to be communicated among the business partners who send or receive documents containing these extensions. I don't use

Listing 9-1   Relaxed `CatalogItem` DTD definition

```
<!ELEMENT CatalogItem.name (#PCDATA | XMI.reference)* >
<!ELEMENT CatalogItem.description (#PCDATA | XMI.reference)* >
<!ELEMENT CatalogItem.listPrice (Money)* >
<!ELEMENT CatalogItem.sku (#PCDATA | XMI.reference)* >
<!ELEMENT CatalogItem.globalIdentifier (#PCDATA | XMI.reference)* >
<!ELEMENT CatalogItem.category (Category)* >
<!ELEMENT CatalogItem.feature (FeatureValue)* >
<!ELEMENT CatalogItem.detail (Resource)* >
<!ELEMENT CatalogItem.supplier (Party)* >

<!ELEMENT CatalogItem (CatalogItem.name | CatalogItem.description |
                       CatalogItem.listPrice | CatalogItem.sku |
                       CatalogItem.globalIdentifier |
                       CatalogItem.category | CatalogItem.feature |
                       CatalogItem.detail | CatalogItem.supplier |
                       XMI.extension)* >
<!ATTLIST CatalogItem
          name CDATA #IMPLIED
          description CDATA #IMPLIED
          sku CDATA #IMPLIED
          globalIdentifier CDATA #IMPLIED
          category IDREFS #IMPLIED
          detail IDREFS #IMPLIED
          supplier IDREFS #IMPLIED
          %XMI.element.att;
          %XMI.link.att;
>
```

this extension element in any CatML examples, but the `XMI.extension` element type must be included in the DTD in order to comply with the XMI standard.

Each UML class defined in the model produces a standard set of XML element type and attribute declarations. The `CatalogItem` class, and the navigable associations from this class, produce the DTD declarations in Listing 9-1.

First, all of the UML attribute and association role elements are produced. Second, the element type corresponding to the class, `CatalogItem`, is produced with a content model that contains all of the elements for attributes and roles. The content model is a choice group (element names separated by '|'), and zero or more instances of the group are allowed in a document ('*' following the choice group). The effective result is that any number of any elements may appear in any order. It can't get much more relaxed than that! Third, the XML attributes are produced for the `CatalogItem` class. All other classes in the UML model follow these same DTD production rules.

For a last example of relaxed DTD generation, consider the DTD produced from the `Product` class, depicted in Listing 9-2. This includes two new features: DTD declarations for enumerated attributes and class inheritance. In the UML

Listing 9-2 Relaxed Product DTD definition

```
<!ELEMENT Product.photoURL (#PCDATA | XMI.reference)* >
<!ELEMENT Product.units EMPTY >
<!ATTLIST Product.units
          xmi.value (each | dozen | meter | kilogram) #REQUIRED
>

<!ELEMENT Product (CatalogItem.name | CatalogItem.description |
               CatalogItem.listPrice | CatalogItem.sku |
               CatalogItem.globalIdentifier |
               CatalogItem.category | CatalogItem.feature |
               CatalogItem.detail | CatalogItem.supplier |
               Product.photoURL | Product.units |
               XMI.extension)* >
<!ATTLIST Product
          name CDATA #IMPLIED
          description CDATA #IMPLIED
          sku CDATA #IMPLIED
          globalIdentifier CDATA #IMPLIED
          category IDREFS #IMPLIED
          detail IDREFS #IMPLIED
          supplier IDREFS #IMPLIED
          photoURL CDATA #IMPLIED
          units (each | dozen | meter | kilogram) #IMPLIED
          %XMI.element.att;
          %XMI.link.att;
>
```

model, the `Product` class includes an attribute named `units` that has the datatype `UnitOfMeasure`. The `UnitOfMeasure` class is defined with a `<<enumeration>>` stereotype. All attributes with enumerated types produce both an XML element and an attribute that include the enumerated list of values.

Because DTDs have no support for inheritance among element types, the XMI specification requires that all attributes and association roles from all superclasses be included in the subclass declarations. So in the case of `Product`, the content model includes all content elements from its superclass, `CatalogItem`. Also, `CatalogItem`'s XML attribute declarations are copied into the attribute list for `Product`.

Strict DTDs

By comparison to relaxed DTDs, the general characteristics of DTDs with *strict validation* may be summarized as follows:

- Multiplicity restricted according to the UML model.
- Ordered content model (sequence) required to enforce multiplicity.
- Only XML elements are generated, not both elements and attributes.

Strict DTDs enforce the attribute and association role multiplicity specified in the UML model. But due to limitations of the DTD language, multiplicity can be enforced only by defining an ordered sequence content model. The only unordered content model allowed in DTDs is the choice group, but elements within a choice group are not allowed to specify multiplicity. This requirement for ordered elements is an unfortunate side effect of strict DTDs for two reasons: the UML model does not require a class's attributes and association roles to appear in any particular sequence nor does it provide a built-in mechanism to specify a desired order.

The strict DTD rules are specified such that a DTD may be generated from any UML class model, without the use of UML stereotype extensions. Given this approach, there is no way for vocabulary designers to specify which UML attributes or association roles should appear as DTD element types and which should appear as DTD attribute declarations. This rule does produce DTDs that are a subset of the relaxed DTD produced from this same UML model, but the restriction to elements is not always desirable. The last section of this chapter describes use of UML stereotypes that enable the designer to control the choice of elements versus attributes.

The following DTD fragment modifies the `Catalog` declaration shown in Figure 9-1 to enforce strict DTD criteria rules.

```
<!ELEMENT Catalog (Catalog.name, Catalog.startDate, Catalog.item*)? >

<!ATTLIST Catalog
    %XMI.element.att;
    %XMI.link.att; >

<!ELEMENT Catalog.name (#PCDATA) >
<!ELEMENT Catalog.startDate (#PCDATA) >
<!ELEMENT Catalog.item (CatalogItem)* >
```

Notice that the content model for `Catalog` uses a sequence group (elements separated by ',' instead of by '|') and that the contained elements specify multiplicity constraints. There must be exactly one `Catalog.name` element; this corresponds to the UML attribute `name`, where a default multiplicity of [1..1] is assumed if not specified in the model. There are no XML attributes from the UML model, only the standard XMI attribute parameter entities.

The production rules for strict DTDs are summarized in Table 9-2. The strict DTD produced from our CatML vocabulary is a straightforward refinement of the relaxed DTD. The DTD declarations generated from the `CatalogItem` class are shown in Listing 9-3, in which I have modified the multiplicity of the association role `CatalogItem.category` to be [1..*] (compared to the UML model which is [0..*]) in order to illustrate the resulting DTD declaration.

Table 9-2 Criteria for strict DTD generation

Criterion	Description
Namespace mapping	Same as for relaxed DTDs.
Element name uniqueness	Same as for relaxed DTDs.
Elements or attributes	Generate an XML element for each UML class attribute and each association role.
Multiplicity constraints	Multiplicity is enforced in the content model, using the DTD designators: blank, ?, *, or +.
	UML attributes with unspecified multiplicity are assumed to be [1..1]
Inheritance	Same as for relaxed DTDs.
Content model	All content models for elements generated from a UML class are produced with a 'sequence' group.
Element order	Elements are required to appear in the order specified in the UML model definition; first the UML class attributes, then followed by the association roles from that class.
Datatypes	Same as for relaxed DTDs.
Linking	Same as for relaxed DTDs.

Listing 9-3 Strict `CatalogItem` DTD definition

```
<!ELEMENT CatalogItem.name (#PCDATA | XMI.reference)* >
<!ELEMENT CatalogItem.description (#PCDATA | XMI.reference)* >
<!ELEMENT CatalogItem.listPrice (Money) >
<!ELEMENT CatalogItem.sku (#PCDATA | XMI.reference)* >
<!ELEMENT CatalogItem.globalIdentifier (#PCDATA | XMI.reference)* >
<!ELEMENT CatalogItem.category (Category)+ >
<!ELEMENT CatalogItem.feature (FeatureValue)* >
<!ELEMENT CatalogItem.detail (Resource)* >
<!ELEMENT CatalogItem.supplier (Party) >

<!ELEMENT CatalogItem (CatalogItem.name, CatalogItem.description,
                       CatalogItem.listPrice, CatalogItem.sku,
                       CatalogItem.globalIdentifier,
                       CatalogItem.category+, CatalogItem.feature*,
                       CatalogItem.detail*, CatalogItem.supplier,
                       XMI.extension? )? >
<!ATTLIST CatalogItem
          %XMI.element.att;
          %XMI.link.att;
    >
```

Generating W3C XML Schemas

XML Schema enables a much more accurate representation of the UML model than is possible with DTDs. The mapping rules presented in this section are not yet standardized as part of the OMG's XMI specification, but a Request for Proposal (RFP) has been issued for such an enhancement.

A mapping from UML to XML Schema is illustrated in Figure 9-2. In order to keep the figure somewhat simpler, a mapping for *strict* XML Schema generation is shown. This strict schema also provides the closest mapping to the UML model; although, like the strict DTD, all UML attributes and association roles are mapped only to XML elements. There are no XML attributes defined in this schema example.

All of the XML Schema elements in this example are prefixed with the "xs:" namespace. For each UML class in this simple model, a `complexType` is defined in the schema, and an `element` is declared whose type is equal to that `complexType`. Each `complexType` is defined using the `<all>` content model, which includes a list of the elements that may be present, subject to their individual multiplicity constraints. But unlike the content model used in strict DTDs, this XML Schema definition validates multiplicity while allowing the elements to be present in any order within a document instance.

Notice that XML Schema enables accurate datatype declarations for the UML class elements. `Catalog.startDate` is declared as type `xs:date`, `Catalog.name` is of type `xs:string`, and `Product.units` is of type `UnitOfMeasure`. `UnitOfMeasure` is defined as a `simpleType` restricted by two enumeration facets. Each element within the content model is declared with `minOccurs` and `maxOccurs` multiplicity. If neither is specified, then they are both equal to 1 by default; if only `minOccurs` is specified, then `maxOccurs` is equal to `minOccurs`, but not less than 1.

Now that we have an overview of the UML to XML Schema mapping, we'll differentiate between the rules for generating relaxed versus strict schemas.

Relaxed Schemas

A *relaxed* XML Schema is produced such that a document instance that is valid with respect to a relaxed XML Schema is also valid with a relaxed DTD. The general characteristics of relaxed XML Schemas are almost identical to those for relaxed DTDs.

- Multiplicity of `minOccurs="0"` for all schema elements
- Unordered content model imposes no restriction on document generation
- Unrestricted choice of elements versus attributes when mapping UML to XML structure

The only difference when compared with relaxed DTDs is that the multiplicity constraints can be relaxed to make each element optional, but they still

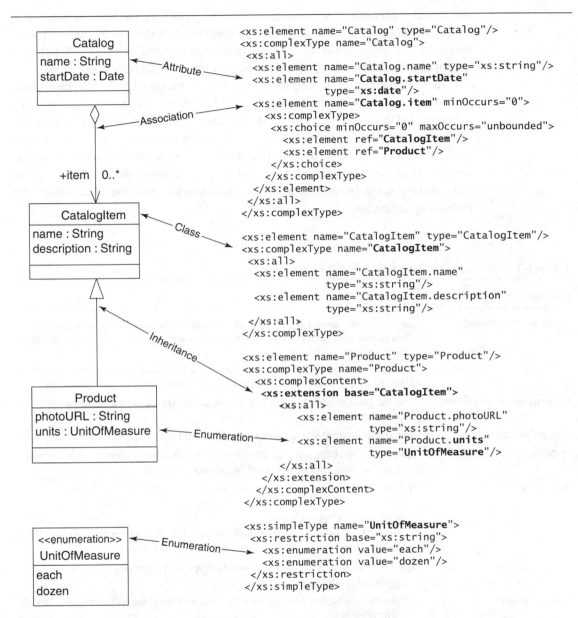

Figure 9-2 Strict XML Schema mapping

enforce the maximum occurrence constraint. This type of definition, not possible with DTDs, is a more accurate interpretation of the intent underlying relaxed schema production. This property is implemented in an XML Schema by adding a `minOccurs="0"` attribute to each element declaration.

Table 9-3 summarizes the production rules for relaxed XML Schemas, classified by the same criteria used to describe DTD production. In order to help you compare DTD generation with XML Schema generation, I will describe the same two classes from `CatML`, which are `CatalogItem` and `Product`. Each class in the UML model produces a standard set of XML Schema `element` declarations, `complexType` definitions, and `attributeGroup` definitions. The `CatalogItem` class, and the navigable associations from this class, produce the XML Schema definitions in Listing 9-4.

Table 9-3 Criteria for relaxed XML Schema generation

Criterion	*Description*
Namespace mapping	An entire UML model is represented in a single schema. But, unlike DTDs, any document instance is free to assign a namespace prefix for elements validated by this schema.
	A simple XML container element is generated for each package that may contain that package's classes and subpackages as child elements.
Element name uniqueness	Use the same production rules as with relaxed DTDs to ensure compatibility of document instances.
Elements or attributes	Use the same production rules as with relaxed DTDs.
Multiplicity constraints	All element declarations have `minOccurs="0"` and the `maxOccurs` constraint is set to the value specified in the UML model.
Inheritance	When a UML class inherits from a single superclass, then generate the `complexType` with an `extension` child element whose `base` attribute is assigned to the superclass name.
	When a UML class inherits from multiple superclasses, then revert to copy-down inheritance as was specified in the DTD production rules.
Content model	Each UML class is generated as a `complexType` definition using the `<all>` unordered model group.
Element order	Unordered content is allowed by `<all>`, but elements are still constrained by the UML multiplicity.
Datatypes	Each UML attribute is generated as an XML attribute declaration, where the XML attribute type is assigned equal to the corresponding UML attribute type.
	If the UML attribute type is not equal to a class defined in the current model, and is not one of the built-in datatypes from XML Schema, then define a `simpleType` derived from `string` whose name is equal to the UML type name.
Linking	Use the same production rules as with relaxed DTDs.

Listing 9-4   Relaxed CatalogItem schema definition

```xml
<xs:element name="CatalogItem" type="CatalogItem"/>
<xs:complexType name="CatalogItem">
  <xs:all>
    <!-- UML class attributes -->
    <xs:element name="CatalogItem.name" type="String" minOccurs="0"/>
    <xs:element name="CatalogItem.description" type="String" minOccurs="0"/>
    <xs:element name="CatalogItem.listPrice" minOccurs="0">
      <xs:complexType>
        <xs:sequence>
          <xs:element ref="Money" minOccurs="0"/>
        </xs:sequence>
      </xs:complexType>
    </xs:element>
    <xs:element name="CatalogItem.sku" type="String" minOccurs="0"/>
    <xs:element name="CatalogItem.globalIdentifier"
                type="String" minOccurs="0"/>

    <!-- navigable association roles -->
    <xs:element name="CatalogItem.supplier" minOccurs="0">
      <xs:complexType>
        <xs:sequence>
          <xs:element ref="Party" minOccurs="0"/>
        </xs:sequence>
      </xs:complexType>
    </xs:element>
    <xs:element name="CatalogItem.feature" minOccurs="0">
      <xs:complexType>
        <xs:sequence>
          <xs:element ref="FeatureValue" minOccurs="0" maxOccurs="unbounded"/>
        </xs:sequence>
      </xs:complexType>
    </xs:element>
    <xs:element name="CatalogItem.detail" minOccurs="0">
      <xs:complexType>
        <xs:sequence>
          <xs:element ref="Resource" minOccurs="0" maxOccurs="unbounded"/>
        </xs:sequence>
      </xs:complexType>
    </xs:element>
    <xs:element name="CatalogItem.category" minOccurs="0">
      <xs:complexType>
        <xs:sequence>
          <xs:element ref="Category" minOccurs="0" maxOccurs="unbounded"/>
        </xs:sequence>
      </xs:complexType>
    </xs:element>
    <xs:element ref="XMI.extension" minOccurs="0"/>
  </xs:all>

  <xs:attributeGroup ref="CatalogItem.att"/>
  <xs:attributeGroup ref="XMI.element.att"/>
  <xs:attributeGroup ref="XMI.link.att"/>
</xs:complexType>
```

continued

Listing 9-4 *continued*

```
<xs:attributeGroup name="CatalogItem.att">
  <xs:attribute name="name" type="String"/>
  <xs:attribute name="description" type="String"/>
  <xs:attribute name="sku" type="String"/>
  <xs:attribute name="globalIdentifier" type="String"/>
  <xs:attribute name="supplier" type="IDREF"/>
  <xs:attribute name="feature" type="IDREFS"/>
  <xs:attribute name="detail" type="IDREFS"/>
  <xs:attribute name="category" type="IDREFS"/>
</xs:attributeGroup>
```

There are three major parts to this schema definition. First, an `element` is declared whose name and type are equal to "CatalogItem." This allows a document instance to include `<CatalogItem>` elements at the root level, where the content and attributes of these elements are validated against the `complexType` with this same name. The element could have a different name than the `complexType`, but using the same name is the most straightforward interpretation of the UML model realized in XML.

Second, the `complexType` definition is produced for this class. Within the `complexType`, there are again three parts: an element for each UML class attribute, an element for each navigable association role, and attribute group references for this class and the standard XMI attributes. Because this is a relaxed schema, each element is defined with `minOccurs="0"`.

A `complexType` definition is therefore equivalent to a class definition in UML, whereas an `element` declaration in the schema allows instance elements of a given type to be included in the XML document. Those instance elements may have tag names equal to the `complexType` name, or the element tags may have a different name as specified in the `element` declaration.

Third, an `AttributeGroup` defines the XML attributes allowed in this element. As described in Chapter 8, an `AttributeGroup` in an XML Schema is analogous to a parameter entity in a DTD; both allow a group of attributes to be defined once and referred to many times. In this example, the `AttributeGroup` is included by reference within the `complexType` definition for `CatalogItem`, and could be included in other `complexType` definitions also.

This example includes two new features of XML Schema that were not explained in Chapter 8. When generating elements for the UML class attributes, the type is set equal to the primitive type used in the UML model. For example, this declaration was included in the above example.

```
<xs:element name="CatalogItem.name" type="String" minOccurs="0"/>
```

Listing 9-5   Java `simpleType` definitions

```
<xs:simpleType name="String">
  <xs:restriction base="xs:string"/>
</xs:simpleType>
<xs:simpleType name="int">
  <xs:restriction base="xs:int"/>
</xs:simpleType>
<xs:simpleType name="float">
  <xs:restriction base="xs:float"/>
</xs:simpleType>
<xs:simpleType name="double">
  <xs:restriction base="xs:float"/>
</xs:simpleType>
<xs:simpleType name="boolean">
  <xs:restriction base="xs:boolean"/>
</xs:simpleType>
<xs:simpleType name="Date">
  <xs:restriction base="xs:date"/>
</xs:simpleType>
```

The type value of "`String`" is not one of the built-in datatypes from XML Schema; the equivalent built-in type is `xs:string`. The UML model was created using standard Java datatypes, but these don't always match those defined in XML Schema. As a result, the standard Java datatypes are included as `simpleType` definitions within the schema. Six common Java types are defined in Listing 9-5.

The result is that "`String`" is equivalent to "`xs:string`", "`double`" is equivalent to "`xs:float`", and so on. Other datatype mappings can be created that correspond to the language datatypes used in the UML model (for example, C++, Visual Basic, and SQL).

Another new schema structure is used, as in this declaration.

```
<xs:element name="CatalogItem.listPrice" minOccurs="0">
  <xs:complexType>
    <xs:sequence>
      <xs:element ref="Money" minOccurs="0"/>
    </xs:sequence>
  </xs:complexType>
</xs:element>
```

This declares an XML element named `CatalogItem.listPrice` that may optionally contain a child element of type `Money`. In XML Schema, this is called an *anonymous* `complexType` that is used within an element to declare the type of its child elements. The element type for `Money` is not defined in this example but must be included in the schema.

Listing 9-6   Relaxed product schema definition

```
<xs:element name="Product" type="Product"/>
<xs:complexType name="Product">
  <xs:complexContent>
    <xs:extension base="CatalogItem">
      <xs:all>
        <!-- UML class attributes -->
        <xs:element name="Product.photoURL" type="String" minOccurs="0"/>
        <xs:element name="Product.units" type="UnitOfMeasure" minOccurs="0"/>
      </xs:all>
      <xs:attributeGroup ref="Product.att"/>
    </xs:extension>
  </xs:complexContent>
</xs:complexType>

<xs:attributeGroup name="Product.att">
  <xs:attribute name="photoURL" type="String"/>
  <xs:attribute name="units" type="UnitOfMeasure"/>
</xs:attributeGroup>


<!-- ~~~~~~~~~~~~~~~~~~~~~~~~~~~~~~~~~~~~~~~~~~~~~~~~~~~~~~~~~~~~~~ -->
<!-- ENUMERATION: UnitOfMeasure -->
<!-- ~~~~~~~~~~~~~~~~~~~~~~~~~~~~~~~~~~~~~~~~~~~~~~~~~~~~~~~~~~~~~~ -->


<xs:simpleType name="UnitOfMeasure">
  <xs:restriction base="xs:string">
      <xs:enumeration value="each"/>
      <xs:enumeration value="dozen"/>
      <xs:enumeration value="meter"/>
      <xs:enumeration value="kilogram"/>
  </xs:restriction>
</xs:simpleType>
```

In our CatML vocabulary model, CatalogItem is the superclass for three other classes: Product, Service, and ProductBundle. Although DTDs do not support definition of class inheritance, XML Schema does support it. The Product class is produced as depicted in Listing 9-6.

This definition has the same structure as that created for CatalogItem, but the Product complexType declares that it is derived by extension from the base class CatalogItem. Thus, only the attributes and association roles for Product are included, and those from CatalogItem are inherited into this element type.

This example also illustrates definition of the UnitOfMeasure enumerated datatype and its use in the units element and attribute of Product. Enumerated datatypes were explained in more detail in Chapter 8.

Strict Schemas

As with strict DTDs, strict Schemas are defined to be a subset of the relaxed form. Any XML document instance that is valid with respect to a strict Schema is also valid with the corresponding relaxed Schema. However, a strict XML Schema may not necessarily validate a document that is validated by a strict DTD. This is true because a strict Schema is able to enforce the UML model multiplicity without requiring an ordered content model. The characteristics of strict Schemas are summarized as follows:

- Multiplicity is restricted according to the UML model.
- Unordered content model is allowed by the <all> element group.
- Only XML elements (not attributes) are generated.

With the exception of unordered content models, these characteristics are the same as those for strict DTDs. The more detailed production rules for strict XML Schemas are listed in Table 9-4.

A strict XML Schema is closer than the strict DTDs are to the original UML model. The UML model multiplicity is directly represented in the minOccurs and maxOccurs attributes for each association role definition. Also, the content model declares which elements may be present as children but doesn't require a particular order. As with strict DTDs, a strict XML Schema defines only elements and no XML attributes for the class. This limitation will be addressed via UML stereotypes described at the end of this chapter. The CatalogItem class is represented in Listing 9-7.

Table 9-4   Criteria for strict XML Schema generation

Criterion	*Description*
Namespace mapping	Same as for relaxed XML Schemas.
Element name uniqueness	Same as for relaxed XML Schemas.
Elements or attributes	Use the same production rules as with strict DTDs.
Multiplicity constraints	The minOccurs and maxOccurs attributes on all element declarations are assigned values equal to those specified in the UML model.
Inheritance	Same as for relaxed XML Schemas.
Content model	Same as for relaxed XML Schemas.
Element order	Same as for relaxed XML Schemas.
Datatypes	Same as for relaxed XML Schemas.
Linking	Same as for relaxed XML Schemas.

Listing 9-7 Strict `CatalogItem` schema definition

```
<xs:element name="CatalogItem" type="CatalogItem"/>
<xs:complexType name="CatalogItem">
  <xs:all>
    <!-- UML class attributes -->
    <xs:element name="CatalogItem.name" type="String"/>
    <xs:element name="CatalogItem.description" type="String"/>
    <xs:element name="CatalogItem.listPrice">
      <xs:complexType>
        <xs:sequence>
          <xs:element ref="Money"/>
        </xs:sequence>
      </xs:complexType>
    </xs:element>
    <xs:element name="CatalogItem.sku" type="String"/>
    <xs:element name="CatalogItem.globalIdentifier" type="String"/>

    <!-- navigable association roles -->
    <xs:element name="CatalogItem.supplier">
      <xs:complexType>
        <xs:sequence>
          <xs:element ref="Party"/>  <!-- element is required -->
        </xs:sequence>
      </xs:complexType>
    </xs:element>
    <xs:element name="CatalogItem.feature" minOccurs="0">
      <xs:complexType>
        <xs:sequence>
          <xs:element ref="FeatureValue" minOccurs="0" maxOccurs="unbounded"/>
        </xs:sequence>
      </xs:complexType>
    </xs:element>
    <xs:element name="CatalogItem.detail" minOccurs="0">
      <xs:complexType>
        <xs:sequence>
          <xs:element ref="Resource" minOccurs="0" maxOccurs="unbounded"/>
        </xs:sequence>
      </xs:complexType>
    </xs:element>
    <xs:element name="CatalogItem.category" minOccurs="0">
      <xs:complexType>
        <xs:sequence>
          <xs:element ref="Category" minOccurs="0" maxOccurs="unbounded"/>
        </xs:sequence>
      </xs:complexType>
    </xs:element>
    <xs:element ref="XMI.extension" minOccurs="0"/>
  </xs:all>

  <xs:attributeGroup ref="CatalogItem.att"/>
  <xs:attributeGroup ref="XMI.element.att"/>
  <xs:attributeGroup ref="XMI.link.att"/>
</xs:complexType>
```

One final topic requires additional description in this example. Notice that the `CatalogItem.supplier` element declaration does not include either `minOccurs` or `maxOccurs` attributes. The same is true of its child element, `Party`. This schema thus requires a `CatalogItem` to contain exactly one `CatalogItem.supplier`, which in turn contains exactly one `Party`. This schema enforces the UML model constraints of an association end role with one object.

On the other hand, the `CatalogItem.feature` element specifies a `minOccurs` attribute value of zero, which means that there may be zero or one of this element in a valid document instance. In addition, there may be zero or more `FeatureValue` elements as children of the `CatalogItem.feature` element. In terms of the UML model, there is an optional element corresponding to the association end role named `feature`, and this association end contains an optional set of `FeatureValue` objects. If there are no linked objects, then the association end is not required.

XLink Support

As described in Chapter 7, the XMI 1.1 specification was created prior to adoption of XLink, so only basic `IDREF` and `href` link attributes are included in the XMI production rules. The previous examples included an attribute group reference to `XMI.link.att` that defines the XMI standard link attributes. This attribute group is defined as follows in an XML Schema:

```
<xs:AttributeGroup name="XMI.link.att">
  <xs:attribute name="xmi.idref" type="xs:IDREF"/>
  <xs:attribute name="href" type="xs:uriReference"/>
</xs:AttributeGroup>
```

Support for simple, unidirectional XLink elements may be added to a schema by creating a similar attribute group definition named `XLink.simple.att`, as shown here.

```
<xs:AttributeGroup name="XLink.simple.att">
  <xs:attribute name="xlink:type" type="xs:string"
                use="fixed" value="simple"/>
  <xs:attribute name="xlink:href" type="xs:uriReference"/>
  <xs:attribute name="xlink:title" type="xs:string"/>
  <xs:attribute name="xlink:role" type="xs:string"/>
  <xs:attribute name="xlink:show" type="ShowKind"/>
  <xs:attribute name="xlink:actuate" type="ActuateKind"/>
</xs:AttributeGroup>

<xs:simpleType name="ShowKind">
  <xs:restriction base="xs:string">
    <xs:enumeration value="new"/>
    <xs:enumeration value="replace"/>
```

```
      <xs:enumeration value="embed"/>
      <xs:enumeration value="other"/>
      <xs:enumeration value="none"/>
    </xs:restriction>
</xs:simpleType>

<xs:simpleType name="ActuateKind">
  <xs:restriction base="xs:string">
    <xs:enumeration value="onLoad"/>
    <xs:enumeration value="onRequest"/>
    <xs:enumeration value="other"/>
    <xs:enumeration value="none"/>
  </xs:restriction>
</xs:simpleType>
```

Two of the attributes, `show` and `actuate`, are defined as enumerated types by the XLink specification, so the corresponding `simpleType` definitions must be included in the schema. In Chapter 7, the `Resource` class was enhanced to become a simple XLink.

A `Resource` is used in CatML as a generic reference to other Web resources; examples include HTML documents, PDF documents, or dynamic resources created on demand by the server from a given URI. By converting the `Resource` element to a simple XLink, any generic XLink processor could read our documents and extract the XLink elements for building cross-reference indexes, presenting reference links in a browser, and so on.

We can convert the `Resource` element to a simple XLink by replacing `XMI.link.att` with `XLink.simple.att` in the schema definition, as follows:

```
<xs:element name="Resource" type="Resource"/>
<xs:complexType name="Resource">
  <xs:attributeGroup ref="XMI.element.att"/>
  <xs:attributeGroup ref="XLink.simple.att"/>
</xs:complexType>
```

We can then use this schema definition to validate document instances, as in this example from Chapter 7.

```
<Product xmi.id="p1">
  <CatalogItem.name>Wizard PC</CatalogItem.name>
  <CatalogItem.detail>
    <Resource xmlns:xlink="http://www.w3.org/1999/xlink"
              xlink:href="/docs/WizardDataSheet.xml"
              xlink:title="Technical specifications for the Wizard PC"
              xlink:role="detail"
              xlink:show="new"
              xlink:actuate="onRequest"/>
  </CatalogItem.detail>
</Product>
```

We need a more generalized, automated solution than manually modifying individual schema entries to support XLink attributes. We could augment the XMI-generated schemas to include both `XMI.link.att` and `XLink.simple.att` in every element, but this is likely overkill and we may not want every element to be a simple XLink. The vocabulary designer must be able to control which elements are XLink enabled. We can gain this control through the use of UML stereotypes.

Controlling Schema Strictness

I described schema strictness as having only two states: relaxed and strict. However, these are in fact the end points of a continuum for strictness in schema validation. The use of UML stereotypes and tagged values enables you to control the degree of strictness deployed in your vocabulary design. In addition, the use of stereotypes enables a vocabulary designer to customize other aspects of schema generation, such as the choice of attributes versus elements and the use of XLink.

UML Extension Profiles

The UML provides a foundation for modeling structure and behavior of most software systems, but there are domain-specific situations that require additional model information to be captured by the analyst beyond what is possible with the UML foundation. For example, generating code from UML for various languages such as Java, EJB, C++, SQL databases, or XML schemas often requires additional information that guides the code-generation syntax or process. These issues are solved through the use of UML extension profiles.

A UML profile has three key items: stereotypes, tagged values, and constraints. A profile provides a definition of these items and explains how they extend the UML in that domain. We had a brief encounter with UML stereotypes in Chapter 6, where the <<enumeration>> stereotype was used to indicate enumerated datatypes in the vocabulary model. `UnitOfMeasure` and `UnitOfTime` are modeled using enumeration in the CatML vocabulary.

The use of a UML profile, with its stereotypes and tagged value definitions, is most easily explained with a simple example. Figure 9-3 shows the `Money` class from our CatML vocabulary, but it is now extended with three different stereotypes.

Recall that the rules for strict DTD and Schema generation specified that all UML attributes and association roles would be produced as XML elements and none as XML attributes. The <<XSDattribute>> stereotype may be assigned to a

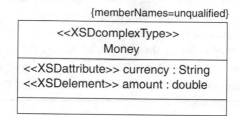

Figure 9-3 Use of UML stereotypes

UML attribute to inform the schema generation tool that this attribute should be generated as an XML *attribute*, not as an element. Similarly, the <<XSDelement>> stereotype specifies an explicit choice to generate a UML attribute as an XML element.

If we wish to instruct the schema generator to create the Money element definition without appending the class name to the beginning of each element name, we can assign the <<XSDcomplexType>> stereotype to the class and then add the *tagged value* memberNames=unqualified to this stereotyped class. Notice that the class is annotated with the tagged value in the diagram. The schema generation tool is responsible for correctly interpreting these stereotypes and tagged values when generating an XML Schema from this UML model. Based on these stereotypes, the following schema would be generated for this class:

```
<xs:complexType name="Money">
  <xs:all>
    <xs:element name="amount" type="double"/>
  </xs:all>
  <xs:attributeGroup ref="Money.att"/>
</xs:complexType>
<xs:attributeGroup name="Money.att">
  <xs:attribute name="currency" type="String"/>
</xs:attributeGroup>
```

Without use of the stereotypes, the same class would be generated as follows according to the strict schema rules:

```
<xs:complexType name="Money">
  <xs:all>
    <xs:element name="Money.currency" type="String"/>
    <xs:element name="Money.amount" type="double"/>
  </xs:all>
</xs:complexType>
```

■ **Purpose and Use of UML Profile Extensions**

Stereotypes—An extension to the UML itself. A stereotype allows a modeler to attach a new meaning to one of the UML foundational elements (for example, Class, Attribute, Association, Package). A stereotype is usually represented on a diagram as the name surrounded by guillements << >>. Alternatively, a stereotyped element can be shown as an icon on the UML diagram.

Tagged values—An extension to the attributes of a UML model element. Each model element has a standard set of attributes (for example, each UML Class has a name, visibility, and so on). A tagged value defines a new attribute that is associated with a stereotyped model element. A tagged value is shown on the diagram as a name/value string: `{tagName=value}`.

Constraints—An extension to the semantics of the UML. A constraint is a rule that defines a valid combination of model elements and/or attribute values. These are referred to as well-formedness rules. A constraint may be written in prose text or using a formal constraint language, such as the Object Constraint Language (OCL). A constraint is shown on the diagram as a string between a pair of braces { }.

The purpose and use of the three UML profile items are summarized in the sidebar. The process for creating a UML profile typically follows these steps.

1. Identify the UML constructs that need to be extended with a specialized meaning. For example, some (but not all) UML *packages* must be identified as distinct XML namespaces; some UML *classes* must be identified as `simpleType` definitions in an XML Schema. A profile for XML includes two stereotypes that are associated with the UML constructs Package and Class, respectively. Each stereotype is assigned a name such as <<XSDschema>> and <<XSDsimpleType>>.

2. For each stereotype defined in the profile, determine if that extended UML element must include additional attributes that further describe its characteristics. For example, our new <<XSDschema>> stereotype requires several additional attributes that will enable us to generate a complete <xs:schema> element in an XML Schema (for example, targetNamespace). Each of these new attributes is defined as a tagged value associated with the stereotype.

3. Given the set of stereotypes and tagged values in the profile, specify any constraints that must be enforced to ensure the validity of this extended model. The constraints might describe either interdependencies among the tagged values of one stereotype or the interdependencies among several

stereotyped elements within the UML model. For example, a class having the stereotype <<XSDsimpleType>> is not allowed to include any UML attributes or associations.

An Extension Profile for XML

A subset of the extension profile for XML schemas is summarized in Table 9-5. The stereotypes are named with an XSD prefix, even though they may be applied to any type of schema generated from the UML model, including DTDs. The prefix serves to reinforce the meaning of these stereotype names based on the XML Schema specification and to ensure unique names for these stereotype definitions within a UML modeling tool. XML Schema generally supports a superset of the features allowed by other schema languages for XML, so this

Table 9-5   UML profile for XML schemas (subset)

UML Construct	Stereotype	Tagged Values
Package	XSDschema	targetNamespace
		targetNamespacePrefix
		version
		attributeFormDefault (qualified | unqualified)
		elementFormDefault (qualified | unqualified)
Class	XSDcomplexType	modelGroup (all | sequence | choice)
		memberNames (qualified | unqualified)
		attributeMapping (attribute | element | both)
		roleMapping (attribute | element | both)
Class	XSDsimpleType	pattern
		length
		minLength
		maxLength
Class	SimpleXLink	role
		arcrole
		show
		actuate
Attribute AssociationEnd	XSDelement	form (qualified | unqualified)
		position
Attribute AssociationEnd	XSDattribute	form (qualified | unqualified)
		use (prohibited | optional | required | default | fixed)
		position

profile may be applied to other commonly used schema languages. A complete definition of this UML profile for XML is provided in Appendix C.

Profile Applied to CatML

We'll now apply this UML profile to two situations in our CatML vocabulary design. First, we may create the UML model to include classes that are not intended to be part of the XML vocabulary for CatML but are integrated into the model to support generation of Java application code. Or, in the case of the FpML package, its schema was generated from a separate UML model and is included here in order to show dependencies. Figure 9-4 is the UML package diagram from Figure 6-6, with the addition of stereotype labels that indicate which packages should be used to generate XML Schemas or DTDs. Table 9-5 lists the tagged values that may be specified for each stereotyped package. The <<XSDschema>> stereotyped package may specify several tagged values that control which namespace this package is generated into as well as other parameters that will be copied into the <xs:schema> element.

As a second example, a subset of the CatML model is reproduced in Figure 9-5 with the addition of several stereotype labels and tagged values. The

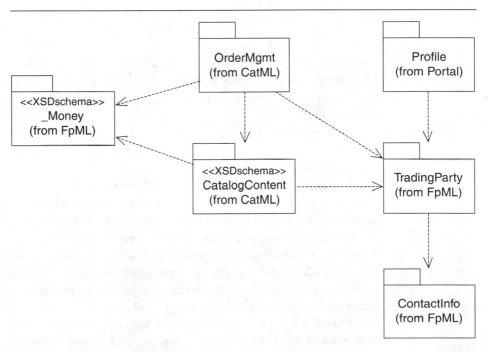

Figure 9-4   CatML package diagram with stereotypes

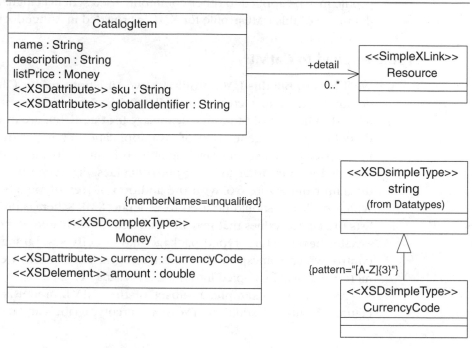

Figure 9-5 CatML model with stereotypes

CatalogItem class includes the <<XSDattribute>> stereotype on two of its UML attributes to indicate that they should be generated as XML attributes in the DTD or XML Schema. The remaining UML attributes will be generated as XML elements.

The Resource class is modified with the <<SimpleXLink>> stereotype label to indicate that this class (but not any others) should be generated with the standard XLink attributes.

The Money class includes the <<XSDcomplexType>> stereotype in order to allow the tagged value memberNames=unqualified, which indicates its generated elements should be unqualified (no prefixed class name).

Finally, stereotyped classes are used to model a new XML Schema simpleType definition for CurrencyCode, which extends the built-in string datatype and adds a pattern facet to restrict the value to three upper-case alphanumeric characters. The pattern facet is specified through the use of a tagged value on the CurrencyCode stereotyped class.

Through use of this UML profile for XML, we can refine the strict XML Schema and the strict DTD that are generated for the CatML vocabulary model.

First, the new `simpleType` for `CurrencyCode` is generated in an XML Schema as follows:

```
<xs:simpleType name="CurrencyCode">
  <xs:restriction base="xs:string">
    <xs:pattern value="[A-Z]{3}"/>
  </xs:restriction>
</xs:simpleType>
```

This `CurrencyCode` datatype is then used to generate a schema for the `Money` class, as follows:

```
<xs:complexType name="Money">
  <xs:all>
    <xs:element name="amount" type="double"/>
  </xs:all>
  <xs:attributeGroup ref="Money.att"/>
</xs:complexType>
<xs:attributeGroup name="Money.att">
  <xs:attribute name="currency" type="CurrencyCode"/>
</xs:attributeGroup>
```

The Resource class includes a <<SimpleXLink>> stereotype, so its schema is generated like this:

```
<xs:complexType name="Resource" content="empty">
  <xs:attributeGroup ref="XMI.element.att"/>
  <xs:attributeGroup ref="XLink.simple.att"/>
</xs:complexType>
```

Finally, the schema for `CatalogItem` is now generated with its attributes `sku` and `globalIdentifier` represented as XML attributes rather than elements as provided in Listing 9-8.

We can use the same CatML model with stereotypes to modify the generation of a strict DTD. However, because DTDs have no ability to define new datatypes like `CurrencyCode`, its definition is substituted as a CDATA type in the DTD. As a result, the `Money` element declaration is generated as follows, with its two attributes represented as XML attributes:

```
<!ELEMENT Money (amount, XMI.extension? )*>
<!ATTLIST Money
          currency CDATA #IMPLIED
          %XMI.element.att;
          %XMI.link.att; >

<!ELEMENT amount (#PCDATA | XMI.reference)* >
```

Listing 9-8   Customized `CatalogItem` schema

```
<xs:complexType name="CatalogItem">
  <xs:all>
    <!-- UML class attributes -->
    <xs:element name="CatalogItem.name" type="String"/>
    <xs:element name="CatalogItem.description" type="String"/>
    <xs:element name="CatalogItem.listPrice">
      <xs:complexType>
        <xs:sequence>
          <xs:element ref="Money"/>
        </xd:sequence>
      </xs:complexType>
    </xs:element>

    <!-- navigable association roles -->
    <xs:element name="CatalogItem.supplier" minOccurs="1">
      <xs:complexType>
        <xs:sequence>
          <xs:element ref="Party" minOccurs="1" maxOccurs="1"/>
        </xd:sequence>
      </xs:complexType>
    </xs:element>
    <xs:element name="CatalogItem.category" minOccurs="0">
      <xs:complexType>
        <xs:sequence>
          <xs:element ref="Category" minOccurs="0" maxOccurs="unbounded"/>
        </xd:sequence>
      </xs:complexType>
    </xs:element>
    <xs:element name="CatalogItem.feature" minOccurs="0">
      <xs:complexType>
        <xs:sequence>
          <xs:element ref="FeatureValue" minOccurs="0" maxOccurs="unbounded"/>
        </xd:sequence>
      </xs:complexType>
    </xs:element>
    <xs:element name="CatalogItem.detail" minOccurs="0">
      <xs:complexType>
        <xs:sequence>
          <xs:element ref="Resource" minOccurs="0" maxOccurs="unbounded"/>
        </xd:sequence>
      </xs:complexType>
    </xs:element>
    <xs:element ref="XMI.extension" minOccurs="0"/>
  </xs:all>

  <xs:attributeGroup ref="CatalogItem.att"/>
  <xs:attributeGroup ref="XMI.element.att"/>
  <xs:attributeGroup ref="XMI.link.att"/>
</xs:complexType>

<xs:attributeGroup name="CatalogItem.att">
  <xs:attribute name="sku" type="String"/>
  <xs:attribute name="globalIdentifier" type="String"/>
</xs:attributeGroup>
```

Listing 9-9 Customized `CatalogItem` DTD

```
<!ELEMENT CatalogItem (CatalogItem.name, CatalogItem.description,
                       CatalogItem.listPrice,
                       CatalogItem.category*, CatalogItem.feature*,
                       CatalogItem.detail*, CatalogItem.supplier,
                       XMI.extension? )* >
<!ATTLIST CatalogItem
          sku CDATA #IMPLIED
          globalIdentifier CDATA #IMPLIED
          %XMI.element.att;
          %XMI.link.att; >

<!ELEMENT CatalogItem.name (#PCDATA | XMI.reference)* >
<!ELEMENT CatalogItem.description (#PCDATA | XMI.reference)* >
<!ELEMENT CatalogItem.listPrice (Money) >
<!ELEMENT CatalogItem.category (Category)* >
<!ELEMENT CatalogItem.feature (FeatureValue)* >
<!ELEMENT CatalogItem.detail (Resource)* >
<!ELEMENT CatalogItem.supplier (Party) >
```

Analogous to the XML Schema generation, the Resource class is produced using a DTD parameter entity that defines a standard set of simple XLink attributes.

```
<!ELEMENT Resource EMPTY>
<!ATTLIST Resource
          %XMI.element.att;
          %XLink.simple.att; >
```

Finally, like the Schema, `CatalogItem` is produced with `sku` and `global-Identifier` represented as XML attributes instead of as elements, as in Listing 9-9.

Although this has been just a brief foray into use of the UML extension profile for XML, it should have whetted your appetite for what is possible. My primary goal when developing this UML profile was to allow vocabulary designers to control the way that strict DTDs and XML Schemas are generated from a UML model. It is important that this control be enabled as a refinement of the schema that remains a subset of the standard XMI relaxed form of schema.

It is also entirely possible for custom schema generators to be written that use this UML profile to guide generation of application-specific schema structures. The companion Web site for this book, at *http://XMLModeling.com*, provides a Web service tool that was used to generate all XML Schemas shown in this book. You may use this tool to experiment with your own ideas for controlling or customizing schema generation from your UML models.

Chapter Summary

- Nine common principles define basic criteria for schema generation. These principles are used to specify and compare four alternative sets of production rules: DTD versus XML Schema, and relaxed versus strict validation.

- Relaxed DTDs are equivalent to the rules specified by the XMI 1.1 standard. Element multiplicity is unrestricted, content models are unordered, and both XML attributes and elements are generated for each UML attribute and association end.

- Strict DTDs restrict element multiplicity but also require sequentially ordered content models in order to enable those restrictions. Only XML elements are generated, not both elements and attributes.

- Relaxed XML Schemas are analogous to relaxed DTDs, but use the new schema language. The XML Schema language includes an <all> construct that allows content models to be unordered while still constraining maximum multiplicity bounds.

- Strict XML Schemas allow unordered content models while constraining both minimum and maximum multiplicity specifications from the UML model. This mapping provides the closest match to UML semantics because UML attributes and association ends are unordered in the model.

- A UML extension profile for XML defines stereotypes and tagged values that allow a vocabulary designer fine-grained control over the schema generation process. Details of this profile are included in Appendix C.

Steps for Success

1. Evaluate the role of XML Metadata Interchange standards both in your application architecture and in the requirements of your business partners for B2B integration. Is a relaxed DTD or Schema sufficient for data interchange requirements? Is a strict DTD or Schema required for data validation or to support authoring tools?

2. Determine whether a DTD, an XML Schema, or both is appropriate for your application. Can all business partners and/or application tools use an XML Schema, or do you need to support DTDs also? How will this situation change over the next several months for your environment?

3. Recognize the different ways in which your UML model datatypes are generated into DTDs and Schemas. Will this affect your choice of DTDs versus Schemas?

4. Determine whether you need to control the degree of strictness either in your DTD or Schema or in subsets of the schema. Do you need to customize the schema-generation process? The UML extension profile for XML will satisfy most needs, or you can further extend the profile with new stereotypes and/or tagged values for custom schema generation.

PART III

Deployment

Chapter 10

Vocabulary Transformation

We now have a robust CatML vocabulary design, plus a DTD and an XML Schema generated from that design. But it's unlikely that the entire global e-business community will select CatML as the single standard for representing catalog data, nor is CatML intended for that purpose. In fact, several XML vocabularies for catalog data are in active use (see references at the end of this chapter). Several of these vocabularies are specialized for particular vertical market segments, such as the information technology supply chain, but there is certainly overlap in vocabulary capabilities. The topic of this chapter is how to enable supply chain and e-marketplace integration, in spite of these differences.

Reasons for XML Transformation

Incompatible XML vocabularies are only one of several reasons for transformation. I'll review four situations that are well suited to the Extensible Stylesheet Language for Transformation (XSLT). After that, I'll summarize the essential characteristics of XSLT from the perspective of system architecture and design; references are provided for books and resources useful to XSLT programmers. Finally, we'll apply these concepts to practical examples of transformations between CatML and RosettaNet.

Alternative Vocabularies

An XML document may be transformed from one schema definition to another if those schemas are fundamentally compatible in their semantics but differ in their grammatical structure and/or use of terms. In most cases a business analyst or developer must determine the transformation rules; if that can be done, XSLT can be applied to automate transformation of documents from one vocabulary to another.

Every XML document has either an explicit or implicit schema. The XML standard does not require a document to be defined by an explicit schema, but the document must be well-formed according to a few basic structural rules. The purpose of such schema-less documents is communicated either informally among developers or in human-readable text documentation. However, even a well-formed document has an implicit schema that *could* be written to define the valid elements and grammatical structure of that document. Transformation rules can be created to read and write any well-formed documents, with or without a schema definition.

There are two common examples of transformation between alternative vocabularies. First, many industry-standard schemas, like RosettaNet, were designed to be compatible with older pre-XML EDI standards and are not intended to be implemented directly as object-oriented models. These vocabularies represent message formats, not business objects. Most organizations have their own proprietary catalog models or are dependent on the models (perhaps CatML) implemented by vendors' products. As a result, documents based on these different schemas must be transformed in one or both directions. Second, because we don't have a single universal standard vocabulary, many businesses will need to participate in e-marketplaces or with supply chain members who are committed to alternative standards. Either each participant or the marketplace manager will transform e-business documents between standard vocabularies.

Filtering Sensitive or Irrelevant Data

It's impractical to design an e-business application that creates different XML documents for each group of users with only slightly different information requirements. And new groups of users with new requirements will continue to be added as customers or suppliers in a growing marketplace. In many cases, all of these documents will be subsets of a larger information set. A better solution is to produce a single XML document that contains all information required by a broad range of user groups, then filter out sensitive or irrelevant data as the document is sent to each user.

XSLT has a powerful set of features for filtering document elements and attributes, either with or without transformation between vocabulary schemas. The input and output documents may be defined by the same schema and differ only in the amount of content.

Presenting XML Documents

One of the most fundamental XML design principles is the separation of data from presentation. We therefore need a standard mechanism for reintroducing presentational format to the XML data. Of course, a programmer can always resort to hacking a few scripts or programs that parse a document into the standard Document Object Model (DOM) and then wrap HTML tags around the data; many thousands of such programs have been written. But such code is expensive to maintain and very difficult to generalize for a broad range of presentation devices, such as mobile phones, pagers, PDAs, and interactive TV.

XSLT is one of several approaches specifically designed for applying presentation stylesheets to XML documents. And, true to its name, this is accomplished by transforming the XML element structure into either HTML for the Web or other presentation languages such as WML for wireless devices.

Other than this brief introduction to transformation of XML into presentation formats, this chapter focuses exclusively on the nonvisual transformation of XML data for exchange in B2B supply chains and e-marketplaces. Chapter 11 focuses on presentation of XML documents.

Exporting Non-XML Data

Many legacy systems have not been updated to accept XML documents as input but continue to require ASCII files using proprietary formats. That format may be a simple set of records with comma-delimited fields, or a position-oriented format inherited from old punch-card mainframe systems. XSLT can produce text files that do not include XML markup, although it may not be able to support production of all required transformations. If the XSLT transformations cannot support a complex text format, then a custom transformation program can be written to parse the XML document and write out the data using the required format.

Introduction to XSLT

XSLT is a general-purpose, nonprocedural language for transforming a source document into one or more output documents. It is *nonprocedural* in the sense that a transformation is defined by a set of *template rules* that can be

> ## ■ XSLT's Primary Strengths
>
> - ■ Declarative (nonprocedural) pattern-matching rules may be added or removed in any order without affecting the other rules.
> - ■ Transformation rules may reorder source elements while producing elements in the output document.
> - ■ Transformation rules may filter elements and attributes from the source document, thus producing summaries or subsets that are free of sensitive or irrelevant information.
> - ■ Transformation rules are free of side effects. A rule cannot modify the source tree, and it cannot modify the results tree produced by other rules; it can only add new nodes to the result tree.

specified in any order. The XSLT processor determines which rule to fire for each element and attribute in the document. Each rule then specifies a *pattern* for the XML elements and/or attributes that it matches and a set of *actions* for what to produce in the output when a match is found. A rule pattern does not simply match elements by name or attributes by value; the rule uses an XPath pattern specifying a complex expression of elements that must occur in a particular context within the source document structure. This XPath pattern language was introduced as part of XPointer locators in Chapter 7, but its design originated as part of the XSLT specification.

Prior to diving into the details of vocabulary transformation, I'll adapt an old adage: XSLT is not a hammer, and every problem is not a nail. Use XSLT where it fits, but don't force it on every situation. XLST's primary strengths relative to other technologies are summarized in the sidebar.

On the other hand, XSLT is less well suited to situations having these characteristics:

- ■ Very large source documents, greater than a few megabytes in size
- ■ Continuous streams of data rather than discrete documents or data sets
- ■ Significant computation or analysis required during transformation

These strengths and weakness will become clearer when supported by an understanding of the standard processing model and language elements that define all XSLT tools.

XSLT Processing Model

XSLT was introduced as a means to transform a source *document* to a result *document*, but this restriction to XML documents is unnecessary. In fact, the

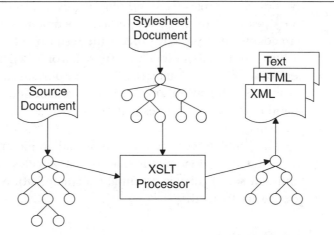

Figure 10-1 XSLT transformation process

XSLT processing model is specified for source and result *trees*, not documents. A tree corresponds to the hierarchical element and attribute structure represented in an XML document, but the source tree may be constructed directly from a nondocument source, such as a legacy system adapter. Or the source tree might be constructed by parsing an XML document file. The point is that an XSLT processor doesn't care how the source tree was created.

The XSLT transformation process is illustrated in Figure 10-1. The figure shows a document-oriented process, where the source document is parsed into a source tree of hierarchically structured nodes corresponding to the XML document's elements and attributes. In the same way, a stylesheet document containing transformation rules is processed into a similar tree based on its elements—after all, the stylesheet is just another XML document. The XSLT processor then selects the best rule applicable to the root node of the source tree and begins to iterate through the source nodes.

The actions contained within each transformation rule produce new nodes in the result tree. The actions also select the next set of source tree nodes to process. Thus, the transformation rules either determine the order of nodes added to the result tree or may omit processing of some source nodes altogether. The rule actions may either create XML element or attribute nodes in the result tree or may create nothing but text nodes. If only text nodes are created, then the transformation will produce a plain-text document as its output. The logic of the transformation rule-matching process is identical, regardless of which output type is produced.

In the default case most commonly applied, the result tree is written to a document file that will contain XML, HTML, or text, depending on how the transformation rules were written. However, as with the source tree, the result tree does not have to be output as a document file. Instead, a customized system adapter may directly process the result tree structure into a legacy system or into a non-XML messaging system. I won't belabor this rather abstract concept of source and result trees, but it's important to think about future possibilities. B2B integration applications often depend significantly on efficient adapters to source and destination systems, and it is critical to optimize their performance.

The XSLT process defines the overall architecture for transformation, but the real work is done by the transformation rules. A stylesheet document containing a set of rules is essentially a specification for transformation of one vocabulary to another.

Transformation Rules

Each XSLT transformation rule specifies a *pattern* of nodes (elements and/or attributes) that must be present in the source tree in order for that rule to be selected for execution. XSLT also defines a set of *actions* that can be included in the body of a rule. When a rule is selected, its actions are processed for a single *context node* from the source tree. An XSLT transformation rule is called a *template* or is sometimes informally referred to as a template rule. This name is appropriate because the typical actions of a rule are to instantiate a new template of result tree nodes (for example, XML or HTML elements) that include data copied from the matched source tree nodes.

The diagram in Figure 10-2 illustrates three simple transformation rules that match patterns of objects shown in a UML class structure diagram. This diagram is a subset of the CatML vocabulary from Figure 7-1. These rules transform CatML documents into a very simple catalog document structure that is determined by the rule action templates. The result document type does not have an associated schema, but this is not unusual for simplified markup languages that are embedded within many applications.

One of the first things you'll notice is that XSLT rules are written using XML syntax. A *transformation stylesheet* is a complete XML document containing one or more transformation rules. The stylesheet document can be validated against the DTD for XSLT, although this is rarely done because most XSLT processors detect errors as part of processing. The term *stylesheet* is historical in that XSLT was initially intended to create stylesheet rules for XML presentation (it was then called XSL). Only later was it generalized as a transformation language.

This stylesheet shown in Figure 10-2 contains three rules, one to match each of the three classes defined in the source vocabulary. A template rule typically contains result tree nodes (for example, `<SalesCatalog>` and `<title>`) as

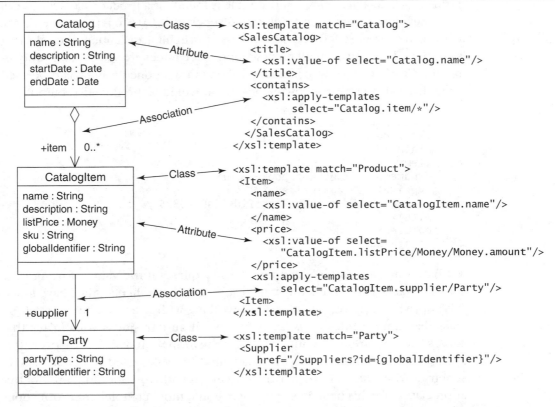

Figure 10-2   XSLT pattern matching on CatML

well as a number of embedded actions. The following action selects the value of an element with type equal to `Catalog.name`, but that element must be a direct child of the current context node, which is `<Catalog>` in this case.

```
<xsl:value-of select="Catalog.name"/>
```

Another common action is one that selects additional child source nodes for processing and then searches for another template rule within the same stylesheet that matches each selected child element. The first template for `Catalog` includes the following action that selects all items within the catalog:

```
<xsl:apply-templates select="Catalog.item/*"/>
```

The XSLT processor then searches for templates that match the elements contained in `Catalog.item` and executes the best fitting rule for each element.

In this example, a matching template rule is found for a `Product` element (recall from previous chapters that `Product` is a subclass of `CatalogItem` in the CatML model). In a larger stylesheet, this process of matching, executing, and selecting is continued recursively until no new source tree nodes are selected for processing. If a CatML document containing a `Catalog` with one `Product` is processed using this stylesheet, the following document would be produced as output:

```
<SalesCatalog>
  <title>June Sale Catalog</title>
  <contains>
    <Item>
      <name>Sony Z505 Notebook</name>
      <price>2495.00</price>
      <Supplier href="Suppliers?id=S34D2-9825"/>
    </Item>
  </contains>
</SalesCatalog>
```

Based on this simple example, you may question the value of using UML class diagrams as a reference when creating XSLT stylesheets; still, I have found this approach to be very helpful when working with large vocabularies. A UML class diagram supplies a *visual* definition of an e-business vocabulary that serves as a reference while writing transformation rules. However, this approach does require that you understand the rules used to generate XML schemas from the UML (described in Chapter 9). You should gain a better appreciation for this benefit as we progress into more complex transformations applied to CatML and RosettaNet vocabularies.

Integrating CatML with RosettaNet

Let's put this theory into practice. Our CatML model and vocabulary was designed as the product catalog structure for a fictitious business, Cheap PCs, Inc. But Cheap PCs must participate in several different supply chains and e-marketplaces used by its customers and suppliers. Consequently, XML documents produced with the CatML vocabulary must be transformed to one or more other industry-standard vocabularies, both when sending and receiving messages. The next several examples illustrate B2B collaboration using the RosettaNet standard,[1] as illustrated in Figure 10-3.

Each of the arrows in this UML collaboration diagram signifies the exchange of an XML document that represents a particular business action message. The

---

1. RosettaNet is an independent, self-funded, nonprofit consortium dedicated to the development and deployment of standard electronic-business interfaces; see *http://www.RosettaNet.org*.

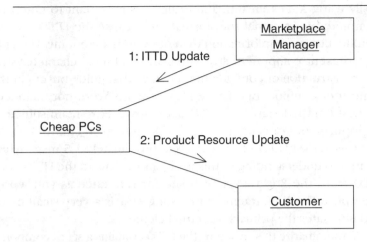

Figure 10-3 Collaboration and message exchange

first message, ITTD Update, contains a standardized RosettaNet IT Technical Dictionary (ITTD) document. This exchange allows Cheap PCs to update the category taxonomy used by its product catalog and to keep its category definitions synchronized with those defined by the RosettaNet standard. The second message, Product Resource Update, includes a standard RosettaNet document structure containing an updated sales catalog requested by a customer. However, Cheap PCs' catalog is represented using CatML, not RosettaNet; so the inbound message must be transformed from RosettaNet to CatML, and the outbound catalog information must be transformed from CatML to RosettaNet.

Refer back to the system integration use case diagram in Figure 4-1. Vocabulary transformation with XSLT fulfills the requirements of the "Transform Message Content" use case shown in that diagram. This chapter's description of transformation focuses on the *message content* vocabularies and not on the vocabularies that define XML document *wrappers* used by various message frameworks.[2] XSLT can, however, transform or filter any XML document.

Importing a RosettaNet Dictionary

The first problem we'll attack is transforming the RosettaNet dictionary of component structures into our CatML taxonomy categories. There are very significant differences in these XML vocabularies, but as you'll see, they are handled quite

---

2. One of the most rapidly growing frameworks used for XML messaging is the Simple Object Access Protocol (SOAP)—see *http://www.w3.org/TR/SOAP*.

easily using XSLT transformation rules. It's important to note that this is not a complete bidirectional transformation because the ITTD document contains significantly more information than our CatML taxonomy. The ITTD is intended to represent component structures and technical characteristics that enable the construction of configuration engines that guide buyers in the assembly of computer components. Those requirements were not included in our more modest CatML design. The ITTD does, however, contain sufficient information to populate our category and feature definitions in CatML.

RosettaNet ITTD version 1.1 is approximately 1.5 megabytes in size. For a complete understanding of this problem, download the ITTD document and its DTD from the RosettaNet Web site for reference as you work through the example.[3] The XML fragment in Listing 10-1 is a very small extract of this file and illustrates the primary structural elements.

To summarize this structure, the ITTD contains a set of component definitions. Each *component* contains specifications and sub-components. The *specifications* contain *feature* elements that describe functional properties of the component and *characteristic* elements that define quantifiable properties. The feature and characteristic elements include different subelements that further specify the kinds of values that can be assigned to those properties. The *sub-components* contain links to other component definitions contained within this ITTD document.

When importing the ITTD into a CatML document, we transform the component structure into a hierarchical definition of Category elements linked by parent and subcategory associations. It would be a good idea to review Figure 7-3, which contains the UML model for CatML. The feature elements in the ITTD map easily onto the CatML Feature elements, but we will ignore all of the characteristic elements from the ITTD.

It's important to mention that the CatML vocabulary was designed without any reference to the RosettaNet ITTD structure, so these transformations are being developed after the fact. This is a realistic situation for many organizations that have preexisting catalog structures but need to enable document interchange with other business partners via RosettaNet standards.

The XSLT stylesheet in Listing 10-2 is a complete set of transformation rules that restructure and filter the RosettaNet ITTD document into a CatML taxonomy document.

All of the code listings from this chapter are available on the companion Web site at *http://XMLModeling.com* so that you can deepen your understanding by running the examples yourself.

---

3. The ITTD XML document and its DTD definition are available from the RosettaNet website. Go to *http://www.rosettanet.org*, and then follow the links to: Standards/Dictionaries/IT Technical Dictionary.

Listing 10-1 Small extract from RosettaNet ITTD

```xml
<?xml version="1.0" encoding = 'ISO-8859-1' ?>
<!DOCTYPE ITTD SYSTEM "ITTD.dtd">
<!--  RosettaNet IT Technical Dictionary copyright 2000  -->

<ITTD version="1.1">
 <component category="Communications"
            definition="A device that performs modulation..."
            dictionary-ref="IEEE Std. 610.7-1995"
            type="component">
  <name>Analog Modem</name>

  <specifications>
    <feature definition="The mode in which data can ...">
      <name>Data Transmission</name>
      <value-domain ordered="No" valuetype="Singlevalued">
        <value>
          <name>Full Duplex</name>
        </value>
        <value>
          <name>Half Duplex</name>
        </value>
      </value-domain>
    </feature>

    <characteristic definition="The rate at which..."
                    dictionary-ref="IEEE 610.10-1994">
      <name>Data Bit Rate</name>
      <dimension>Rate</dimension>
      <units>
        <unit system="OTHER">bits per second (bps)</unit>
      </units>
      <domain>X is a real</domain>
    </characteristic>
  </specifications>

  <sub-components>
    <component-link link="Power Adapter"/>
    <component-link link="Battery"/>
    <component-link link="Port"/>
    <component-link link="Cable"/>
    <component-link link="Microphone"/>
    <component-link link="Headset"/>
    <component-link link="Speaker"/>
  </sub-components>
 </component>
</ITTD>
```

Listing 10-2   XSLT transformation from ITTD to CatML taxonomy

```
<?xml version="1.0"?>
<xsl:stylesheet
    xmlns="http://www.XMLmodeling.com/2000/CatML"
    xmlns:xsl="http://www.w3.org/1999/XSL/Transform"
    xmlns:date="/java.util.Date"
    exclude-result-prefixes="date"
    version="1.0" >

<!-- select XML as the output type and set the DTD name -->

<xsl:output method="xml" indent="yes"
            doctype-system="CatML.dtd"/>
<xsl:strip-space elements="*"/>

<!-- Match the root element <ITTD> and produce a
     complete XMI document in the result tree.
     The actions in this template select which ITTD
     sub-elements to process, and in what order. -->

<xsl:template match="ITTD">
  <XMI xmi.version="1.1" timestamp="{date:new()}">
    <XMI.header>
      <XMI.metamodel xmi.name="CatML" xmi.version="1.0"/>
    </XMI.header>
    <XMI.content>

      <!-- Top-level category names are represented in
           the @category attribute of each RosettaNet
           <component> element. -->
      <xsl:comment> Primary categories </xsl:comment>
      <!-- extract a sorted list of unique category names
           from all components. -->
      <xsl:for-each select=
          "component[not(@category=preceding::component/@category)]">
        <xsl:sort select="@category" order="ascending"/>
        <!-- create a valid ID by replacing ' ' with '_' -->
        <Category xmi.id="{translate(@category,' ','_')}">
          <Category.name>
            <xsl:value-of select="@category"/>
          </Category.name>
          <Category.subcategory>
            <!-- Iterate through all components whose @category
                 is equal to the current primary category.
                 Transform each to an xmi.idref link. -->
            <xsl:for-each select="//component[@category=current()/@category]">
              <Category xmi.idref="{translate(name,' ','_')}"/>
            </xsl:for-each>
          </Category.subcategory>
        </Category>
      </xsl:for-each>
```

```xml
      <!-- Process each <component> in the dictionary. -->
      <xsl:comment> Secondary categories </xsl:comment>
      <xsl:apply-templates select="component"/>
    </XMI.content>
  </XMI>
</xsl:template>

<!-- For each component in the ITTD, create a <Category> -->

<xsl:template match="component">
  <!-- create a valid ID attribute by replacing spaces -->
  <Category xmi.id="{translate(name,' ','_')}">
    <Category.name>
      <xsl:value-of select="name"/>
    </Category.name>
    <Category.description>
      <xsl:value-of select="@definition"/>
    </Category.description>
    <Category.parent>
      <!-- The component's parent category is the one
           created for its @category attribute -->
      <Category xmi.idref="{translate(@category,' ','_')}"/>
    </Category.parent>
    <Category.subcategory>
      <!-- process all <component-link> children -->
      <xsl:apply-templates select="sub-components"/>
    </Category.subcategory>
    <Category.feature>
      <!-- process all feature and characteristic children -->
      <xsl:apply-templates select="specifications"/>
    </Category.feature>
  </Category>
</xsl:template>

<!-- For each <component-link> child of a component,
     create a Category proxy element with xmi.idref -->

<xsl:template match="component-link">
  <Category xmi.idref="{translate(@link,' ','_')}"/>
</xsl:template>

<!-- For each <feature> in the ITTD, create a <Feature> -->

<xsl:template match="feature">
  <!-- ID = component ID + '.' + feature ID -->
  <Feature xmi.id=
   "{translate(ancestor::component/name,' ','_')}.{translate(name,' /','_')}">
    <Feature.name><xsl:value-of select="name"/></Feature.name>
    <Feature.description>
      <xsl:value-of select="@definition"/>
    </Feature.description>
```

continued

Listing 10-2 *continued*

```
        <!-- Map multivalued type spec from ITTD to CatML -->
        <xsl:choose>
          <xsl:when test="value-domain/@valuetype='Multivalued'">
            <Feature.multivalued xmi.value='true'/>
          </xsl:when>
          <xsl:otherwise>
            <Feature.multivalued xmi.value='false'/>
          </xsl:otherwise>
        </xsl:choose>
      </Feature>
    </xsl:template>

    <!-- Filter out a subset of <feature> elements, selecting
         only those whose <name> child has specified value. -->
    <xsl:template match="feature
                          [name= 'Name'
                           or name= 'Product Name'
                           or name= 'Manufacturer Name'
                           or name= 'Manufacturer Part Number'
                           or name= 'Global Product Identification'
                           or name= 'Component Category'
                           or name= 'Abbreviated Description'] ">
      <!-- This template has no actions,
           so features with these names are ignored. -->
    </xsl:template>

    <!-- All <characteristic> elements are ignored. -->
    <xsl:template match="characteristic"/>

</xsl:stylesheet>
```

This stylesheet contains six template rules that match elements from the ITTD source document. I won't attempt to explain all of the XSLT syntax used by these rules but instead emphasize the overall transformation process. For details on XSLT development, see the programming references at the end of this chapter.

The first transformation rule matches the ITTD root element of the source document and produces a complete XMI wrapper element to contain the CatML category element (see Chapter 6 for details). A bit of trickery is required to extract the top-level category names from the ITTD because they are only referenced in the category attribute of each component element. Thus, we need to extract a unique list of category names from the hundreds of components in the dictionary. This is accomplished by this rather clever XPath expression:

```
component[not(@category=preceding::component/@category)]
```

This expression may be paraphrased this way: for each component within ITTD, filter out those where the @category attribute value is not equal to the @category value of any preceding component. This relatively small list of components then produces a set of top-level Category elements in the result tree. Then, for each of these top-level categories, we produce a subcategory Category element in the result tree corresponding to the component in the source tree.

We next process all of the component elements in the source tree to extract their sub-components. We produce a Category for each component and a Category proxy element for each component-link defined within the sub-components in the source document.

Finally, we process all child elements of the specifications in the source component. The specification elements are either a feature or characteristic. The stylesheet includes a transformation rule that matches each feature element and produces a corresponding Feature element in the result tree. Notice that there are *two* rules that match the feature element. The second rule contains an additional filter within its XPath expression, so the XSLT processor will select this second rule *instead of the first rule* for features that have one of the specified names. The second rule has no actions, so these features are filtered out of the results. A template rule is also provided that matches the characteristic element; this rule contains no actions, so the characteristics are effectively ignored in the output.

When the previous ITTD document fragment is processed by these transformation rules, the CatML document in Listing 10-3 is produced.

CatML was designed independent of RosettaNet, and the two vocabularies are based on fundamentally different requirements. However, these transformation rules have allowed us to import RosettaNet's component specification dictionary into our CatML category taxonomy. This book's companion Web site includes a downloadable copy the XSLT stylesheet used in this example, plus a complete CatML taxonomy document produced from the ITTD. You will gain a better understanding for XSLT by running this example yourself and customizing the transformation rules to suit your own ideas. Be creative and explore the possibilities!

Exporting a RosettaNet Sales Catalog

Now that you've mastered the basic principles of XSLT, this second example will be straightforward. The UML collaboration diagram shown in Figure 10-3 shows a Product Resource Update message sent from Cheap PCs to a customer. Because the customer is expecting a standard RosettaNet document for this

Listing 10-3   CatML taxonomy produced by the transformation

```xml
<?xml version="1.0" encoding="utf-8" ?>
<!DOCTYPE XMI
  SYSTEM "CatML.dtd">
<XMI xmlns="http://www.XMLmodeling.com/2000/CatML"
     xmi.version="1.1"
     timestamp="Fri Aug 11 14:53:02 MDT 2000">
  <XMI.header>
    <XMI.metamodel xmi.name="CatML" xmi.version="1.0"/>
  </XMI.header>
  <XMI.content>
    <!-- Primary categories -->
    <Category xmi.id="Communications">
      <Category.name>Communications</Category.name>
      <Category.subcategory>
        <Category xmi.idref="Analog_Modem"/>
      </Category.subcategory>
    </Category>
    <!-- Secondary categories -->
    <Category xmi.id="Analog_Modem">
      <Category.name>Analog Modem</Category.name>
      <Category.description>
        A device that performs modulation...
      </Category.description>
      <Category.parent>
        <Category xmi.idref="Communications"/>
      </Category.parent>
      <Category.subcategory>
        <Category xmi.idref="Power_Adapter"/>
        <Category xmi.idref="Battery"/>
        <Category xmi.idref="Port"/>
        <Category xmi.idref="Cable"/>
        <Category xmi.idref="Microphone"/>
        <Category xmi.idref="Headset"/>
        <Category xmi.idref="Speaker"/>
      </Category.subcategory>
      <Category.feature>
        <Feature xmi.id="Analog_Modem.Data_Transmission">
          <Feature.name>Data Transmission</Feature.name>
          <Feature.description>
            The mode in which data can...
          </Feature.description>
          <Feature.multivalued xmi.value="false"/>
        </Feature>
      </Category.feature>
    </Category>
  </XMI.content>
</XMI>
```

Listing 10-4   CatML catalog document

```
<?xml version = '1.0' encoding = 'ISO-8859-1' ?>
<!DOCTYPE XMI SYSTEM "CatX.dtd">
<XMI xmi.version="1.1" timestamp="Sun Jun 11 2000">
  <XMI.header>
    <XMI.metamodel xmi.name="CatML" xmi.version="1.0"/>
  </XMI.header>
  <XMI.content>
    <Catalog>
      <Catalog.name>May Specials</Catalog.name>
      <Catalog.startDate>May 1, 2000</Catalog.startDate>
      <Catalog.endDate>June 30, 2000</Catalog.endDate>
      <Catalog.item>
        <Product href="Products.xml#sku-Z505JE"/>
        <Product href="Products.xml#sku-1200XL118"/>
        <Product href="Products.xml#sku-CP14479"/>
      </Catalog.item>
    </Catalog>
  </XMI.content>
</XMI>
```

message type, we must transform our CatML catalog into a RosettaNet sales catalog representation.

RosettaNet defines Partner Interface Processes (PIP) for each standardized exchange between business partners. For this example, we are concerned with the "PIP2A1 Distribute New Product Information" specification. For a complete understanding, download the PIP specification, including the corresponding DTD, from RosettaNet.[4] However, I suggest that you work through the following example before becoming immersed in the lengthy RosettaNet specifications.

In Chapter 7, I described how many different catalogs could be created for particular customers, market segments, or promotions and that each catalog could refer to a common set of product definitions. Based on this design the CatML catalog document in Listing 10-4 includes references to three products, using `Product` proxy elements with `href` linking attributes.

The `Products.xml` document referred to in the catalog links is shown in Listing 10-5. Only one `Product` element is included for brevity, but the others are similar.

---

4. The RosettaNet PIP specifications are available from the RosettaNet Web site. Go to *http://www.rosettanet.org*, and then follow the links to: Standards/PIPs/Cluster 2/Segment 2A/PIP 2A1.

Listing 10-5 CatML document named Products.xml

```
<?xml version = '1.0' encoding = 'ISO-8859-1' ?>
<!DOCTYPE XMI SYSTEM "CatX.dtd">
<XMI xmi.version="1.1" timestamp="Sun Jun 11 2000">
  <XMI.header>
    <XMI.metamodel xmi.name="CatML" xmi.version="1.0"/>
  </XMI.header>
  <XMI.content>
    <Product xmi.id="sku-Z505JE">
      <CatalogItem.name>Sony VAIO Z505</CatalogItem.name>
      <CatalogItem.description>
        500MHz Sony VAIO Superslim Notebook with Windows 98
      </CatalogItem.description>
      <CatalogItem.listPrice>
        <Money currency="USD">
          <Money.amount>2499</Money.amount>
        </Money>
      </CatalogItem.listPrice>
      <CatalogItem.sku>Z505JE</CatalogItem.sku>
      <CatalogItem.category>
        <Category href="Taxonomy.xml#Laptop_Computer_System"
                  xmi.label="Laptop Computer System"/>
      </CatalogItem.category>
      <CatalogItem.detail>
        <Resource href="http://www.ita.sel.sony.com/jump/z505/"
                  xmi.label="Product Specifications"/>
      </CatalogItem.detail>
      <CatalogItem.supplier>
        <Party href="Suppliers.xml#Sony" xmi.label="Sony"/>
      </CatalogItem.supplier>
    </Product>
  </XMI.content>
</XMI>
```

The XSLT stylesheet in Listing 10-6 includes six transformation rules. This is not a complete definition of all transformations required to produce a valid RosettaNet sales catalog from CatML, but a sufficient subset is provided to illustrate how such transformations would be written. If you were to complete this example, you could check the accuracy of your results by validating the output document against the RosettaNet DTD for this PIP. The RosettaNet DTDs are analogous to the strict DTD described in Chapter 9, so proper element sequence must be maintained for successful validation.

Listing 10-6   XSLT transformation from CatML to RosettaNet

```xml
<?xml version="1.0"?>
<xsl:stylesheet
    xmlns:xsl="http://www.w3.org/1999/XSL/Transform"
    xmlns:date="/java.util.Date"
    exclude-result-prefixes="date"
    version="1.0" >

<xsl:output method="xml" indent="yes"
            doctype-system="Pip2A1ProductResourceUpdateGuideline.dtd"/>
<xsl:strip-space elements="*"/>

<!-- Match the root <XMI> element of the CatML catalog document
     and produce a complete RosettaNet document wrapper for
     the Pip2A1ProductResourceUpdate. The CatML catalog
     elements are inserted at the end of this template. -->

<xsl:template match="XMI">
  <Pip2A1ProductResourceUpdate>
    <fromRole>
      <xsl:comment> omitted in example </xsl:comment>
    </fromRole>
    <toRole>
      <xsl:comment> omitted in example </xsl:comment>
    </toRole>
    <thisDocumentGenerationDateTime>
      <DateTimeStamp>
        <xsl:value-of select="date:new()"/>
      </DateTimeStamp>
    </thisDocumentGenerationDateTime>
    <thisDocumentIdentifier>
      <ProprietaryDocumentIdentifier>
        <xsl:comment> add identifier here </xsl:comment>
      </ProprietaryDocumentIdentifier>
    </thisDocumentIdentifier>
    <GlobalDocumentFunctionCode>
        <xsl:comment> add code here </xsl:comment>
    </GlobalDocumentFunctionCode>
    <xsl:apply-templates select="XMI.content/Catalog"/>
  </Pip2A1ProductResourceUpdate>
</xsl:template>

<!-- The CatML <Catalog> element is transformed to a
     <SalesCatalog> in the result tree. -->

<xsl:template match="Catalog">
  <SalesCatalog>
    <xsl:apply-templates select="Catalog.item"/>
    <effectiveDate>
      <DateStamp>
        <xsl:value-of select="Catalog.startDate"/>
      </DateStamp>
    </effectiveDate>
```

continued

Listing 10-6 *continued*

```
      </SalesCatalog>
</xsl:template>

<!-- If the <Product> has an href attribute, then it is a
     proxy element that refers to an external resource.
     The XSLT document() fuction is used to retrieve
     this resource, then this stylesheet is recursively
     applied to the corresponding Product element
     in that external document. -->

<xsl:template match="Product[@href]">
  <xsl:variable name="prod-id" select="substring-after(@href, '#')"/>
  <xsl:apply-templates select="document(@href)//Product[@xmi.id=$prod-id]"/>
</xsl:template>

<!-- For each <Product> element matched in the source,
     produce a <ProductLineItem> in the result tree.
     Transform appropriate sub-elements from the source
     to the result, if the data is available.
     (Note: this example intentionally omits some elements. -->

<xsl:template match="Product">
  <ProductLineItem>
    <productUnit>
      <ProductPackageDescription>
        <ProductDescription>
          <TextualDescription>
            <primary>
              <FreeFormText>
                <xsl:value-of select="CatalogItem.description"/>
              </FreeFormText>
            </primary>
            <detail>
              <FreeFormText>
                <xsl:value-of select="CatalogItem.detail/Resource/@href"/>
              </FreeFormText>
            </detail>
          </TextualDescription>
          <productName>
            <FreeFormText>
              <xsl:value-of select="CatalogItem.name"/>
            </FreeFormText>
          </productName>
          <ProprietaryProductIdentifier>
            <xsl:value-of select="CatalogItem.sku"/>
          </ProprietaryProductIdentifier>
        </ProductDescription>
      </ProductPackageDescription>
    </productUnit>
    <unitPrice>
```

```
      <!-- Because the child element is <Money>, this will
            cause the separate template to be invoked. -->
      <xsl:apply-templates select="CatalogItem.listPrice"/>
    </unitPrice>
  </ProductLineItem>
</xsl:template>

<!-- By creating a separate element for <Money>, we can
      reuse this template in any other situation where
      the <Money> element occurs in the source document. -->

<xsl:template match="Money">
  <FinancialAmount>
    <GlobalCurrencyCode>
      <xsl:value-of select="@currency"/>
    </GlobalCurrencyCode>
    <MonetaryAmount>
      <xsl:value-of select="Money.amount"/>
    </MonetaryAmount>
  </FinancialAmount>
</xsl:template>

</xsl:stylesheet>
```

Unlike the stylesheet for transforming the ITTD categories, there is no trickery or major restructuring required by this catalog content transformation. The transformation rules retain the same hierarchical document structure and are only required to map one vocabulary onto another. When these rules are applied to the previous document fragment from the CatML catalog, the RosettaNet document in Listing 10-7 is produced.

As commented in this document, the <fromRole> and <toRole> content is omitted in order to prevent the example from becoming too unwieldy. The content of these elements in the RosettaNet DTD is similar to that included in the Party class of our CatML vocabulary. If you were to extend this example, it would be useful to create a general transformation rule that matches Party and produces the required RosettaNet definitions in the result. The source would be extended to include hyperlinks to Suppliers.xml and Customers.xml resources, similar to the way we included a link from the catalog to Products.xml.

If catalog vocabulary standards other than RosettaNet must be supported by your application, the transformation rules would be similar to those created in this example. As long as an analyst can correctly map the vocabulary semantics to or from CatML, it's likely that XSLT can be applied to execute the transformation in a deployed system.

Listing 10-7 RosettaNet document produced by the transformation

```xml
<?xml version="1.0" encoding="utf-8" ?>
<!DOCTYPE Pip2A1ProductResourceUpdate
  SYSTEM "Pip2A1ProductResourceUpdateGuideline.dtd">

<Pip2A1ProductResourceUpdate>
  <fromRole><!-- omitted in example --></fromRole>
  <toRole><!-- omitted in example --></toRole>
  <thisDocumentGenerationDateTime>
    <DateTimeStamp>Sun Aug 13 09:52:37 MDT 2000</DateTimeStamp>
  </thisDocumentGenerationDateTime>
  <thisDocumentIdentifier>
    <ProprietaryDocumentIdentifier>
      <!-- add identifier here -->
    </ProprietaryDocumentIdentifier>
  </thisDocumentIdentifier>
  <GlobalDocumentFunctionCode>
    <!-- add code here -->
  </GlobalDocumentFunctionCode>
  <SalesCatalog>
    <ProductLineItem>
      <productUnit>
        <ProductPackageDescription>
          <ProductDescription>
            <TextualDescription>
              <primary>
                <FreeFormText>
                 500MHz Sony VAIO Superslim Notebook with Windows 98
                </FreeFormText>
              </primary>
              <detail>
                <FreeFormText>
                 http://www.ita.sel.sony.com/jump/z505/
                </FreeFormText>
              </detail>
            </TextualDescription>
            <productName>
              <FreeFormText>Sony VAIO Z505</FreeFormText>
            </productName>
            <ProprietaryProductIdentifier>Z505JE</ProprietaryProductIdentifier>
          </ProductDescription>
        </ProductPackageDescription>
      </productUnit>
      <unitPrice>
        <FinancialAmount>
          <GlobalCurrencyCode>USD</GlobalCurrencyCode>
          <MonetaryAmount>2499</MonetaryAmount>
        </FinancialAmount>
      </unitPrice>
    </ProductLineItem>
    <effectiveDate>
      <DateStamp>May 1, 2000</DateStamp>
    </effectiveDate>
  </SalesCatalog>
</Pip2A1ProductResourceUpdate>
```

Chapter Summary

- XSLT may be used to transform an XML document from one schema to another, as long as those schemas are fundamentally compatible in their semantics and differ only in their grammatical structure.

- XSLT template rules can filter document content by specifying which elements and attributes are copied into the result document, with or without structural transformation.

- XSLT can also transform document content for a variety of presentation devices, including to non-XML output such as HTML.

- XSLT transformation may not be suitable for very large documents or for processing continuous streams of input data.

- An XSLT stylesheet is composed of a set of template rules, where each rule specifies a pattern of element and/or attribute nodes and a set of actions applied to the matched nodes. The processing engine selects the best rule for each element or attribute node in the source document.

- A RosettaNet dictionary can be imported into our CatML vocabulary by transforming its category/component/feature structure into a category/ sub-category/feature structure.

- A RosettaNet sales catalog can be exported from CatML by mapping the `CatalogItem` and its subclasses into the elements and attributes required by RosettaNet.

Steps for Success

1. Evaluate all the ways in which XSLT can contribute to your application architecture. There are many situations where XSLT transformations may be applied to your XML source data. We have focused on the more difficult problem of transformation between alternative vocabularies, but the same process applies to the simpler problem of filtering subsets of a document.

2. Evaluate vendor products for their architecture and efficiency of XSLT integration. The XSLT transformation rules are based on an adopted W3C Recommendation, and there is a growing list of open source tools and commercial products that implement this standard. The most important difference will be the way in which the transformation engine is integrated with other application services.

3. As these XSLT products mature, watch for new entrants that enable nonprogrammers to apply graphical tools that map one vocabulary to another and generate the necessary XSLT transformation rules; also beware of proprietary transformation tools versus those based on the XSLT standard.

Bibliography

The first item will be helpful when you're learning to develop complex XSLT transformation rules.

- World Wide Web Consortium. *XSL Transformations (XSLT)*, W3C Recommendation—see *http://www.w3.org/TR/xslt*.
- Kay, Michael. *XSLT Programmer's Reference*. Birmingham, UK: Wrox Press, 2000.
- Bradley, Neil. *The XSL Companion*. Boston: Addison-Wesley, 2000.

There is no single preferred standard for representing product catalog data in XML, but several choices will offer trade-offs with industry specialization. These catalog vocabulary proposals are offered for your consideration.

- RosettaNet—see *http://www.rosettanet.org*.
- XML Common Business Library (xCBL)—see *http://www.xcbl.org*.
- eCatalog XML (eCX)—see *http://www.ecx-xml.org*.
- Open Catalog Format (OCF)—see *http://www.martsoft.com/ocp*.

Chapter 11

B2B Portal Presentation

Each B2B market can be viewed holistically as a unified global Web of information. This idealized view can be applied to a supply chain, e-marketplace, or other extended enterprise relationship. One or more portals are created to provide customized views into subsets of this Web, and communication messages move information around from place to place within the distributed content locations. An alternative perspective is to view B2B information as a collection of independent applications that must export and import information to synchronize their content, and each application is responsible for providing its own client applications for viewing content. Granted, the latter perspective is a more realistic view of actual implementation, but the idealized viewpoint of a holistic Web often yields more creative ideas about how to benefit from B2B connectivity.

This holistic view is built around the vocabularies that define how information content is created, communicated, transformed, and presented to all actors participating in the global system. Over the past several chapters we have considered techniques and design criteria for using the UML to specify XML vocabularies. Chapter 10 described how XSLT is used to transform documents from one vocabulary to another. In the ideal world this transformation is embedded in the fabric of communication so that the exchange appears seamless. This is not unlike the newspaper and media industry in which information is moved around a global network and translated between human natural languages as necessary to support a relatively complete understanding of world events.

Just as the *New York Times* provides a printed portal into world news (and as many Web portals are now doing with on-line news), a B2B portal presents a view into the world of business data and information relevant to a particular e-marketplace or supply chain.

This chapter's goal is twofold. First, we'll apply UML modeling techniques to design a B2B portal, then we'll work through two examples using XSLT to present this data within portlets that are available to an array of wired and wireless devices.

Portal Analysis Model

We'll approach portal analysis more systematically than simply reading a variety of XML documents and converting them into HTML for presentation in portlets, but we won't become overly involved with analysis models and risk falling victim to paralysis by overanalysis.

Success in the hyperaccelerated e-business marketplace requires moving quickly through iterative design and development. I addressed the overall development requirements for B2B portals in Chapter 5 and provided a use case diagram in Figure 5-1. This chapter now probes more deeply into the design of portlets and the transformation of XML content into HTML presentation.

The concept of portals and portlets introduced in Chapter 5 deserves a brief review. Most Web portals divide the screen interface into subregions, or portlets, each of which is dedicated to a specific topic or content source. A portlet's content may be provided by an XML document formatted by a stylesheet—that is the focus of this chapter. However, a portlet's content also may be provided dynamically by JavaServer Pages (JSP) or other similar component technology. This chapter uses the Apache Jetspeed server for examples, but BEA Systems and Oracle provide similar portal/portlet architectures in their products; the list of portal products is growing quickly.

Figure 11-1 illustrates a UML analysis model for a subset of the MyCat portal. (An analysis model is quite simply a high-level UML class diagram analogous to those used for vocabulary design in Chapters 6 and 7.) But the emphasis is shifted to specification of how the domain objects are associated with control and interface objects used by the system's actors.

You'll notice that the five classes shown on the right side of this diagram are a subset of those specified in the CatML vocabulary model. The attributes are hidden in most of the classes in order to focus attention on the associations between classes in this view of the model. These are called *entity* classes in an analysis model. The three classes positioned in the middle of the figure are called *control* classes and those on the left are called *boundary* classes. These

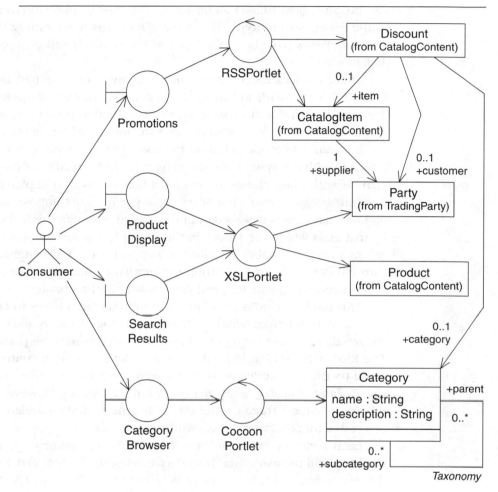

Figure 11-1   UML portal analysis model

are all ordinary classes within the UML model, and each may include attributes, operations, and associations in their definitions. However, to improve the visual interpretation of analysis models, alternative display icons may be assigned to each type of class.

When creating this model in a UML tool, the analysis role of each class is assigned through use of a stereotype. For example, we used an <<enumeration>> stereotype in Chapter 6 to specify classes containing enumerated lists of terms. Similarly, the model shown in Figure 11-1 assigns a <<boundary>> stereotype to four classes on the left, and a <<control>> stereotype to the three classes in the middle. The stereotype labels are not shown because most UML modeling tools can be configured to alter automatically the class display icon to an alternative shape for each stereotype. The seven class icons representing boundary and control classes have been modified in the figure based on their stereotype assignments.

These particular stereotypes and icons are defined as part of the Rational Unified Process (RUP) and are specified in a UML profile for business modeling. The profile includes more stereotypes than the two used here; see RUP documentation for additional detail and explanation [Kruchten, 2000].

In an analysis model, a boundary class represents a point at which an actor interacts with the system, and the class definition specifies constraints or associations with other classes in the model that are used to implement that interface. But assignment of a boundary class type does not impose any restrictions on how that class is designed or implemented; it signifies only the role fulfilled by that class within the model. In this example, the four boundary classes represent portal interfaces required to support a CatX Consumer. We'll work through details of implementing the first two boundary classes using XSLT stylesheets and Apache Jetspeed portlets later in this chapter.

This model includes associations from boundary classes to control classes that guide the interface behavior. By separating the boundary and control classes, we are able to reuse common behavior provided within the portal framework. The RSSPortlet, XSLPortlet, and CocoonPortlet are generic control classes provided by the Apache Jetspeed portal server, and we use them to very quickly specify (and ultimately implement) our CatX interfaces. However, the behavior provided by these three control classes is generic, and equivalent classes could be created for other portal frameworks.

Each control class includes associations with one or more entity classes used to fulfill the associated boundary classes, so the RSSPortlet controls how the Promotions boundary class gains access to the Discount, CatalogItem, Category, and Party entities. This relatively simple analysis model specifies a substantial amount of information about how a portal framework controls the boundary classes by serving as an intermediary with the CatML entity classes.

Transforming XML Documents into Portlets

In the remainder of this chapter we'll work through an implementation scenario for this analysis model. The first two boundary classes from Figure 11-1 are implemented using XSLT stylesheets deployed within the Apache Jetspeed portal server. Our focus is on implementing the Create Stylesheet use case shown in Figure 5-1, not on the configuration and layout of the portlets within a portal. Although the examples are described using Jetspeed deployment, the same concepts could be applied to any other Web application architecture or portal product.

This chapter is mostly independent of the vocabulary transformations described in Chapter 10. However, if you are reading this chapter prior to Chapter 10, you should read the "Introduction to XSLT" section from that chapter before continuing. The XSLT processing model and transformation rules described there apply in an identical way to producing HTML from an XML vocabulary. XSLT is designed for general-purpose transformation of XML documents and is currently the most widely used approach for producing HTML from XML documents.

Unlike Chapter 10 where the only output was additional XML documents, this chapter has a more tangible visual output showing the fruits of our labor. We begin with XML documents containing product, supplier, and promotional discount data that are compliant with the CatML vocabulary. In the first example, we apply a relatively simple XSLT stylesheet that creates an HTML document, which presents product data within a table structure. This resulting HTML document is then displayed in Jetspeed as the content of a portlet, exactly as was described in Chapter 5. The same HTML document could, however, be displayed alone or embedded within any other nonportal Web application.

The sequence of actions required to produce a portlet from an XML document is most easily explained in a UML sequence diagram. Figure 11-2 illustrates an informal specification of the messages that are exchanged among portal components, starting with the Consumer's request for a Product Display boundary object. These messages are informal because they are specified using a combination of English language and operations specified in the design of each participating object.

A UML sequence diagram illustrates the time-ordered interactions between objects that are required to fulfill the goal of a use case or operation. The time order is organized top to bottom in the diagram, and each vertical line represents an instance of a class from the analysis model. The label on each message arrow signifies the operation that is invoked on the destination object. This sequence diagram is specified as part of a high-level analysis that is independent of a particular portal framework, so most messages are defined using informal names. Although the examples in this chapter are illustrated using Jetspeed, the same analysis model and message sequences can be applied to other commercial portal products. After selecting a portal product for your project, you can add additional detail to this diagram by formalizing the message labels to match operations and parameters for the portal's components.

The diagram is mostly self-explanatory. The only new concept is that there are two control objects serving as intermediaries between the boundary class and the entities. The XSLT Processor is shown in the sequence diagram as a control object that is used by the XSL Portlet to transform the Product and

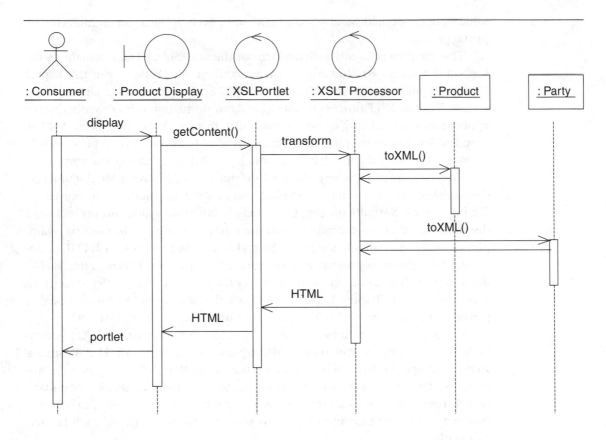

Figure 11-2   Product Display sequence diagram

Party entity objects. The XSLT Processor could have been added to the analysis model in Figure 11-1 and shown with associations to XSLPortlet, Product, and Party. But the class was omitted from this analysis model view to avoid unnecessary distraction at the higher level and is included now for more precise specification in the sequence diagram. A complete UML analysis should create a refinement diagram that expands on these points.

The Product and Party objects are shown in the diagram as being accessed by the XSLT Processor using the toXML() message. In this high-level specification, it is not known how those entities are stored (they could be stored either as records in a relational database, as objects in a content-management repository, or in simple text files). For our example, the entities are represented in files containing XML document instances. At this abstract level, the toXML() message simply means that the Product and Party entities are responsible for returning their content represented as XML, and that content is then input to the XSLT Processor object.

In the final steps, the XSLT Processor returns HTML output after having applied a stylesheet of transformation rules to the Product and Party entities. The XSLPortlet wraps this HTML with additional HTML that displays the portlet's title bar, control buttons, and "skin" style, then it returns the final HTML for display to the Consumer.

In the next section, we'll review the XSLT stylesheet used to transform Product and Party entities to HTML and then take a quick look at the final portlet presentation.

A Portlet for Product Display

The Product Display boundary class, as shown in Figure 11-1, is controlled by an XSLPortlet, which in turn depends on an XSLT Processor to transform the Product and Party class definitions. In this example, the Product and Party object instances are represented in two separate XML documents, named Products.xml and Suppliers.xml, respectively. The XSLT transformation rules merge these data into an HTML presentation of the product, including a hyperlink to the supplier's Web site.

We've seen many examples of CatML products over the past several chapters, so first XML document in Listing 11-1 requires little introduction. It contains one product instance for a Sony VAIO notebook computer. This product element is wrapped inside of standard XMI document elements.

Notice that the supplier reference (shown in bold font) is included as a proxy element using an href attribute to link to a Party element contained within a separate document. This document link must be resolved by the XSLT transformation rules to display additional supplier data. As explained in Chapter 7, the locator fragment included after the '#' character specifies either an ID or an XPointer expression that selects elements within the referenced document.

The referenced Suppliers.xml document is shown in Listing 11-2. This document contains one Party element that includes data about Sony Corporation. The Party element is wrapped within standard XMI elements. In order to keep the example small, some of the subelements of Party are not fully expanded. For example, CorporateInformation.corporateAddress and CorporateInformation.primaryContact are shown as empty elements, but they should contain address and personal contact data.

The XSLT stylesheet (Listing 11-3) required to process these documents is much simpler than the examples described in Chapter 10. There are only two template rules, one of which contains a single line in its body. The only piece of tricky code is the one required to process the link from a product to a supplier. It's beyond the scope of this book to explain each piece of syntax used in these templates; the best current XSLT programmer's reference is Michael Kay's

Listing 11-1   CatML document with one Product

```xml
<?xml version = '1.0' encoding = 'ISO-8859-1' ?>
<!DOCTYPE XMI SYSTEM "CatX.dtd">
<XMI xmi.version="1.1" timestamp="Sun Jun 11 2000">
 <XMI.header>
   <XMI.metamodel xmi.name="CatML" xmi.version="1.0"/>
 </XMI.header>
 <XMI.content>
  <Product xmi.id="sku-Z505JE">
    <CatalogItem.name>Sony VAIO Z505</CatalogItem.name>
    <CatalogItem.description>
      The small size and weight of the Sony VAIO Z505...
    </CatalogItem.description>
    <CatalogItem.listPrice>
     <Money currency="USD">
      <Money.amount>2499</Money.amount>
     </Money>
    </CatalogItem.listPrice>
    <CatalogItem.sku>Z505JE</CatalogItem.sku>
    <Product.photoURL>/examples/images/SonyZ505.jpg
    </Product.photoURL>
    <CatalogItem.category>
      <Category href="Taxonomy.xml#Laptop_Computer_System"
                xmi.label="Laptop Computer System"/>
    </CatalogItem.category>
    <CatalogItem.detail>
      <Resource href="http://www.ita.sel.sony.com/jump/z505/"
                xmi.label="Product Specifications"/>
    </CatalogItem.detail>
    <CatalogItem.supplier>
      <Party href="Suppliers.xml#Sony" xmi.label="Sony"/>
    </CatalogItem.supplier>
  </Product>
 </XMI.content>
</XMI>
```

book, which explains all of this syntax in great detail, including the tricks required to resolve IDs in linked documents [Kay, 2000].

The template that matches `Product` does all of the work in this stylesheet. This template sets up the content template for an HTML table, then populates the table's cells with data from a `Product` element in the XML source document. The HTML table contains three rows and two columns. The first row contains a product name and sku in the first cell, and the product's list price in the second cell. The second cell has right-justified alignment. The second row of the table contains the product description in the first cell, followed by a link to the product's photo in the second cell. Finally, the third row contains a hyperlink to the supplier's Web site.

Listing 11-2   Suppliers.xml document with one Party

```
<!DOCTYPE XMI SYSTEM "CatX.dtd">
<XMI xmi.version="1.1" timestamp="Sun Jun 11 2000">
 <XMI.header>
   <XMI.metamodel xmi.name="CatML" xmi.version="1.0"/>
 </XMI.header>
 <XMI.content>
  <Party xmi.id="Sony">
    <Party.corporateInformation>
      <CorporateInformation>
        <CorporateInformation.shortName>
          Sony
        </CorporateInformation.shortName>
        <CorporateInformation.longName>
          Sony Computing
        </CorporateInformation.longName>
        <CorporateInformation.website>
          http://www.ita.sel.sony.com/
        </CorporateInformation.website>
        <CorporateInformation.corporateAddress/>
        <CorporateInformation.primaryContact/>
      </CorporateInformation>
    </Party.corporateInformation>
  </Party>
 </XMI.content>
</XMI>
```

Listing 11-3   XSLT transformation from CatML to HTML

```
<?xml version="1.0"?>
<xsl:stylesheet
    xmlns:xsl="http://www.w3.org/1999/XSL/Transform"
    version="1.0" >

<xsl:output method="html" indent="yes"/>

<!-- This variable is used later as a way to find the supplier
     document in the same path used by the source document. -->
<xsl:variable name="sourceRoot" select="/"/>

<!-- Match the root XMI element and process all
     Product elements contained within XMI.content -->
<xsl:template match="XMI">
  <xsl:apply-templates select="XMI.content/Product"/>
</xsl:template>

<xsl:template match="Product">
  <!-- Until XPointer is supported, we need to dissect the URL
       and split out the #fragment ID -->
  <xsl:variable name="suppliersURL"
```

continued

Listing 11-3 *continued*

```
                    select="substring-before(
                        CatalogItem.supplier/Party/@href, '#')"/>
    <xsl:variable name="suppliersID"
                    select="substring-after(
                        CatalogItem.supplier/Party/@href, '#')"/>

    <!-- If there is more than 1 product, add a thin gray line
         before all products, except the first -->
    <xsl:if test="position() > 1">
      <hr size="1" style="color: #cccccc"/>
    </xsl:if>

    <table width="100%">
      <tr>
        <td align="center">
          <b><xsl:value-of select="CatalogItem.name"/></b>
          <span style="color: gray">
            (<xsl:value-of select="CatalogItem.sku"/>)
          </span>
        </td>
        <td align="right" style="color: red">
          $<xsl:value-of
               select="CatalogItem.listPrice/Money/Money.amount"/>
        </td>
      </tr>
      <tr>
        <!-- Using xsl:copy-of instead of xsl:value-of allows the
             product description to contain HTML markup tags -->
        <td>
          <xsl:copy-of select="CatalogItem.description/*
                          | CatalogItem.description/text()"/>
        </td>
        <td align="right">
          <img border="0" src="{Product.photoURL}"/>
        </td>
      </tr>
      <tr><td>
        <!-- Retrieve the suppliers document, then look up the
             supplier ID.  We must use xsl:for-each to change
             the XSLT current node before calling id().
             The $sourceRoot causes XSLT to look in the same
             directory that contains the products document.
             Fetch the long supplier name and website URL. -->
        <xsl:for-each select="document($suppliersURL, $sourceRoot)">
          <xsl:variable name="supplier" select="id($suppliersID)"/>
          <a href="{$supplier//CorporateInformation.website}">
            <xsl:value-of select="$supplier//CorporateInformation.longName"/>
          </a>
        </xsl:for-each>
      </td></tr>
    </table>
  </xsl:template>

</xsl:stylesheet>
```

This stylesheet for product display implements two of the use cases, Design Content Template and Create Stylesheet, shown in Figure 5-1. As described in Chapter 5, both use cases may be realized by XSLT. When an XSLT processor executes this stylesheet using the first product list document as its source, the HTML document in Listing 11-4 is produced as output. During processing, the stylesheet rule reads the second source document containing supplier data and merges selected elements into the result.

This stylesheet does not produce a complete HTML document, principally because it does not include the HTML wrapper elements, for example, <html> and <body>. The wrapper elements are not necessary because the stylesheet's output is embedded within a portlet, which is in turn embedded within the portal Web page. The required HTML elements are provided as part of the portal page. When Jetspeed displays this HTML document within a portal, it appears as shown in Figure 11-3.

The title bar, control buttons, and border surrounding this portlet are created by the Jetspeed portal framework using additional configuration information that is specified as part of portlet design and layout. The specific detail of this configuration is not important in this discussion because this chapter is not

Listing 11-4 HTML produced by the transformation

```
<table width="100%">
  <tr>
    <td align="center">
      <b>Sony VAIO Z505</b>
      <span style="color: gray">  (Z505JE)</span>
    </td>
    <td align="right" style="color: red">
      $2499
    </td>
  </tr>
  <tr>
    <td>
      The small size and weight of the Sony VAIO Z505...
    </td>
    <td align="right">
      <img border="0" src="/examples/images/SonyZ505.jpg">
    </td>
  </tr>
  <tr>
    <td>
      <a href="http://www.ita.sel.sony.com/">Sony Computing</a>
    </td>
  </tr>
</table>
```

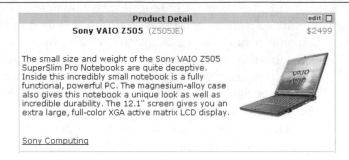

Figure 11-3 Product Display portlet

a tutorial for any one particular portal framework. This book's companion Web site does, however, present the complete Jetspeed portal along with its configuration details.

A Portlet for Promotional Discounts

This second example of presenting XML content adds a new twist to the product display portlet. The presentation of promotional discounts from the catalog is accomplished in a two-stage process. First, an XML document containing `Discount` objects from the CatML vocabulary is processed by an XSLT stylesheet into a Rich Site Summary (RSS) channel. Second, the RSS document is transformed into HTML for display in the portal. This is a useful approach because we can take advantage of a preconfigured Jetspeed portlet that includes an RSS-to-HTML stylesheet able to display any RSS channel document.

The RSS vocabulary was introduced in Chapter 2 as an informal standard for exchanging channels of headline summaries. Although RSS is most often used for news headlines, any content items can be listed with titles, links, and descriptions within a channel. We'll leverage this generality to produce an RSS channel of promotional discounts from our product catalog. After creating a valid RSS document, we can publish, distribute, or display this channel in any of the Internet portals that accept RSS content—for example, our RSS channel could be published to the *My Netscape Network* for anyone to add to their customized portal.

To help you follow the discussion in this section, I have reproduced a condensed version of the RSS sample from Chapter 2. Use this sample as a rough template for creating an XSLT stylesheet to transform Discount and Product objects into a valid RSS document.

```
<rss version="0.91">
  <channel>
    <title>CatX special discounts</title>
    <!-- more channel elements here -->
    <item>
      <title>News item title</title>
      <link>URL for the full news item</link>
      <description>News item abstract</description>
    </item>
    <!-- more item elements here -->
  </channel>
</rss>
```

Each promotional discount from the catalog must be transformed into an
`<item>` element in the RSS document. An item has only three child elements, so
we will need either to omit some attributes from the Discount class or combine
several attributes into a single text field in RSS. A subset of the CatML vocabulary from Figure 7-1 is reproduced in Figure 11-4. We are primarily concerned

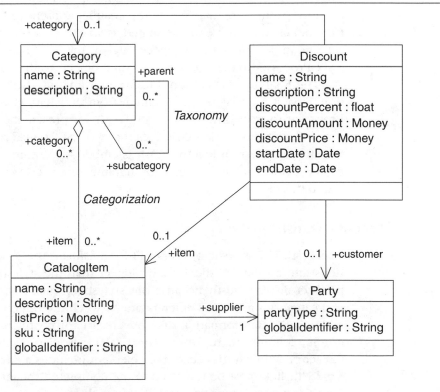

Figure 11-4 Subset of CatML showing Discount class

with instances of the Discount class, where each Discount includes a link to a Category or CatalogItem defining the subject of the promotion.

Listing 11-5 contains four Discount definitions. The first discount is associated with a category and specifies that all catalog items in that category have a 10 percent discount. The second discount is associated with one specific product that is discounted by $100. The third and fourth discounts are also associated with specific products, but they specify a new discount price rather than a discount amount to be deducted from the product's list price.

Now that an XML document for promotional discounts has been created and the requirement for distributing these discounts as an RSS channel has been specified, how are these features designed into a portal framework? The sequence diagram for the Product Display portlet, shown in Figure 11-2, is revised and extended to include these new requirements. A two-stage transformation sequence in shown in Figure 11-5.

A new entity class named RSS Channel is introduced in this diagram. At this relatively high level of analysis, the implementation detail of this class is not specified, but it should support an operation named getChannel() that returns a valid RSS document. When the design is completed, this operation will need one or more parameters that specify the channel content to be returned. The RSS Channel class could be implemented as an EJB, Java servlet, or other dynamic server component. In the sequence diagram, the RSS Channel object invokes the XSLT Processor to transform the Discount objects to the RSS vocabulary.

The RSSPortlet is responsible for coordinating the two-stage transformation. First, it requests the RSS content from the channel, then it uses the XSLT Processor to transform the RSS into HTML for presentation in the portlet. The remainder of this section describes the two XSLT transformations. The second transformation, from RSS to HTML, is embedded within a reusable RSSPortlet class provided by the Jetspeed portal framework used to produce the final output in this example.

Discount Transformation

This first XSLT stylesheet (Listing 11-6) transforms the product discount definitions into a valid RSS file. It's a bit longer than the stylesheet used to create a product display, mostly because this stylesheet must transform both products and categories as well as differentiate between the three kinds of discounts. In addition, the transformation rules traverse the proxy references used in the discount elements to represent the CatML associations to CatalogItem and Category. When a Discount.item element includes a CatalogItem proxy, the href URI link must be traversed to the complete Product definition that contains the name, description, and listPrice values.

Listing 11-5   CatML document with four Discounts

```xml
<?xml version = '1.0' encoding = 'ISO-8859-1' ?>
<!DOCTYPE XMI SYSTEM "CatX.dtd">
<XMI xmi.version="1.1" timestamp="Sun Jun 11 2000">
  <XMI.header>
    <XMI.metamodel xmi.name="CatML" xmi.version="1.0"/>
  </XMI.header>
  <XMI.content>
    <Discount>
      <Discount.category>
        <Category href="Taxonomy.xml#Accessories"/>
      </Discount.category>
      <Discount.discountPercent>10</Discount.discountPercent>
    </Discount>
    <Discount>
      <Discount.item>
        <CatalogItem href="Products.xml#Z505JE"/>
      </Discount.item>
      <Discount.discountAmount>
        <Money currency="USD">
          <Money.amount>100.00</Money.amount>
        </Money>
      </Discount.discountAmount>
    </Discount>
    <Discount>
      <Discount.item>
        <CatalogItem href="Products.xml#1200XL118"/>
      </Discount.item>
      <Discount.discountPrice>
        <Money currency="USD">
          <Money.amount>999.00</Money.amount>
        </Money>
      </Discount.discountPrice>
    </Discount>
    <Discount>
      <Discount.item>
        <CatalogItem href="Products.xml#3CRWE737A"/>
      </Discount.item>
      <Discount.discountPrice>
        <Money currency="USD">
          <Money.amount>149.95</Money.amount>
        </Money>
      </Discount.discountPrice>
    </Discount>
  </XMI.content>
</XMI>
```

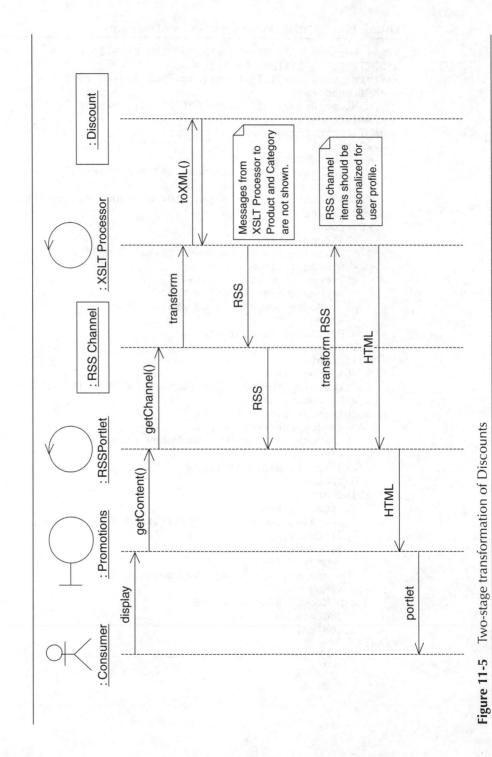

Figure 11-5 Two-stage transformation of Discounts

Each of the transformation templates is preceded by a comment that introduces its purpose; to help you navigate the stylesheet structure, each of the template elements is shown in bold font and the actions within those templates that apply other templates are also shown in bold.

It is beyond the scope of this book to explain the details of XSLT syntax; references for XLST programming resources are provided at the end of Chapter 10. Although you might not follow every detail of these examples on first reading, referring to them later will help you understand how a comprehensive XML application is deployed.

Listing 11-6   XSLT transformation from CatML to RSS

```
<?xml version="1.0"?>
<xsl:stylesheet
    xmlns:xsl="http://www.w3.org/1999/XSL/Transform"
    version="1.0" >

<!-- The current version of RSS in use at this time is 0.91
     so the PUBLIC and SYSTEM identifiers are assigned
     in the stylesheet for output to the result document. -->
<xsl:output method="xml" indent="yes"
    doctype-public="-//Netscape Communications//DTD RSS 0.91//EN"
    doctype-system="http://my.netscape.com/publish/formats/rss-0.91.dtd"/>

<xsl:variable name="sourceRoot" select="/"/>

<!-- When the root XMI element is matched in the input document,
     then the stylesheet outputs a standard RSS header for
     this news channel of CatX product specials.
     All of the child Discount elements are then processed
     to create RSS <item> elements in the output. -->

<xsl:template match="XMI">
  <rss version="0.91">
    <channel>
      <title>CatX special discounts</title>
      <link>http://XMLModeling.com:81</link>
      <description>
        RSS newsfeed of price discounts from CatX
      </description>
      <language>en-us</language>
      <image>
        <title>Catalog Exchange Service (CatX)</title>
        <url>/images/CatX.jpg</url>
        <link>http://XMLModeling.com:81</link>
        <width>85</width>
        <height>37</height>
```

continued

Listing 11-6 *continued*

```
          <description>News, Articles, Resources, etc</description>
        </image>

        <xsl:apply-templates select="XMI.content/Discount"/>
      </channel>
    </rss>
  </xsl:template>

<!-- Create an RSS <item> for each <Discount> in the source -->

  <xsl:template match="Discount">
    <item>
      <xsl:apply-templates select="Discount.item/*
                              | Discount.category/Category">
        <xsl:with-param name="discount">
          <xsl:apply-templates select="Discount.discountPrice
                                  | Discount.discountAmount
                                  | Discount.discountPercent"/>
        </xsl:with-param>
      </xsl:apply-templates>
    </item>
  </xsl:template>

<!-- Match a CatalogItem or any of its subclasses, and output
     the RSS <title>, <link>, and <description> elements.
     Because the Discount only contains proxy elements for
     these catalog items, we must follow the proxy's href
     URI to get the product details. -->

  <xsl:template match="CatalogItem | Product | Service | ProductBundle">
    <xsl:param name="discount"/>

    <xsl:variable name="itemURL" select="substring-before(@href, '#')"/>
    <xsl:variable name="itemSKU" select="substring-after(@href, '#')"/>

    <!-- open the products list document. -->
    <xsl:for-each select="document($itemURL, $sourceRoot)">
      <!-- find the proxy item in the products list. -->
      <xsl:variable name="item" select="id(concat('sku-',$itemSKU))"/>

      <title>
        <xsl:value-of select="$item/CatalogItem.name"/>
        <xsl:text> </xsl:text>
        <xsl:value-of select="$discount"/>
      </title>
      <link>
        <xsl:text>/Catalog.jsp?sku=</xsl:text>
        <xsl:value-of select="$itemSKU"/>
      </link>
      <description>
        <!-- We'll leave the RSS description empty for now -->
        <!-- <xsl:value-of select="$item/CatalogItem.description"/> -->
```

```
      </description>
    </xsl:for-each>
</xsl:template>

<!-- If a Discount is associated with a Category, then this
     template matches the Category proxy element and reads
     the Taxonomy file to retrieve the category name.
     The amount of discount is passed to this template as
     a parameter. -->

<xsl:template match="Category">
  <xsl:param name="discount"/>

  <xsl:variable name="categoryURL" select="substring-before(@href, '#')"/>
  <xsl:variable name="categoryID" select="substring-after(@href, '#')"/>
  <xsl:for-each select="document($categoryURL, $sourceRoot)">
    <title>
      <xsl:text>All </xsl:text>
      <xsl:value-of select="id($categoryID)/Category.name"/>
      <xsl:text> </xsl:text>
      <xsl:value-of select="$discount"/>
    </title>
    <link>
      <xsl:text>/Catalog.jsp?category=</xsl:text>
      <xsl:value-of select="$categoryID"/>
    </link>
    <description/>
  </xsl:for-each>
</xsl:template>

<!-- The next three templates are used to match the
     discountPrice, discountAmount, or discountPercent.
     Each Discount element should have only one of these.
     These templates transform the discount data into
     a display string that will be added to the output. -->

<xsl:template match="Discount.discountPrice">
  <xsl:text>$</xsl:text>
  <xsl:value-of select="Money/Money.amount/text()"/>
</xsl:template>

<xsl:template match="Discount.discountAmount">
  <xsl:text>$</xsl:text>
  <xsl:value-of select="Money/Money.amount/text()"/>
  <xsl:text> off</xsl:text>
</xsl:template>

<xsl:template match="Discount.discountPercent">
  <xsl:value-of select="text()"/>
  <xsl:text>% off</xsl:text>
</xsl:template>

</xsl:stylesheet>
```

Listing 11-7 RSS document produced by the transformation

```
<?xml version="1.0" encoding="utf-8" ?>
<!DOCTYPE rss
  PUBLIC "-//Netscape Communications//DTD RSS 0.91//EN"
  "http://my.netscape.com/publish/formats/rss-0.91.dtd">
<rss version="0.91">
  <channel>
    <title>CatX special discounts</title>
    <link>http://XMLModeling.com:81</link>
    <description>
      RSS newsfeed of price discounts from CheapPCs, Inc.
    </description>
    <language>en-us</language>
    <image>
      <title>Catalog Exchange Service (CatX)</title>
      <url>/images/catx.jpg</url>
      <link>http://XMLModeling.com:81</link>
      <width>97</width>
      <height>34</height>
      <description>Products, Services, etc</description>
    </image>
    <item>
      <title>All Accessories 10% off</title>
      <link>/Catalog.jsp?category=Accessories</link>
      <description/>
    </item>
    <item>
      <title>Sony VAIO Z505 $100.00 off</title>
      <link>/Catalog.jsp?sku=Z505JE</link>
      <description/>
    </item>
    <item>
      <title>COMPAQ Presario 1200 $999.00</title>
      <link>/Catalog.jsp?sku=1200XL118</link>
      <description/>
    </item>
    <item>
      <title>3Com AirConnect LAN PC Card $149.95</title>
      <link>/Catalog.jsp?sku=3CRWE737A</link>
      <description/>
    </item>
  </channel>
</rss>
```

When this stylesheet is applied to the previous XML document containing discount definitions, the RSS document in Listing 11-7 is produced. Note that the DOCTYPE declaration at the beginning of this document is required for the document to be recognized as a version 0.91 RSS vocabulary, which is the most current version in use at this time. The declaration also enables the receiver to validate this document against the DTD located at the referenced URI location.

The first fourteen lines following the `<channel>` element define attributes of the channel itself, and the remaining lines in the document define four items contained in the channel. Each item link is a URI constructed to retrieve the complete product definition using a dynamic JSP, which receives the product `sku` as a URI parameter. This product detail is displayed in a portlet created by the first example from this chapter. Except for the first item, in which the category name is appended with the string `10% off` defined by the associated discount, the title of each RSS item was constructed in the stylesheet by combining the product's name with the discount amount or price.

This RSS channel could be used for many purposes that may or may not include presentation in a portal. If the channel is published to an open Internet audience, then it's up to the receiver to determine how to process the RSS content. However, one benefit of using RSS is that many portal frameworks include support for these channels and are able to display our new channel content without modification or customization.

RSS Transformation

Because RSS documents have a very simple structure, the XSLT transformation needed to produce an HTML display is straightforward. A stylesheet for transforming RSS to HTML was described in Chapter 2. No additional description of the stylesheet is included in this chapter; instead this discussion focuses on how the RSS transformation is provided by an RSSPortlet within Jetspeed. Other portal frameworks could easily provide the same functionality.

The Promotions portlet, as created by Jetspeed, is shown in Figure 11-6. As described for the Product Display portlet, the title bar, control buttons and border are configured as part of the Jetspeed portlet design and layout. The content is produced by an XLST stylesheet applied to our RSS channel.

Jetspeed is configured in a way that makes it easy for anyone deploying the portal to customize the RSSPortlet presentation. At the most general level, the portlet "skin" defines the title bar color and background color for the content area. The XSLT stylesheet can be modifed to customize the channel display. For

Figure 11-6 Promotions portlet

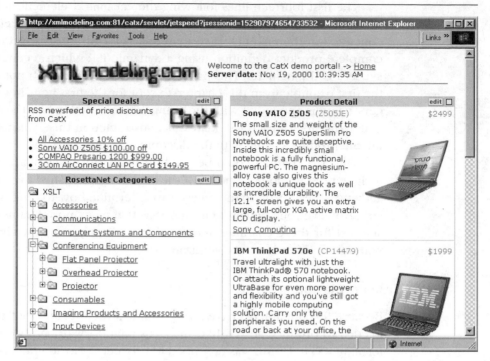

Figure 11-7 MyCat portal with three CatML portlets

example, each item within an RSS channel may have an image and description. Although both of these were omitted from this portlet display to create a more compact view, the stylesheet can be easily modified to incorporate these additional elements into the HTML display.

Finally, pulling together all of the topics from this chapter, the complete Jetspeed portal for MyCat is shown in Figure 11-7. In addition to the portlets for Product Display and Promotions, there is also a portlet titled RosettaNet Categories. This is an implementation of the Category Browser boundary class shown in Figure 11-1. The details of its XSLT stylesheet implementation are available on this book's companion Web site.

Chapter Summary

- The UML allows alternative icons to be substituted for stereotyped model elements. The RUP business modeling profile is used to create a high-level analysis diagram by assigning class stereotypes for boundary, control, and entity roles.

- A sequence diagram models the application behavior by specifying interactions between these analysis classes. Two sequence diagrams were created to illustrate how portlet content is produced using an XSLT processor.

- A product display portlet transforms CatML catalog items into HTML for inclusion in a Jetspeed portal.

- A promotional discount portlet transforms CatML discounts into an RSS channel, then transforms the RSS channel into HTML for inclusion in a Jetspeed portal. This promotional discount RSS channel could be distributed to any Internet portal that supports RSS display.

- The complete Jetspeed portal for MyCat can be extended to include many other portlets related to the CatX marketplace.

Steps for Success

1. Define your portal analysis model with clear separation between boundary, control, and entity classes. Responsibilities are summarized as follows:

   - Entity classes define sources of XML content.
   - Control classes transform, filter, and summarize the content.
   - Boundary classes display the transformed content.

2. Boundary classes may be specialized for alternative display devices, such as PC, mobile phone, or PDA. The control classes should support dynamic run-time adaptation to produce the best presentation format for the current client device.

3. Use these models as evaluation criteria for portal frameworks. Consult the use case diagram from Chapter 5 and the analysis model and sequence diagrams from this chapter when evaluating XML-enabled design features.

Chapter 12

e-Business Architecture

This chapter is the last step of our journey through modeling XML applications with UML. It is therefore appropriate to assemble the previously described requirements and XML vocabularies within an adaptable Web-based architecture. A Web-based architecture allows for flexible deployment of the requirements described in Chapters 5, 7, and 11, where a portal provides views into a globally distributed information network. This same Web-based architecture provides for deployment of inter-enterprise e-business integration, as described in Chapters 4 and 10. The vocabularies used for messages exchanged within this architecture are defined by UML models and XML schemas and are transformed as necessary for communication and presentation.

The term *Web Services* has emerged as a general category for loosely coupled, dynamically connected, Web-based services. These services use XML to encode both the message wrapper and the content of the message body. As a result, the integration is completely independent of operating system, language, or other middleware product used by each component participating in the service. The only fundamental requirement is that each component have the ability to process XML documents and that each node connected in a distributed system supports HTTP as a default transport layer. These Web Services are most commonly used to invoke remote application services using a Remote Procedure Call (RPC) interaction, implemented using only XML messages.

We begin this final chapter by reviewing common business and technical requirements that are driving and guiding the development of Web Services. Then, three key subsystems that are required when deploying scalable Web

Service architectures are summarized. These subsystem requirements are described generally, but specific examples are provided for the Simple Object Access Protocol (SOAP). Finally, a concrete example is presented for a CatX component architecture.

Requirements for e-Business Architecture

Most changes to system architecture are driven by new or evolving business requirements. This motivation is very clear in our current business environment where both e-commerce and the broader e-business integration strategies are demanding faster deployment of new systems; in addition, those systems must integrate a wide range of existing business systems and information in a global marketplace. This broad-based integration, including inter-enterprise system integration, has proven to be difficult in the loosely coupled chaos of incompatible platforms and information that are a common reality.

Approaches for development and deployment of Web Services have been created in response to these new demands. The solution must be delivered quickly or companies will fall behind in the accelerated competitive race. The primary business requirements for Web Services architecture are summarized as follows:

- Web-based information and services
- Rapid time-to-market
- Dynamic configuration and reconfiguration of business models
- Just-in-time integration
- Loosely coupled services
- Minimal coordination and control of service end points
- Platform and language independent

In addition to meeting these business requirements, the new architectures must accommodate a set of common technical requirements that although not unique to this new environment must be reinterpreted or reassessed in this new context. A partial list includes

- Security, including both encryption and authentication
- Network management, monitoring, and control
- Plus the standard "-ilities:" scalability, reliability, durability, and so on

Neither the business nor technical requirements make specific reference to which network transports are used for communication. However, the general requirements for Web-based services and platform independence strongly suggest use of the ubiquitous HTTP transport that forms the backbone of the Web. Other protocols, such as FTP, SMTP e-mail, or Java Message Service (JMS) implementations, might be used in specific situations or as alternative transport protocols for a particular service. Additional descriptions of transport bindings are included in the following section.

Deploying Web Services

Although there are currently no adopted standards for Web Service integration and messaging based on XML, numerous specification proposals and early implementations are available on the Internet. Several of these specifications are reviewed in this section. In addition, both the W3C[1] and the OMG[2] have formed working groups to develop XML messaging standards. Check this book's companion Web site for updates and current references.

Based on the preliminary specifications, three major categories of infrastructure are required for deploying Web Services in scalable e-business architectures. Separate, but interdependent, specification proposals are described for each category.

Message Protocols in XML

Distributed system connectivity ultimately requires some kind of standard or agreement about how messages will be formatted and coordinated. Many of these message protocols have been developed in the past, some as standards and others as proprietary specifications used by one vendor's product. But because they impose requirements or constraints on platform, vendor, or capability, most of these existing protocols have limitations when deployed in a very large-scale Web-based environment.

The open extensibility of XML has been widely embraced as a solution for next-generation message protocols. That's not to say that XML should be applied to every messaging system requirement; in fact, XML's verbose syntax may be unacceptable for high-performance systems. But for many e-business applications, the openness and extensibility of XML vocabularies applies equally well to content and message protocol structure. At this early stage of development, a rough guideline suggests that XML message protocols are best suited for the non-real time integration commonly found in B2B e-commerce exchange.

---

1. W3C XML Protocol Activity—see *http://www.w3.org/2000/xp/*.
2. OMG CORBA semantics over SOAP—see *http://www.omg.org*.

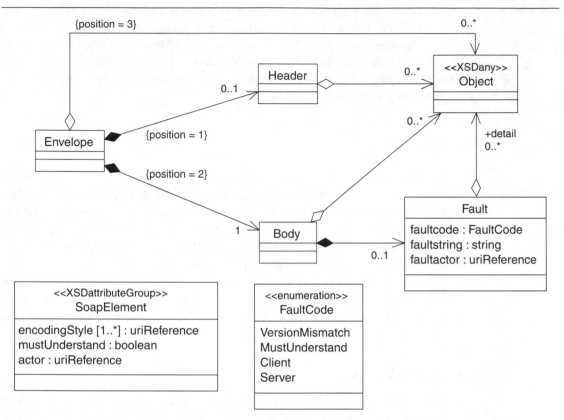

Figure 12-1   Generic SOAP message structure

Numerous alternative XML message protocols are under development at this time. Some are specialized by application area, and others are pet projects of particular vendors or industry groups. However, one of these proposals has begun to rise above the others in terms of generality and widespread acceptance. I'll describe the SOAP[3] as a representative candidate among the current alternatives.

By this point, you should be getting comfortable with the use of UML class diagrams as a means to define and document XML vocabularies. The SOAP specification is not defined using UML, so I've reverse-engineered the core model into the UML diagram shown in Figure 12-1.

A quick review of the diagram reveals that SOAP is a generic message structure composed of an Envelope that contains a Header, Body, and any other

---

3. Simple Object Access Protocol 1.1, W3C Note, 8 May 2000—see *http://www.w3.org/TR.SOAP.*

optional objects. The Object class is assigned a UML stereotype of <<XSDany>>, which specifies that this class allows any XML element in the generated schema. The Header and Body may contain any objects, and the Body may contain an optional Fault element. The SoapElement class defines three attributes that are mapped to global attributes in the generated XML schema. These attributes may be added to any of the other elements in an XML document. Most association end roles in this diagram are anonymous because the SOAP schema directly embeds the aggregated classes in the content model without use of an additional container element.

It's important to note that DTD-generation tools based strictly on the XMI standard would reject this model because it requires all navigable association ends to have a role name. It's also true that an XMI-compliant DTD-generation tool could not duplicate the SOAP DTD if generated from a UML model. The UML profile for XML described in Appendix C uses stereotypes and tagged values to customize DTD and Schema generation beyond what is possible with XMI. Using that profile, I have implemented a Schema generation tool that could duplicate the SOAP Schema from the model shown in Figure 12-1.

The following XML document illustrates a SOAP message instance, where the Header contains an element used for transaction management, and the Body contains a Product instance defined according to the CatML vocabulary. Notice the use of XML namespaces to designate three vocabulary schemas used for the SOAP envelope, the transaction element, and the CatML product element. Each namespace is assigned a prefix: SOAP-ENV, t, and cml, respectively.

```
<SOAP-ENV:Envelope
  xmlns:SOAP-ENV="http://schemas.xmlsoap.org/soap/envelope/"
  SOAP-ENV:encodingStyle="http://schemas.xmlsoap.org/soap/encoding/"/>
  <SOAP-ENV:Header>
     <t:Transaction
        xmlns:t="http://xmlmodeling.com/schemas/transaction"
        SOAP-ENV:mustUnderstand="1">
           53987
     </t:Transaction>
  </SOAP-ENV:Header>
  <SOAP-ENV:Body>
     <cml:Product xmlns:cml="http://xmlmodeling.com/schemas/CatML">
        <cml:CatalogItem.name>VAIO Z505JE</cml:CatalogItem.name>
        <cml:CatalogItem.listPrice>
          <cml:Money currency="USD">2499.00</cml:Money>
        </cml:CatalogItem.listPrice>
     </cml:Product>
  </SOAP-ENV:Body>
</SOAP-ENV:Envelope>
```

It is sometimes necessary to include additional information in a message that is not part of the service definition itself but is required by the system infrastructure. This kind of information is included in a SOAP message header. An example of this header element is shown in the above listing, where a transaction identifier is included as part of an embedded `Transaction` child element. By adding this element to the header using an agreed upon vocabulary definition for transactions, the transaction manager on the receiving side can extract the transaction identifier and use it without affecting the encoding of catalog information in the message body using CatML.

This message might be sent by a CatX server in response to a prior request that includes a similar SOAP message containing a product catalog query in its Body element. SOAP messages are often combined either in request-response pairs or in larger sequences of messages that implement a business process. These types of process definitions were described as part of the e-business integration requirements in Chapter 4. Each step of such processes might be implemented using a SOAP message exchanged between process participants.

This SOAP message could be sent using many different network transports. The most obvious transport candidate is HTTP, especially when used for large-scale inter-enterprise marketplaces. These messages are simply included in the content of an HTTP request message or in the content of an HTTP response. But the same message could either be attached to an e-mail message using the SMTP transport or included in the content of other vendor- or platform-specific asynchronous messaging systems. As the SOAP specification matures, alternative binding standards will be defined for these other common transport mechanisms. At this time, most emphasis is placed on HTTP.

Web Service Description

If we are to achieve the just-in-time integration and dynamic configuration promised by a Web Services architecture, then the services must be self-describing and available from any location on the Web. The service description must enable any calling application to create valid messages and deliver them to the service provider. And the caller must correctly interpret any messages that are returned. These service descriptions are also referred to as a *service contract*. A complete service description must include the following specifications.

- Named Web services, each with a set of one or more operations
- Definition of each operation in terms of its request and response messages
- The XML vocabularies used within those messages
- One or more bindings for each operation, relating it to specific transport protocols, such as HTTP, FTP, or SMTP.

Several proposals have been put forth by IBM, Microsoft, and others for solving this problem of Web service description. One possible candidate is the Web Service Description Language (WSDL),[4] which, not surprisingly, is an XML vocabulary for describing and exchanging information about Web services. It's too early to provide recommended solutions at this time, but WSDL is representative of the required solution.

It will be relatively easy to automate the generation of WSDL documents from a UML class model. These production rules must be specified in a manner that is very similar to the schema productions examined in Chapter 9. But the Web Services description is based on the *behavior* of classes in the model rather than on the model structure used to define an XML vocabulary. In order to generate these Web service descriptions for our CatX model, we need to extend the class model to include operations on the classes. For example, we might add a findProduct() operation to the Catalog class. These operation definitions, including their parameters and return types, would be used to generate a WSDL document that enables a SOAP-based service interface for CatX. This CatX architecture is examined in more detail later in this chapter.

Web Service Discovery

After we have created a WSDL document describing the services available from our CatX marketplace, how would other suppliers and customers discover these Web-based services? Conversely, how would our MyCat portal server discover services from other suppliers and information sources that can be integrated as portlets?

This idea of discovering system components is not new. For example, the CORBA standard includes a Trader service (*not* a Web-based service) that allows other CORBA client applications to discover components that satisfy a set of property/value search criteria. The trader returns a set of object references that may be invoked by the client. Similarly, the Java Naming and Directory Interface (JNDI) is part of the Java 2 Enterprise Platform, where it enables Java client applications to find EJB components.

But a Web Services architecture cannot depend on CORBA or Java platforms or on any other similar restriction. The goal of Web Services is to enable truly ubiquitous discovery, description, and messaging for globally distributed applications. There have been several proposals for responding to this requirement. One of the most noteworthy proposals is the Universal Description, Discovery,

---

4. Web Services Description Language 1.0, September 25, 2000—see *http://msdn.microsoft.com/ xml/general/wsdl.asp.*

and Integration (UDDI) specification.[5] Like WSDL, however, this UDDI specification is very preliminary and is subject to change.

The goals of UDDI are wide ranging. First, it hopes to enable a registry of business entities and contact information that are classified by several different industry taxonomies. For example, you might search for all businesses that are assigned to a particular UNSPC product classification code. Second, you can request a list of services offered by a business or search the services and then ask which businesses offer the desired service. Third, you can request specific binding information for a service that would enable you to invoke that service at a given URL access point. The specifics of a service description would be returned as a WSDL document discovered through use of the UDDI business registry. Finally, the UDDI specification draft describes about 30 SOAP message-based services that define the entire interface for accessing the business registry.

A directory like that proposed by UDDI provides a critical component in the dynamic infrastructure for Web Services. Its success will depend on political and economic factors among prospective business partners as well as on the technical design for offering a scalable, secure directory service. But a "universal" directory is neither universal nor useful unless it is used by a critical mass of business partners. This milestone has yet to be achieved; but the puzzle pieces are beginning to take shape, even while there are many details yet to be worked out.

CatX Component Architecture

Our final challenge before concluding this discussion is to apply the Web Services architecture to the CatX example application. Parts of this architecture have been described for RSS newsfeeds in Chapters 2 and 3, for supplier catalog integration in Chapters 4 and 10, and for portal design in Chapters 5 and 11. These design elements will be used here, along with incorporation of SOAP-based Web Services.

When specifying system architecture, it is important to trace the design back to the initial system requirements. The Unified Process introduced in Chapter 3 is both use case driven and architecture centric. The balance between use case requirements and architecture is well summarized in a recent title [Jacobson, 1999, p. 6].

How are use cases and architecture related? Every product has both function and form. One or the other is not enough. These two forces must be balanced

---

5. The UDDI specification and related information can be found at *http://www.uddi.org*.

to get a successful product. In this case function corresponds to use cases and form to architecture. There needs to be interplay between use cases and architecture. It is a "chicken and egg" problem. On the one hand, the use cases must, when realized, fit in the architecture. On the other hand, the architecture must allow room for realizations of all the required use cases, now and in the future. In reality, both the architecture and the use cases must evolve in parallel.

As a means to establishing the interrelationship between requirements and architecture, the CatX deployment architecture is described in seven subsections. Each of these process-oriented subsections is superimposed on the architecture diagram in order to identify their fulfillment. The seven requirements are as follows:

1. Display portal content
2. Update newsfeed
3. Query catalog content
4. Integrate supplier catalog
5. Execute currency trade
6. Query schema repository
7. Query service registry

The CatX system architecture is shown as a UML deployment diagram in Figure 12-2. A deployment diagram specifies the assignment of components to processing nodes as well as the dependencies among these components. When a component dependency spans two nodes, an implied network communication is required for deployment. A processing node is illustrated using a three-dimensional box in UML deployment diagrams, and the components assigned to those nodes are illustrated using the same symbols introduced as part of UML component diagrams in Chapter 3.

The dependency arrows indicate the source and target of a dependency relationship between deployed system components but not necessarily the direction of information flow. The diagram includes dependencies between components that span nodes in the distributed architecture, and dependencies are shown between components within one node. For example, a dependency is shown between nodes from Mozilla to Portal Server, and within the Portal node from Portal Server to SOAP Requester. In this architecture, all internode dependencies are specified to use the HyperText Transport Protocol (HTTP) as a default transport binding, but intranode dependencies may use either HTTP or another platform-specific connection made available by that node's design.

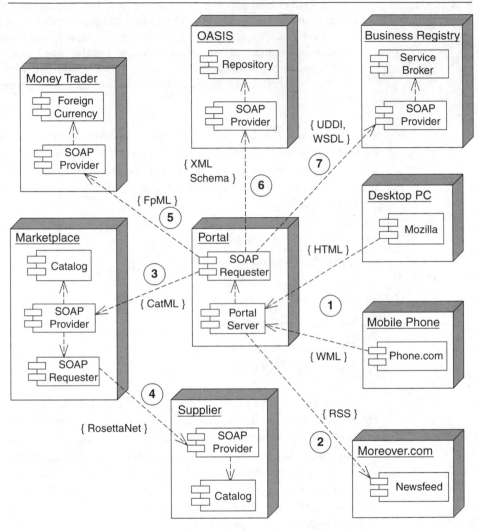

Figure 12-2 Distributed components and SOAP services

(I do not describe intranode communication in this chapter because the emphasis is on architecture for distributed Web Services.)

Although not explicitly shown in the diagram, each of the seven server nodes must support an HTTP application interface (for example, an Apache Web server instance). The two client nodes representing Desktop PC and Mobile Phone are excluded from this requirement because they participate only as HTTP requesters in the architecture. Each of the internode dependency arrows can be interpreted as indicating the direction of an HTTP Request message; the property label on the arrow denotes the vocabulary required for the contents of the HTTP Response message.

This architecture diagram is centered on the Portal node, which aggregates information content and services provided to the user client devices. The Portal also serves as a requester of information or an intermediary for services provided by other nodes in the distributed system. In fulfilling this broker role, the Portal is responsible for transforming content vocabularies as necessary to create a unified, integrated presentation to users.

Rather than describe these architectural components and their integration from the abstract technical perspective, I'll organize their descriptions along the lines of the seven functional requirements that are numbered in the diagram. The fulfillment of each requirement is described in terms of the Web Services architecture that was introduced in the previous section.

Display Portal Content

A portal server translates its content into the presentation vocabulary required by each user client device. The diagram illustrates two types of clients: a desktop PC and a mobile phone. Each of these client nodes is shown containing one component that encapsulates its Web browser functionality. Each browser component is shown with a dependency to the Portal Server component, and each dependency arrow is labeled with a property indicating the vocabulary used for response to the respective client.

The analysis model shown in Figure 11-1 and described by the transformation portlets in Chapter 11 summarizes a partial design for the Portal Server component. The detailed specification of these component interactions was also illustrated using UML sequence diagrams in that chapter. SOAP messages are not required for these interactions because they are handled by simple HTTP requests.

One additional processing node was omitted from the architecture diagram to avoid excessive complexity. To be more precise, a WAP Gateway node is required as an intermediary between the Portal Server and the Mobile Phone. The WAP Gateway is responsible for converting the Wireless Application Protocol (WAP) used by the mobile phone network to the Hypertext Transport Protocol used by the Web application network. However, from the perspective of our application architecture, the WAP Gateway is better hidden behind the simple dependency.

Update Newsfeed

The use of RSS newsfeeds was described in detail in Chapters 2, 3, and 11. Retrieving an updated newsfeed document is usually a very simple matter of sending a URL request to the news server and receiving the RSS document in response. There is no process or dialog between the client and server, and the news server expects no confirmation in return. As a result of this simplicity, no XML message protocol is required, only a basic HTTP connection.

This HTTP-based update is shown in Figure 12-2 as a dependency between the Portal Server and Newsfeed components. In the Apache Jetspeed portal server, the RSS update is built into the server configuration and is automatically executed at regular intervals using a daemon server thread. No additional implementation is required. On the news server, the RSS document may be dynamically generated from a Java servlet querying a news database; the RSS document can also be manually authored by a human editor.

One could, however, imagine an alternate world where the newsfeed provider (Moreover.com in this example) offers a standard set of SOAP services for querying and filtering their large catalog of news sources. They already use URL parameters on the HTTP request to specify which news channel to retrieve and what format to return (including RSS, among other formats). Using a Web Services architecture, the query interface could be expanded to allow a requester to determine the maximum number of items returned or the date range of items in a channel. In fact, I'll make a prediction that one or more news providers will offer a SOAP interface within the next several months—maybe before this book hits the shelves.

Query Catalog Content

This next requirement uses SOAP Web Services to define the interface from the Portal Server to the Marketplace catalog (shown as dependency #3 in Figure 12-2). In this scenario, the Portal Server calls upon a SOAP Requester component to initiate the remote service request to the Marketplace server, where a SOAP Provider receives the request for catalog content. The interchange between Requester and Provider is structured as a SOAP message containing the catalog query parameters as a XML document within the message body. This Provider implements a service that queries the Catalog component and then returns a CatML document encapsulated within a SOAP message to the original Requester.

When the Portal Server receives the CatML document, that content can be presented to a user in any number of different ways. As described in Chapter 11, the CatML can be transformed into an HTML product display portlet whose detail "skin" style characteristics are customized for each user's profile. Alternatively, a WML stylesheet can be applied to the same source document for presentation on a mobile phone.

Integrate Supplier Catalog

This next scenario combines Figure 12-2 dependencies #3 and #4. If all catalog data is not present within the Marketplace server, then a request for product information must be forwarded to another supplier server. The reply from that supplier may be simply returned to the original requester, or it may be combined with additional data from the Marketplace catalog. This is sometimes referred to as a *virtual catalog* because the Marketplace contains metadata about other catalogs and redirects each buyer's query to one or more suppliers.

To make this example more interesting, assume that the supplier is able only to respond to catalog queries using the RosettaNet vocabulary. The Marketplace redirects the buyer's query to the Supplier using a new SOAP service request, and the Supplier returns a SOAP response containing a RosettaNet document. The Marketplace server must transform the RosettaNet catalog content to CatML before forwarding that result back to the Portal Server. The transformation from RosettaNet to CatML is very similar to the detailed example provided in Chapter 10, but the transformation is done in the opposite direction.

This example provides a good illustration of the *contracts* that are implemented by Web Services. A service implementation must advertise both the vocabulary required by its inbound request (for example, catalog query parameters) and the vocabulary used to define its returned documents. This two-stage request is constructed as a composite of two services that are invoked serially. When the services are assembled, each service's contract is analyzed to determine if its inputs and outputs are compatible or if an output can be transformed into the vocabulary required by the following service.

Execute Currency Trade

This next scenario, illustrated as #5 in Figure 12-2, is directly analogous to interaction #3, where catalog queries are processed by the Marketplace. In this case, however, the foreign currency trade service returns an FpML document instead of a CatML document. This service also requires an FpML document in the body of its Web Service request sent from the Portal Server. A small subset of the Financial Products Markup Language (FpML) was introduced in Chapter 6 and presented as a UML model in Appendix A.

When the Portal Server component invokes the Foreign Currency component, it does so through a pair of SOAP service end points. The diagram shows the same SOAP Requester being used for both catalog queries and currency trades. Although it's more likely that two distinct requesters are implemented within the Portal server, this is an implementation decision. It's only important that the requester is able to send two different SOAP messages and that the corresponding returned vocabularies, CatML and FpML, are handled appropriately.

Query Schema Repository

Given the plethora of XML vocabularies used by these services, it would be useful if a shared repository were available where the Portal Server could find and retrieve all vocabulary schemas that are required by its services. There are several such schema repositories being created, but all are still in the formative stages in early 2001. Two of the most widely publicized repositories are OASIS (*www.xml.org*) and Biztalk (*www.biztalk.org*).

A consistent architecture for deployment of the repository would use SOAP messages to invoke query services provided by the OASIS or BizTalk server. If a common Web Service interface were defined, then the Portal Server could query either repository in an identical manner. This interaction is shown as #6 in Figure 12-2.

Because the new W3C XML Schema recommendation represents a schema using an XML document instance, those schemas can be exchanged in the body of SOAP messages just as with any other XML document. The XML Schema recommendation also specifies a "schema for schemas," which is an XML Schema that defines the valid vocabulary for XML Schema documents. So, when exchanged using SOAP, the schema for XML Schemas is used to specify the valid content types for these SOAP messages. This recursive structure creates a very elegant design for using XML to define, exchange, and manipulate XML.

Query Service Registry

Just as we benefit from a repository of schema definitions, we can also benefit from a registry of Web Service definitions. This is the purpose of the UDDI and WSDL specifications that were introduced in the previous section of this chapter. Like the schema repository, this registry employs SOAP messages to implement the service interface used to query and update the business entity and service descriptions. As shown by interaction #7 in Figure 12-2, the SOAP message replies from the registry contain documents defined by the UDDI and/or WSDL vocabularies.

The requirements described for querying catalog content and integrating supplier catalogs offer a good illustration for use of the service registry. As described previously, a virtual catalog should enable just-in-time integration of many suppliers' catalogs into a unified view from the marketplace catalog. For the most flexible integration, the marketplace could use a business registry to search for suppliers in the desired industry but select only those offering a

SOAP interface to their catalog services. A supplier's service description specifies which vocabulary is used for its catalog representation. If that vocabulary is different from CatML, then the marketplace would again query the registry in search of services to transform the foreign vocabulary (for example, Rosetta-Net) into CatML. This scenario clearly illustrates the benefits of loosely coupled services requiring little coordination among service providers.

The MyCat portal also offers a good illustration of the service registry benefits. Most portals allow each user to search and browse a wide array of information sources that can be added to that user's view. The ultimate pinnacle of portal flexibility might be achieved if a user could search a global business registry for desired sources and add any of them to the portal's view. The Portal Server would need to query the selected service descriptions and determine which vocabularies are used. After also considering the user's device type (for example, desktop PC or mobile phone), the Portal Server must find a service that can transform the source vocabulary into the required presentation language.

These examples of dynamic configuration and just-in-time integration are still beyond the reach of current Web integration technology (in spite of some vendors' claims to the contrary). But the examples create a worthy goal that is realistic, even if requiring a bit of a stretch. Start with a more limited range of services and vocabularies that offer a service platform analogous to the CatX marketplace and MyCat portal. Use the UML to establish a clear definition of requirements and vocabulary models. And strive for the next-generation Semantic Web that integrates a global network of information and services.

Chapter Summary

- Web Services are emerging as a general-purpose architecture for loosely coupled, dynamically connected, Web-based services. Deployment of this architecture is being driven by business requirements for rapid time-to-market and response to competition.

- Message protocols in XML are a critical ingredient in Web Services, enabling the broadest platform and vendor connectivity. A basic message structure is composed of a Header and a Body, each containing one or more XML elements.

- There are several proposals for XML messaging, but the Simple Object Access Protocol is gaining the most attention at this time.

- The Web Service Description Language is a proposed XML vocabulary used to describe other Web Services, thus enabling their dynamic integration. A service description includes specification of the available messages, the URI end points where those messages are sent, the required vocabularies used by those messages, and the binding of messages to one or more transport protocols.

- The Universal Description, Discovery, and Integration standard is proposed as a set of Web Services used to register businesses and the definition of their available services.

- A CatX component architecture uses both simple HTTP requests and SOAP-based messages to integrate a variety of distributed services into a Web portal. This architecture is summarized from the perspective of seven process-oriented requirements.

Steps for Success

Of all the chapters in this book, this one is farthest out on the bleeding edge and therefore its content is most subject to change. But in spite of any changes, the overall deployment architecture should remain viable in the future, even if the specific details of SOAP, WSDL, and UDDI are modified. The concepts of Web Services and XML message protocols are here to stay because they respond to fundamental business requirements in our new networked economy.

1. Separate fact from fantasy. Dynamic configuration and just-in-time integration is a wonderful vision, but we're not there yet. I'd settle for flexible configuration and pretty quick integration.

2. Watch for vacuous claims of "SOAP-compliant" systems. SOAP is a general message specification, and many very significant details must be specified about a particular vendor's use of SOAP. The use of Header content is likely to be the most common difference among vendor implementations.

3. Security is still an issue. The ease of embedding application messages in HTTP requests is attractive because HTTP is often not blocked by firewall security. But HTTP-based messages are hazardous to security because they aren't blocked by firewalls. Firewall products and configuration will become more selective. Check your own configuration before opening the floodgates with these new message types.

4. Begin experimenting, even though the future is uncertain. Web Services specifications are subject to change, so it's not time to bet your company on them (at least not when this was written). But designs similar to the CatX component architecture are worthy of focused early-stage development.

PART IV

Appendixes

Appendix A

Reuse of FpML Vocabulary

The Financial Products Markup Language (FpML)[1] was originally specified by its standards committee in the form of XML DTDs, without the use of UML modeling. The architectural guidelines for FpML do, however, follow a very clear object-oriented design approach, so the mapping to UML is straightforward. The earlier beta versions of FpML[2] had a broader content coverage than the final standard, and they also made extensive use of XML namespaces to separate and differentiate the subvocabularies. However, because XML Schemas were not yet adopted when FpML was drafted, and because DTDs and the current XML parsers were not able to support the use of multiple namespaces, the final specification version dramatically reduced its scope. The final specification is defined in a single namespace.

The primary objective of this appendix is to illustrate the benefits of using UML diagrams to communicate the design of a moderately complex vocabulary. I will not attempt to describe the use of FpML in e-business transactions, as the description of many elements in this vocabulary requires knowledge of financial derivative terminology. But the overview of these high-level elements is sufficiently self-explanatory. I will also emphasize the reuse of a few FpML elements within our CatML vocabulary design.

---

1. The complete FpML 1.0 specification and architecture guideline is available at *http://www.FpML.org*.

2. As of early 2001, the FpML 1.0 beta 2 draft specification was still available for downloading.

I have manually reverse-engineered the high-level elements from a DTD in the final draft of FpML 1.0. The UML diagram shown in Figure A-1 covers approximately 20% of the content in FpML 1.0.

Four of the classes in this diagram are shown with light-gray shading: Trade-Header, Fra, Swap, and Free. These classes are placeholders in this diagram—their attributes and associations to other classes represent the remaining 80 percent of FpML definitions. (For those who are curious, "Fra" represents the trade content of a forward rate agreement, and "Swap" refers to the trade content of an interest rate swap.) Two other classes are shown with dark-gray shading: Money and Party. These classes are reused in the CatML vocabulary described in Chapter 7.

This diagram also demonstrates the use of two different UML stereotypes. <<XSDchoice>> on the Product class specifies that either Fra or Swap, but not both, may be embedded in the content model of Trade. <<XSDsimpleType>> indicates that string is an XML Schema datatype definition. Because Currency and PartyId are specializations of a simpleType definition, their corresponding XML elements may contain string content. A detailed description of these stereotypes is provided as part of the UML profile for XML in Chapter 9 and Appendix C.

In addition to the subset of FpML 1.0, I have also reverse-engineered two modules from the previous beta 2 specification. Although these definitions are no longer part of the latest FpML 1.0, they may be reintroduced in a future specification based on XML Schema and defined using multiple namespaces. I have created two UML packages, named TradingParty and ContactInfo. The ContactInfo package is independent of any other FpML modules, whereas the TradingParty package depends only on the ContactInfo package. These dependencies are illustrated in the UML package diagram shown in Figure A-2.

Because the FpML specification was developed independent of the CatML vocabulary, we should use XML namespaces to merge these vocabularies in a single XML document instance. The document instance on page 290 declares three namespaces. The CatML vocabulary is declared as the default, anonymous namespace; TradingParty is declared as a namespace with the prefix pty; and, FpML is declared with the prefix m (representing our use of its Money element).

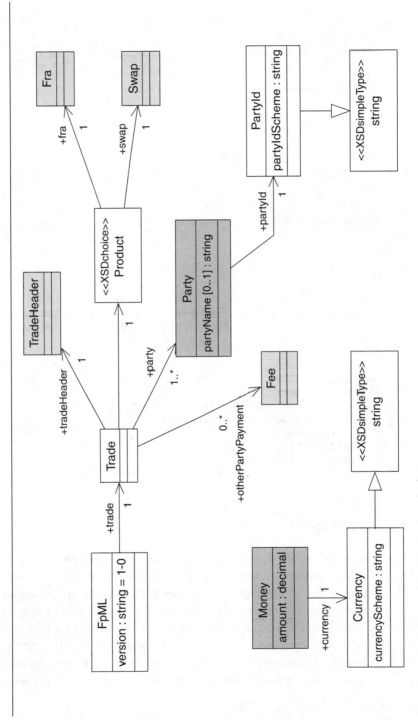

Figure A-1 Subset of FpML 1.0 vocabulary

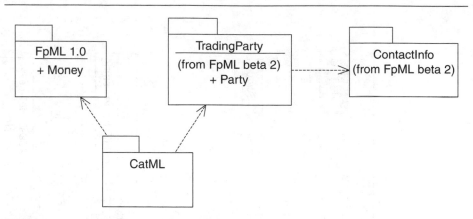

Figure A-2   FpML package dependencies

```
<Catalog xmlns="http://xmlmodeling.com/schemas/CatML"
   xmlns:pty="http://xmlmodeling.com/schemas/TradingParty"
   xmlns:m="uri://www.fpml.org/spec/2000/fpml-dtd-1-0-2000-06-01">
 <Catalog.item>
  <Product xmi.id="p1">
    <CatalogItem.name>Wizard PC</CatalogItem.name>
    <CatalogItem.listPrice>
      <m:Money>
        <m:currency>USD</m:currency>
        <m:amount>799.00</m:amount>
      </m:Money>
    </CatalogItem.listPrice>
    <CatalogItem.supplier>
      <pty:Party href="/Suppliers?name=Wizard"/>
    </CatalogItem.supplier>
  </Product>
 </Catalog.item>
</Catalog>
```

In this document, the Party element is a simple proxy for its complete instance definition, which can be obtained from the href location attribute. This is a common design practice in XML applications when an element value is either used in more than one context or is contained in a separate XML resource. In this case, the Party element is identified by a URI and is likely generated from a dynamic query to a catalog database. But the storage format of the referenced element is irrelevant, as long as the URI returns an XML document fragment that is valid with respect to the TradingParty vocabulary.

Trading Party Model

The TradingParty model described here is based on the FpML beta 2 specification and is not included in the final FpML 1.0 recommendation. The Party class as defined in the final recommendation is limited to the simple specification shown in Figure A-1. These additional definitions might be used to add further detail to a Party element within an exchanged XML document. The CatML vocabulary borrows a very small part of this model for trading party definitions, but I have reverse-engineered the entire module into UML to provide a complete example. If you consult the FpML beta 2 specification document for its DTD definition, you will find that the UML class diagram provides a much more intuitive presentation of this vocabulary. The trading party package is shown in Figure A-3.

This diagram does not contain any new UML concepts other than those used in previous CatML diagrams. Composition associations (with a solid diamond) indicate ownership of values that will be represented as child elements in XML. Thus, you can see at a glance that the Party class will be the primary XML parent element because it is composed of most other elements in the model. The relationship from Party to CorporateInformation was modeled as a regular association (not a composition) because I assumed that the CorporateInformation element might be referenced by multiple Party elements. In this situation, CorporateInformation cannot be owned by value in a composition. This does not, however, prevent an XML document from including CorporateInformation as a child element if desired; this is allowed by the current XMI production rules.

The current CatML examples only use two classes from this diagram: Party and CorporateInformation. Notice that CorporateInformation refers to two additional classes in its attribute types. Contact and Address are both defined in the ContactInfo package. This package was also reverse-engineered from the FpML beta 2 specification and is illustrated in Figure A-4.

The ContactInfo is a straightforward model containing three classes, ultimately composed into a Contact object. I have not added my own modeling ideas into either TradingParty or ContactInfo; the models are a faithful reproduction of the FpML definitions mapped into UML. The FpML specification was not intended for use outside of financial information interchange, so one could easily identify refinements or extensions that would improve its reuse. However, as an educational exercise, I believe that the reuse is successful.

As a final step, I'll use these models to create an XML document instance for a Party object. This description of the Wizard PCs party would be linked as a supplier for the products included in other product catalog documents (see page 293).

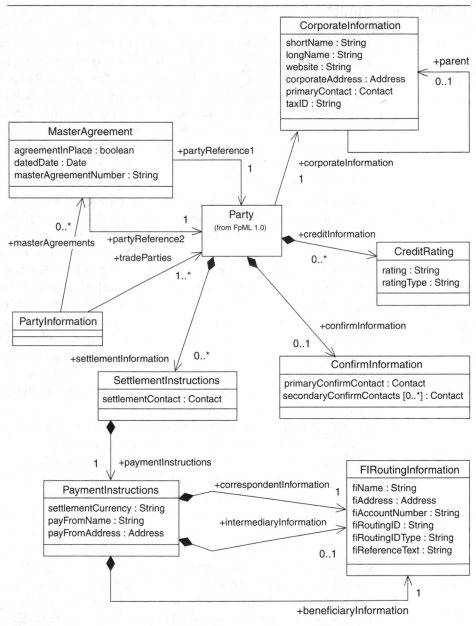

Figure A-3 Trading party model

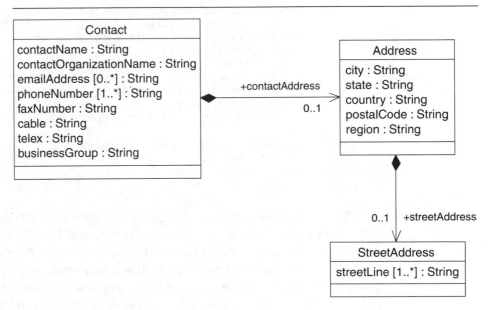

Figure A-4 ContactInfo model

```
<Party>
  <Party.corporateInformation>
    <CorporateInformation>
      <CorporateInformation.shortName>
        Wizard PCs</CorporateInformation.shortName>
      <CorporateInformation.longName>
        Wizard PCs, Inc.</CorporateInformation.longName>
      <CorporateInformation.website>
        http://www.wizard-PCs.com</CorporateInformation.website>
      <CorporateInformation.corporateAddress>
        <Address>
          <Address.streetAddress>
            <StreetAddress>
              <StreetAddress.streetLine>
                100 Austin Street</StreetAddress.streetLine>
              <StreetAddress.streetLine>
                Suite 210</StreetAddress.streetLine>
            </StreetAddress>
          </Address.streetAddress>
          <Address.city>New York</Address.city>
          <Address.state>NY</Address.state>
          <Address.country>USA</Address.country>
          <Address.postalCode>10001</Address.postalCode>
        </Address>
      </CorporateInformation.corporateAddress>
      <CorporateInformation.primaryContact>
        <Contact>
```

```
            <Contact.contactName>Joe Smith</Contact.contactName>
            <Contact.contactOrganization>
              Wizard PCs</Contact.contactOrganization>
            <Contact.emailAddress>
              joe.smith@wizard-PCs.com</Contact.emailAddress>
            <Contact.phoneNumber>212-235-9999</Contact.phoneNumber>
            <Contact.faxNumber>212-235-9998</Contact.faxNumber>
            <Contact.businessGroup>
              Corporate Purchasing Dept.</Contact.businessGroup>
          </Contact>
        </CorporateInformation.primaryContact>
      </CorporateInformation>
    </Party.corporateInformation>
</Party>
```

This example has a slightly different syntax than what was described in the FpML beta 2 specification. The *structure* is identical, but the elements in this example use longer, qualified names that include class and attribute names from the UML model (for example, `Contact.phoneNumber` is used instead of `phoneNumber`). The XML element names in this example are generated according to the XMI version 1.1 standard, whereas the FpML working group handcrafted their XML DTDs. They were careful not to use the same child element name (class attribute in our UML model) more than once within the same vocabulary package.

Appendix B
MOF and XMI

In Part II, XML Metadata Interchange (XMI) plays a central role as a standard both for generating XML documents from objects and generating XML DTDs and Schemas from UML class structure models. But there are many more ways in which XMI is used and more detail underlying XMI's relationship to UML. This appendix offers a sampling of these broader horizons and references for your continued learning.

I'll first review the Meta Object Facility (MOF) and then explain XMI's relationship to the MOF. Both of these specifications are adopted standards of the Object Management Group (OMG).

Meta Object Facility

It is most straightforward to think about the MOF[1] as a more abstract, specialized form of UML. The MOF is more specialized because it addresses only core class structure and package models from UML and omits the behavioral models such as interaction or use case models. It is more abstract because it is intended as a metametamodel that can represent other metamodels. The MOF has a specific objective to provide a rigorous metamodeling framework for development of metadata repositories, metadata interchange, and software engineering tools. On the other hand, UML was designed to support a wide array of software engineer-

---

1. MOF version 1.3 specification is available at *ftp://ftp.omg.org/pub/docs/formal/00-04-03.pdf*.

ing tasks covering the entire development lifecycle, including requirements analysis, domain modeling, and code generation for implementation.

UML is a metamodel for software development. In other words, UML is a model for creating software models. The MOF Model is a metametamodel intended for representing other metamodels, so UML is modeled as an instance of the MOF Model. This relationship is illustrated in Figure B-1 as part of a four-layer architecture for metamodeling; it's common practice to label these layers M0 through M3. These four layers are useful in many situations, but it is not essential to have exactly four layers; there may be more or fewer layers required in other situations. An article by Cris Kobryn provides a good summary of the four-layer metamodel architecture applied to design of the UML [Kobryn, 1999].

As shown on the left side of Figure B-1, the UML metamodel defines UML models, so the elements of our CatML model are defined as instances of the corresponding UML metamodel classes. The UML metamodel defines metaclasses, such as Model, Package, Class, Attribute, and Association, implemented by UML modeling software tools. In CatML, a `CatalogItem` class is an instance of the UML metaclass `Class`, and the `description` attribute is an instance of the UML metaclass `Attribute`, and so on.

Other OMG standard metamodels are also defined as instances of the MOF Model.

- Common Warehouse Metamodel (CWM).[2] The same concepts of four-layer metamodel architectures apply to CWM, where a particular database schema's tables, attributes, and datatypes are instances of the CWM's classes that represent elements of database schemas. This relationship is illustrated in Figure B-1.

- CORBA Component Model (CCM).[3] This metamodel is analogous to the Enterprise JavaBeans (EJB) specification and defines a standard for server-side components integrated with the CORBA family of standards. Instances of the CCM metamodel represent application-specific component models.

- Unified Process Model (UPM).[4] Just as the UML metamodel is used by many vendors to implement compatible software modeling tools, the UPM will be used by vendors to implement tools that define software development processes. A tool based on the UPM metamodel would be a tool for process authoring and customizing. For example, if the Rational Unified Process (RUP) were defined as a model of the UPM, then companies could

---

2. The CWM specification is available at *http://www.omg.org/technology/cwm/*.

3. The CCM specification is available at *ftp://ftp.omg.org/pub/docs/orbos/99-02-05.pdf*.

4. The UPM draft specification is available at *ftp://ftp.omg.org/pub/docs/ad/00-05-05.pdf*.

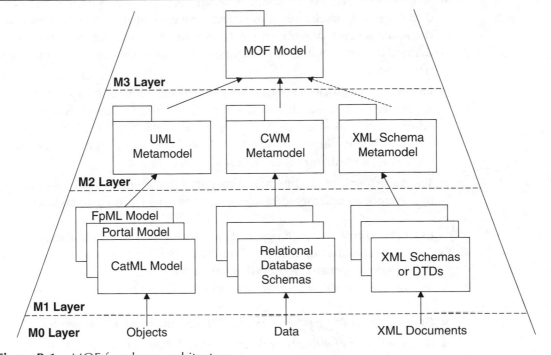

Figure B-1 MOF four-layer architecture

use this new authoring tool to refine or customize RUP for their unique development processes.

■ The XML Schema Metamodel[5] is shown in Figure B-1 with a dotted-arrow to the MOF Model. This is because XML Schema is not currently defined as an instance of the MOF, but it could be. I'm toying with this idea during my contemplative coffeehouse time. . . .

So, why is this abstract discussion of metamodels relevant to the development and deployment of XML applications? There are several reasons.

■ Enterprise and B2B portals require integration of data across heterogeneous models and metamodels. The MOF framework provides a common architecture for designing this integrated view of many diverse information sources. The integration of these sources is accomplished using XML.

---

5. World Wide Web Consortium. XML Schema Part 1: Structures, W3C Candidate Recommendation, 24 October 2000—see *http://www.w3.org/TR/xmlschema-1*.

- XML data interchange between applications (layer M0) is defined by metadata (layer M1), exchange of metadata between software tools is based on the metamodels that define those tools (layer M2), and the metamodels are defined by the common MOF Model, which lies at the top of the pyramid (layer M3).

- Metadata repositories are becoming increasingly common as a way to aggregate these disparate sources of metadata and metamodels within an enterprise and as shared repositories of metadata that define the vocabularies for B2B e-commerce. The MOF Model was specifically designed as the model for holding other metamodels in a repository.

- The MOF four-layer architecture provides a framework for transformation of metamodels and metadata across the domains within a given layer.

For example, consider two types of data transformation within the M0 layer: (1) convert relational data to or from XML documents, and (2) serialize/deserialize Java objects to/from XML documents.

Models may also be transformed within the M1 layer:

- Generate a database schema or an XML schema from a UML model.

- Reverse-engineer a database schema or XML schema into a UML model.

- Generate a database schema from an XML schema, or the reverse.

- Generate EJB or CCM entity bean classes from database schemas.

XML Metadata Interchange

Given this MOF architecture, we need a standard way of exchanging metamodels and models between applications. The XML Metadata Interchange (XMI) standard[6] was developed by the OMG to enable easy interchange of metadata among modeling tools, repositories, and applications in a distributed heterogeneous environment. The following two objectives summarize the key contribution of the XMI specification.

- The XMI specification includes standard production rules for generating DTDs from instances of the MOF Model (for example, models at the M2 layer).

- Production rules are defined for encoding and decoding models at the M1 layer to and from XML document instances.

---

6. The XMI version 1.1 specification is available at *ftp://ftp.omg.org/pub/docs/ad/99-10-02.pdf*.

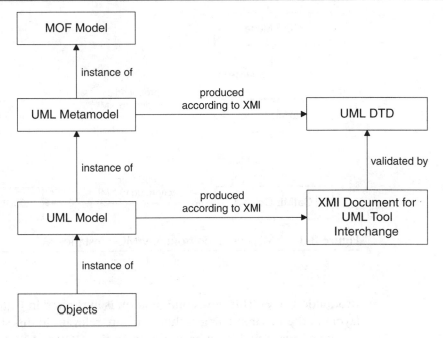

Figure B-2 XMI production from MOF metamodels

These features of XMI are illustrated in Figure B-2, but with a new twist not described in Part II. Because the UML metamodel is an instance of the MOF, XMI is used to produce a DTD for UML. XMI is also used to serialize UML models into XML documents, based on this generated DTD. This is a direct analogy to our extensive discussion of CatML models, schemas, and documents; but the model is the UML itself. The same process is applied to any other MOF metamodels, including the CWM. Thus, XMI is used to exchange both UML models between different vendors' tools and database schemas between different vendors' data warehouse products.

One last piece remains in this puzzle. Because we modeled the CatML vocabulary in UML, how can we apply XMI to generate a DTD? I just stated that XMI is applied to metamodels at the M2 layer, but a UML model is at the M1 layer. CatML is not a metamodel; it's an M1 layer application model, as shown in Figure B-1. The puzzle is solved with a simple trick of transforming the UML model (for example, CatML) into an instance of the MOF Model.

As stated previously, the MOF Model can be viewed as a restricted subset of the UML metamodel for class static structures. We therefore take an instance of the UML metamodel (CatML again) and transform it to become a direct instance of the MOF Model in the M2 layer, after which we can apply the XMI

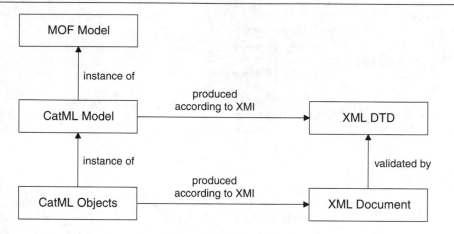

Figure B-3 XMI generation from any MOF instance

production rules. This new configuration is illustrated in Figure B-3. Only three layers of the metamodeling architecture are relevant in this situation.

If you want additional background on the MOF and XMI but don't want to jump into the deep end of the conceptual pool, read the conceptual overview in section 2 of the MOF 1.3 specification, plus the design rationale in section 4 of the XMI 1.1 specification.[7]

---

7. The XMI version 1.1 specification is available at *ftp://ftp.omg.org/pub/docs/ad/99-10-02.pdf*.

Appendix C
UML Profile for XML

Introduction

A UML profile defines a set of stereotypes, tagged values, and constraints that extend the UML core constructs with new meaning and properties. Although UML profiles are often written either as informal specification documents or vendor-specific scripts that extend existing UML tools, the OMG is working toward a standard definition for profiles.[1] Additional UML profiles are being standardized by the OMG[2] or have been proposed by other authors [Conallen, 2000].

The primary purpose of this UML profile for XML is to guide the generation of XML schemas from UML class structure models. The profile design is aligned with the W3C XML Schema specification but is sufficiently general to guide generation of other XML schema variants, including the original standard DTD. In cases where other schemas include specialized features, adding additional tagged values to the existing stereotypes can often accommodate the extensions. Additional stereotypes can be added as well.

Most of the stereotype names are derived from the core constructs of the XML Schema specification, such as schema, complexType, and simpleType. The prefix 'XSD' (short for XML Schema Definition) is added to all stereotypes based

---

1. *White Paper on the Profile Mechanism*, OMG Analysis and Design Platform Task Force, April 1999—see OMG document at *ftp://ftp.omg.org/pub/docs/ad/99-04-07.pdf*.

2. *UML Profile for CORBA*, Version 1.0, 14 February 2000—see OMG document at *ftp://ftp.omg.org/pub/docs/ad/00-02-02.pdf*.

on the specification. Two other stereotypes are derived from the XLink specification: SimpleXLink and ExtendedXLink. For each stereotype, several tagged values are taken directly from the attributes of the constructs in XML Schema or XLink. These standards-based tagged values are listed using a normal font. Other tagged values have been added to guide implementation of an XML Schema generator. These additional tagged values are listed using an italic font. Many of the tagged value names are followed by an enumerated list; default values are underlined in the list.

If the default values are accepted for each stereotype, then the schema will be generated following the *relaxed* definitions outlined in Chapter 9. Modifying several of the tagged values for <<XSDschema>> can generate a strict schema. Or, you can modify the tagged values for individual model constructs to control the schema strictness between the extreme end points. It is *not* required to assign a stereotype to every UML class, attribute, association, and so on; assign a stereotype only if you need to override the default behavior for schema generation.

Following presentation of the stereotype specifications, an example is provided that uses several of the more advanced extensions to generate a customized XML Schema for a bibliography.

Stereotypes

The OMG white paper describes an enhanced UML profile mechanism that will be incorporated into UML 1.4. It was still in draft stage in late 2000, but one of its enhancements is a standard approach for representing UML profiles as UML class diagrams. Using this approach, the UML profile for XML is shown in Figure C-1. Each stereotype definition is modeled as a class with a <<stereotype>> stereotype, and the attributes defined for the class become tagged values in the profile. Each stereotype definition is associated with one or more UML metaclasses, which determine the model elements that may be assigned with this new stereotype.

Each of these new stereotypes is described in the following tables, including a brief description of the stereotype's purpose and intended use of its tagged values.

<<XSDschema>>

UML Constructs	Package Component
Description	In an XML Schema document, the root element <schema> contains all of the definitions for a particular namespace. This is analogous to a UML package. When a UML package is marked with this stereotype, then all of that package's elements will be placed within one XML schema. When a UML component is marked with this stereotype, then all of its assigned classes are added to a schema definition. The schema is further specified by the tagged values.
Tagged Values	targetNamespace—A URI representing a unique XML namespace that will contain this schema's definitions. *targetNamespacePrefix*—The prefix associated with the target XML namespace. version—The version of this schema. elementFormDefault (qualified | <u>unqualified</u>)—Global default specifying whether document instance elements must be qualified with a namespace prefix. attributeFormDefault (qualified | <u>unqualified</u>)—Global default specifying whether document instance attributes must be qualified with a namespace prefix. *modelGroup* (all | sequence | <u>choice</u>)—Indicates the default model group used when generating complexType definitions for this schema. Changing this value to 'all' would correspond to the strict schema production rules. *attributeMapping* (element | attribute | <u>both</u>)—Indicates the default for generating UML attributes as either elements, attributes, or both within complexType definitions for this schema. A value of 'both' corresponds to the XMI 1.1 specification requirement for compliance.[3] *roleMapping* (element | attribute | <u>both</u>)—Indicates the default for generating UML association roles as either elements, attributes, or both within complexType definitions for this schema. *memberNames* (<u>qualified</u> | unqualified)—Determines whether the UML attribute and association role names are qualified by the UML class name. Must be qualified for XMI compliance. *anonymousType* (true | <u>false</u>)—Default setting for all Attributes and AssociationEnds. See <<XSDelement>> for additional description. *anonymousRole* (true | <u>false</u>)—Default setting for all Attributes and AssociationEnds. See <<XSDelement>> for additional description. *elementDerivation* (<u>true</u> | false)—Determines whether the XML Schema will be generated using derived complexType definitions (with extension) or copy-down inheritance. *relaxedMultiplicity* (<u>true</u> | false)—Determines whether all association roles should be generated with minOccurs=0, corresponding to the relaxed schema production rules. *xmiCompliant* (<u>true</u> | false)—Determines whether the required XMI attributes and wrapper elements are generated for this schema.
Constraints	None.

---

3. XML Metadata Interchange (XMI) version 1.1 specification is available at *ftp://ftp.omg.org/pub/docs/ad/99-10-02.pdf*.

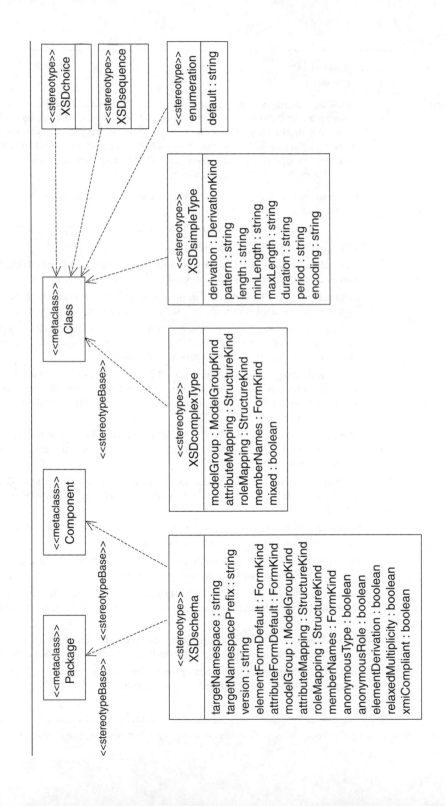

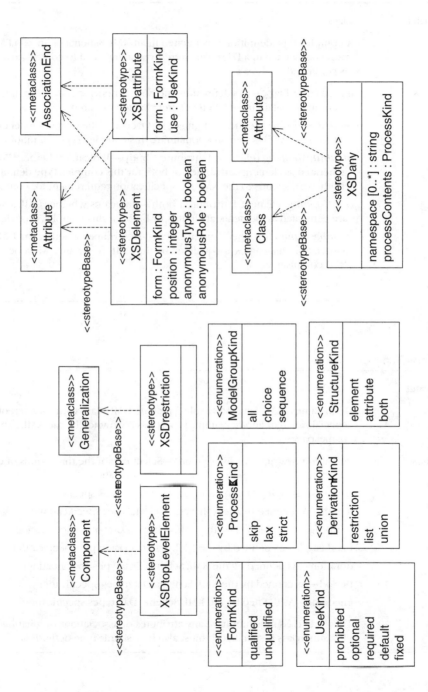

Figure C-1 Stereotype and tagged value definitions for XML profile

305

<<XSDcomplexType>>

UML Construct	Class
Description	A complexType definition is generated in an XML Schema or an <!ELEMENT > definition is generated in a DTD. This stereotype allows you to control how this definition is generated.
Tagged Values	*mixed* (true | <u>false</u>)—As defined by the XML Schema specification. If true, this element may contain mixed element and character content.
	modelGroup (all | sequence | <u>choice</u>)—Overrides the default model group selection set for the <<XSDschema>> containing this complexType definition.
	attributeMapping (element | attribute | <u>both</u>)—Indicates whether UML attributes are generated as elements, attributes, or both for this complexType definition. A value of 'both' corresponds to the XMI 1.1 specification requirement for compliance.
	roleMapping (element | attribute | <u>both</u>)—Indicates whether UML association roles are generated as elements, attributes, or both for this complexType definition.
	memberNames (<u>qualified</u> | unqualified)—Determines whether the UML attribute and association role names are qualified by the UML class name. Must be qualified for XMI compliance.
Constraints	None.

<<XSDsimpleType>>

UML Construct	Class
Description	Define a new XML Schema simpleType. The UML class with this stereotype is usually a specialization of another simpleType, possibly owned by the XML Schema Datatypes namespace.
Tagged Values	derivation (<u>restriction</u> | list | union)—Select one of the three kinds of derivation, as defined by the XML Schema Datatypes specification.
	pattern—As defined by the XML Schema Datatypes specification.
	length—As defined by the XML Schema Datatypes specification.
	minLength—As defined by the XML Schema Datatypes specification.
	maxLength—As defined by the XML Schema Datatypes specification.
	duration—As defined by the XML Schema Datatypes specification.
	period—As defined by the XML Schema Datatypes specification.
	encoding—As defined by the XML Schema Datatypes specification.
Constraints	This UML class must not have any attributes or associations originating from this class. If a superclass is specified, it must also be a simpleType definition.

<<enumeration>>

UML Construct	Class
Description	This stereotype was intentionally named equal to the one defined within the UML specification standard. Other XMI tools already use this stereotype for DTD generation, and the same stereotype is often used for non-XML application models. Its use in this profile will generate an XML Schema simpleType with enumeration facets or a DTD enumeration definition as specified in the XMI 1.1 standard.
Tagged Values	*default*—This optional tagged value selects the default value from the enumerated list.
Constraints	If the attributes defined for this class include datatype specifications, they will be ignored.

<<XSDsequence>>

UML Construct	Class
Description	A UML class that is marked with this stereotype represents a *sequence* model group, contained within a higher-level model group of a complexType definition.
Tagged Values	None.
Constraints	The class with this stereotype must be the destination of unidirectional associations in the UML model.

<<XSDchoice>>

UML Construct	Class
Description	A UML class that is marked with this stereotype represents a *choice* model group, contained within a higher-level model group of a complexType definition.
Tagged Values	None.
Constraints	The class with this stereotype must be the destination of unidirectional associations in the UML model.

<<SimpleXLink>>

UML Construct	Class
Description	By assigning this stereotype to a UML class, the generated complexType definition will include a standard set of XML attributes for simple XLink. The optional tagged values will assign values to the corresponding XLink attributes.
Tagged Values	role—As defined by the XLink specification. arcrole—As defined by the XLink specification. show (new | replace | embed | other | <u>none</u>)—As defined by the XLink specification. actuate (onLoad | onRequest | other | <u>none</u>)—As defined by the XLink specification.
Constraints	None.

<<ExtendedXLink>>

UML Construct	Association
Description	By assigning this stereotype to a UML association, a new complexType definition will be created that includes a standard set of XML attributes for extended XLink.
Tagged Values	None.
Constraints	None.

<<XSDrestriction>>

UML Construct	Generalization
Description	This stereotype marks a UML generalization as being a restriction of the superclass, overriding the default behavior of extension. The child class will be generated as a complexType with a `<restriction>` child element.
Tagged Values	None.
Constraints	Parent and child elements must by UML classes.

<<XSDelement>>

UML Constructs	Attribute AssociationEnd
Description	This stereotype may be assigned to either a UML Attribute or an AssociationEnd to indicate that the corresponding UML construct should be generated as an *element* definition within the parent complexType and not generated as an *attribute* definition.
Tagged Values	form (qualified | unqualified)—Overrides the elementFormDefault selection set for the <<XSDschema>> containing this definition.
	position—A value, if assigned, indicates the position of this element within the sequence model group of the parent complexType.
	anonymousType (true | <u>false</u>)—The class type of this Attribute or AssociationEnd will be anonymous for XML documents defined by the generated schema (that is, the element defined by the attribute or role name will contain child elements from the class, but not the class element type) This value must be false when generating XMI 1.1 compliant schemas.
	anonymousRole (true | <u>false</u>)—The class type of this Attribute or AssociationEnd will be directly embedded within the complexType definition for the owner class, omitting the role or attribute name element type wrapper. This value must be false when generating XMI 1.1-compliant schemas.
Constraints	None.

<<XSDattribute>>

UML Constructs	Attribute AssociationEnd
Description	This stereotype may be assigned to either a UML Attribute or an AssociationEnd to indicate that the corresponding UML construct should be generated as an *attribute* definition within the parent complexType and not generated as an *element* definition.
Tagged Values	form (qualified | unqualified)—Overrides the attributeFormDefault selection set for the <<XSDschema>> containing this definition.
	use (prohibited | <u>optional</u> | required | default | fixed)—As defined by the XML Schema specification.
Constraints	The attribute datatype may not refer to a class specification.

<<XSDtopLevelElement>>

UML Construct	Component
Description	When this stereotype is assigned to a UML component, an XML Schema top-level element will be declared with its name equal to the component name and the type equal to the UML class name assigned to the component.
Tagged Values	None.
Constraints	This component must be assigned to exactly one class.

<<XSDany>>

UML Constructs	Class Attribute
Description	The stereotyped Class or Attribute will be replaced by an <any> or <anyAttribute> element, respectively, in the generated schema. The tagged values are copied into the corresponding attributes of the generated element to provide additional constraints on the XML document elements or attributes.
Tagged Values	namespace—As defined by the XML Schema specification. processContents (skip | lax | <u>strict</u>)—As defined by the XML Schema specification.
Constraints	None.

Bibliography Example

The above stereotypes are used with a UML model for the bibliography example presented in Chapter 8. The schema example in that chapter is not compliant with the XMI 1.1 specification rules but was designed to illustrate more advanced features of schema content models that are not possible when using XMI. Using stereotypes, you can override several rules of schema generation in order to produce the same advanced schema structures. You can also generate an XMI-compliant schema, either relaxed for strict, by ignoring the stereotypes when executing the schema generator tool. The UML profile for XML gives you control over the generation process so that you can satisfy the requirements of your application.

The best way to gain a full understanding of this example is to use the XML Schema generation tool from this book's companion Web site. You can then modify the stereotypes and/or tagged value and regenerate the schema to see the results.

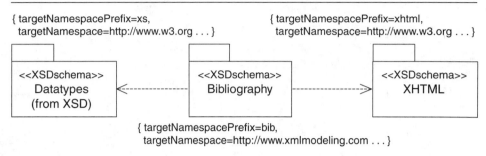

Figure C-2 Package diagram with stereotypes

A UML package diagram is shown in Figure C-2. The Bibliography package is dependent both on XML Schema Datatypes, as well as on a schema for XHTML. XHTML is a recent W3C standard that reformulates HTML to be compliant with XML. As you'll see in the following model, we now use XHTML markup for the content of the book's abstract. Each of these packages is assigned the <<XSDschema>> stereotype in order to enable specification of the XML target namespace URI and prefix used when generating the schema. These values are added as tagged values assigned to each package.

The class structure model from the Bibliography package is shown in Figure C-3. If a stereotype is assigned to a class, then the tagged values are shown immediately above that class, enclosed by { }. Don't forget, however, that you can generate an XMI-compliant schema from this same model without using *any* stereotypes or tagged values!

And finally, the following XML Schema is generated from this model, using the stereotypes and tagged values to override the default rules for strict schemas.

```
<xs:schema
  xmlns:xs = "http://www.w3.org/2000/10/XMLSchema"
  xmlns:xhtml = "http://www.w3.org"
  targetNamespace = "http://xmlmodeling.com/schemas/bibliography" >

<!-- ~~~~~~~~~~~~~~~~~~~~~~~~~~~~~~~~~~~~~~~~~~~~~~~~~~~~~~~~~~~~~~ -->
<!-- DATATYPE: PhoneNumber -->
<!-- ~~~~~~~~~~~~~~~~~~~~~~~~~~~~~~~~~~~~~~~~~~~~~~~~~~~~~~~~~~~~~~ -->

    <xs:simpleType name="PhoneNumber">
       <xs:restriction base="xs:string"/>
    </xs:simpleType>
```

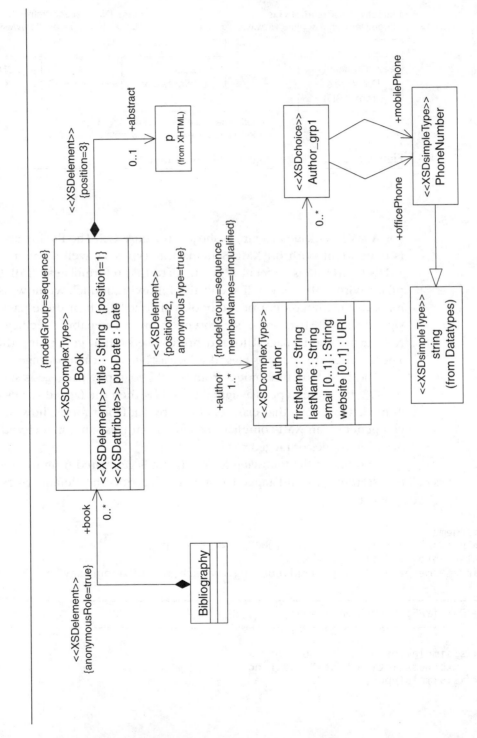

Figure C-3 Bibliography model with stereotypes

```
<!-- ~~~~~~~~~~~~~~~~~~~~~~~~~~~~~~~~~~~~~~~~~~~~~~~~~~~~~~~~~~~~ -->
<!-- CLASS: Bibliography -->
<!-- ~~~~~~~~~~~~~~~~~~~~~~~~~~~~~~~~~~~~~~~~~~~~~~~~~~~~~~~~~~~~ -->

    <xs:element name="Bibliography" type="Bibliography"/>
    <xs:complexType name="Bibliography">
        <xs:all>
          <xs:element ref="Book" minOccurs="0" maxOccurs="unbounded"/>
        </xs:all>
    </xs:complexType>


<!-- ~~~~~~~~~~~~~~~~~~~~~~~~~~~~~~~~~~~~~~~~~~~~~~~~~~~~~~~~~~~~ -->
<!-- CLASS: Book -->
<!-- ~~~~~~~~~~~~~~~~~~~~~~~~~~~~~~~~~~~~~~~~~~~~~~~~~~~~~~~~~~~~ -->

    <xs:element name="Book" type="Book"/>
    <xs:complexType name="Book">
        <xs:sequence>
            <xs:element name="Book.title" type="String"/>
            <xs:element name="Book.author" type="Author"
                        minOccurs="1" maxOccurs="unbounded"/>
            <xs:element name="Book.abstract">
                <xs:complexType>
                  <xs:sequence>
                    <xs:element ref="xhtml:p" minOccurs="0" maxOccurs="1"/>
                  </xs:sequence>
                </xs:complexType>
            </xs:element>
        </xs:sequence>
        <xs:attributeGroup ref="Book.att"/>
    </xs:complexType>
    <xs:attributeGroup name="Book.att">
        <xs:attribute name="pubDate" type="Date"/>
    </xs:attributeGroup>


<!-- ~~~~~~~~~~~~~~~~~~~~~~~~~~~~~~~~~~~~~~~~~~~~~~~~~~~~~~~~~~~~ -->
<!-- CLASS: Author -->
<!-- ~~~~~~~~~~~~~~~~~~~~~~~~~~~~~~~~~~~~~~~~~~~~~~~~~~~~~~~~~~~~ -->

    <xs:element name="Author" type="Author"/>
    <xs:complexType name="Author">
        <xs:sequence>
            <xs:element name="firstName" type="String"/>
            <xs:element name="lastName" type="String"/>
            <xs:element name="email" type="String"
                        minOccurs="0" maxOccurs="1"/>
            <xs:element name="website" type="URL"
                        minOccurs="0" maxOccurs="1"/>
            <xs:choice minOccurs="0" maxOccurs="unbounded">
              <xs:element name="officePhone" type="PhoneNumber"/>
              <xs:element name="mobilePhone" type="PhoneNumber"/>
            </xs:choice>
        </xs:sequence>
    </xs:complexType>
```

```
<!-- _____ -->
<!-- _____ -->
<!-- JAVA: Standard Java simpleType definitions -->
<!-- _____ -->

    <xs:simpleType name="String">
        <xs:restriction base="xs:string"/>
    </xs:simpleType>
    <xs:simpleType name="int">
        <xs:restriction base="xs:integer"/>
    </xs:simpleType>
    <xs:simpleType name="float">
        <xs:restriction base="xs:float"/>
    </xs:simpleType>
    <xs:simpleType name="double">
        <xs:restriction base="xs:float"/>
    </xs:simpleType>
    <xs:simpleType name="Date">
        <xs:restriction base="xs:date"/>
    </xs:simpleType>
    <xs:simpleType name="URL">
        <xs:restriction base="xs:uriReference"/>
    </xs:simpleType>

</xs:schema>
```

The following XML document instance may be validated by this schema:

```
<?xml version="1.0" ?>
<Bibliography
    xmlns:xsi='http://www.w3.org/2000/10/XMLSchema-instance'
    xsi:noNamespaceSchemaLocation='bibliography.xsd'>
 <Book pubDate = "2000-03-01">
  <Book.title>Modeling XML Applications with UML</Book.title>
  <Book.author>
    <firstName>David</firstName>
    <lastName>Carlson</lastName>
    <email>dcarlson@ontogenics.com</email>
    <website>http://www.XMLModeling.com</website>
    <officePhone>303-555-1212</officePhone>
    <officePhone>415-555-1212</officePhone>
  </Book.author>
  <Book.abstract>
    <p xmlns:xhtml="http://www.w3.org/1999/xhtml">
      This book presents the <b>benefits and concepts</b>
      required for successful use of the <i>Unified Modeling
      Language (UML)</i> in XML application development.
    </p>
  </Book.abstract>
 </Book>
</Bibliography>
```

References

[Berners-Lee, 1999]   Tim Berners-Lee. *Weaving the Web*. New York: HarperCollins, 1999.

[Booch, 1999]   Grady Booch, James Rumbaugh, and Ivar Jacobson. *The Unified Modeling Language User Guide,* Reading, MA: Addison-Wesley, 1999.

[Bradley, 2000]   Neil Bradley. *The XSL Companion.* Boston: Addison-Wesley, 2000.

[Conallen, 2000]   James Conallen. *Building Web Applications with UML.* Boston: Addison-Wesley, 2000.

[Fowler, 2000]   Martin Fowler, Kendall Scott. *UML Distilled: A Brief Guide to the Standard Object Modeling Language*, Second Edition. Boston: Addison-Wesley, 2000.

[Jacobson, 1999]   Ivar Jacobson, Grady Booch, and James Rumbaugh. *The Unified Software Development Process.* Reading, MA: Addison-Wesley, 1999.

[Kay, 2000]   Michael Kay. *XSLT Programmer's Reference*. Birmingham, UK: Wrox Press, 2000.

[Kobryn, 1999]   Cris Kobryn. UML 2001: A standardization odyssey. *Communications of the ACM*. October 1999.

[Kruchten, 2000]   Philippe Kruchten. *The Rational Unified Process: An Introduction*, Second Edition. Boston: Addison-Wesley, 2000.

[Maler, 1996]   Eve Maler, Jeanne El Andaloussi. *Developing SGML DTDs*. Upper Saddle River, NJ: Prentice-Hall, 1996.

[St. Laurent, 1999]   Simon St. Laurent. *XML Elements of Style.* New York: McGraw-Hill, 1999.

[Schneider, 1998]   Geri Schneider, Jason P. Winters, and Ivar Jacobson. *Applying Use Cases: A Practical Guide.* Reading, MA: Addison-Wesley, 1998.

Index

Note: Italicized page locators indicate figures/tables.

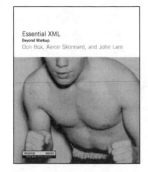

Essential XML: *Beyond Markup*

Don Box, Aaron Skonnard, and John Lam
The DevelopMentor Series

Essential XML provides a solid understanding of XML's inner workings. Readers will come to see how XML's platform, language, accessibility, and vendor independence make it an effective solution for software interoperation. This book covers the key issues, technologies, and techniques involved in using XML as the adhesive between disparate software components and environments. The authors explain the fundamental abstractions and concepts that permeate all XML technologies, primarily those documented in the XML Information Set (Infoset). XML-based approaches to metadata, declarative, and procedural programming through transformation, and programmatic interfaces are covered in detail.

0-201-70914-7 • Paperback • 400 pages • ©2000

The XML Companion, Second Edition

Neil Bradley

If you're a current or potential XML user looking for just one reference to get you up to speed on XML with clarity, comprehensive coverage and precision, then this book will be your essential and constant companion. Building on the success of the first edition, Neil Bradley has updated this accessible, in-depth reference to release 1.0 of the XML standard. This edition contains the complementary standards that have been released, including detailed coverage of DOM 1.0, SAX 1.0, CSS 2 and NameSpaces 1.0, as well as describing the latest, most stable drafts of XSL & XSLT, Xlink & Xpointer.

0-201-67486-6 • Paperback • 576 pages • ©2000

Building Web Applications with UML

Jim Conallen
Addison-Wesley Object Technology Series

Building Web Applications with UML is a guide to building robust, scalable, and feature-rich web applications using proven object-oriented techniques. Written for the project manager, architect, analyst, designer, and programmer of web applications, this book examines the unique aspects of modeling web applications with the Web Application Extension (WAE) for the industry standard UML. Using UML allows developers to model their web applications as a part of the complete system and the business logic that must be reflected in the application. Readers will gain not only an understanding of the modeling process, but also the ability to map models directly into code.

0-201-61577-0 • Paperback • 320 pages • ©2000

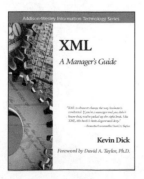

XML: *A Manager's Guide*

Kevin Dick
Addison-Wesley Information Technology Series

This book serves as a concise guide for technical managers, as well as a starting point for developers interested in taking advantage of XML. It uses clear explanations of XML essentials as a foundation to demonstrate how this technology can substantially benefit your organization. Designed to let you access exactly the information you require, this book clearly delineates different paths through the chapters based on your needs, provides executive briefings for every chapter, and includes fast-track summaries of major points in the margins.

0-201-43335-4 • Paperback w/CD-ROM • 208 pages • ©2000

Enterprise Modeling with UML
Designing Successful Software through Business Analysis
Chris Marshall
Addison-Wesley Object Technology Series

Written for business engineering practitioners coming from both the ranks of business and the software industry, this book fuses object technology, workflow, data warehousing, and distributed systems concepts into a single coherent system model that has been successfully implemented worldwide. It describes specific methods for modeling large, complex, and adaptable enterprises, using the object-based Unified Modeling Language (UML) for designing model components. The accompanying CD-ROM contains Java and XML implementations of many of the ideas and models in the book, demonstrating how software components are created to reflect business specifications.

0-201-43313-3 • Paperback with CD-ROM • 288 pages • ©2000

XML and Java™
Developing Web Applications
Hiroshi Maruyama, Kent Tamura, and Naohiko Uramoto

XML and Java™ is a tutorial that will teach Web developers, programmers, and system engineers how to create robust XML business applications for the Internet using the Java technology. The authors, a team of IBM XML experts, introduce the essentials of XML and Java development, from a review of basic concepts to thorough coverage of advanced techniques. Using a step-by-step approach, this book illustrates real-world implications of XML and Java technologies as they apply to Web applications. Readers should have a basic understanding of XML as well as experience in writing simple Java programs.

0-201-48543-5 • Paperback with CD-ROM • 400 pages • ©1999